Grose Francis

The Antiquities of England and Wales

Volume 1

Grose Francis

The Antiquities of England and Wales
Volume 1

ISBN/EAN: 9783337321413

Printed in Europe, USA, Canada, Australia, Japan

Cover: Foto ©ninafisch / pixelio.de

More available books at **www.hansebooks.com**

THE

Antiquities

OF

ENGLAND

AND

Wales

By FRANCIS GROSE, Esq. F. A. S.

VOL. I. New Edition.

London Printed for S: HOOPER, N°. 212, High-Holborn, facing *Southampton Street, Bloomsbury-Square.*

THE

ANTIQUITIES

OF

ENGLAND and WALES:

BEING A

COLLECTION of VIEWS

OF THE

Moſt remarkable Ruins and antient Buildings,

ACCURATELY DRAWN ON THE SPOT.

TO EACH VIEW IS ADDED

An Hiſtorical Account of its Situation, when and by whom built, with every intereſting Circumſtance relating thereto.

COLLECTED FROM THE BEST AUTHORITIES:

By FRANCIS GROSE, Eſq; F. A. S.

VOL. I.

THE SECOND EDITION, CORRECTED AND ENLARGED.

LONDON:

PRINTED BY C. CLARKE,

For S. HOOPER, N° 188, the Corner of Arundel Street, Strand.

M.DCC.LXXXIII.

INTRODUCTION.

As in the courſe of the enſuing work many terms and alluſions may occur, unintelligible to perſons who have not made the antiquities of this country their immediate ſtudy; and who would, for information, be obliged to turn over a variety of books; to theſe a general hiſtory of ancient caſtles, explaining the terms relative to their conſtruction, garriſons and privileges, with the machines uſed for their attack and defence, will be uſeful, if not neceſſary: the ſame may be ſaid on the ſubject of abbies and other monaſtic foundations.

Illustrative accounts of both are therefore here given, compiled from the beſt authorities; and as moſt of theſe buildings are either of the Saxon architecture, or of that ſtile commonly called Gothic, ſome characteriſtic marks and principles of the firſt are pointed out, and an inveſtigation of the origin of the latter attempted. Domeſday-book being quoted in ſeveral deſcriptions, ſome particulars of that ancient record, with a ſpecimen of the hands in which it is written, will, it is hoped not improperly, be inſerted.

The

The author begs to have it underſtood, that he does not herein pretend to inform the veteran antiquary; but has drawn up theſe accounts ſolely for the uſe of ſuch as are deſirous of having, without much trouble, a general knowledge of the ſubjects treated of in this publication; which they will find collected into as ſmall a compaſs as any tolerable degree of perſpicuity would permit. In order to render every article as clear as poſſible, the verbal deſcriptions, where capable, are illuſtrated by drawings.

PREFACE.

PREFACE.

CASTLES.

CASTLES, (a) walled with ſtone, and deſigned for reſidence as well as defence, ſuch as thoſe whoſe remains make a conſiderable part of the following work, are, for the moſt part, of no higher antiquity than the conqueſt; (b) for although the Saxons, Romans, and even, according to ſome writers on antiquity, (c) the ancient Britons had caſtles built with ſtone; yet theſe were both few in number, and, at that period, through neglect or invaſions, either deſtroyed, or ſo much decayed, that little more than their ruins were remaining. This is aſſerted by many of our hiſtorians and antiquaries, and aſſigned as a reaſon for the facility with which William made himſelf maſter of this country.

(a) LARGER caſtles were in Latin called caſtra; the ſmaller by the diminutive, caſtella. Julius Ferettus has this ridiculous etymology of the word caſtrum. Caſtra dicta ſunt a caſtitate, quia ibi omnes caſtè vivere debent. They were likewiſe ſtiled arx, turris, foſſa, maceria, mota, firmitas, & munitio: as in the charter made between King Stephen and Henry II. Caſtrum de Wallingford, Caſtellum de Belencomber, Turris London, Mota Oxenford, Firmitas Lincolniæ, Munitio Hamptoniæ. Pile, Peel and Baſtile, alſo ſignify a ſmall caſtle or fortreſs.

(b) AGARD, in his Diſcourſe of Caſtles, ſays, "For I read in the Hiſtorye of Normandye, wrytten in Frenche, that when Sweyne, King of Denmark, entered the realme againſte Kinge Alred or Allured, to revenge the night ſlaughter of the Danes, done by the Saxons in Englande, he ſubdued all before him, becauſe there were no fortes or caſtles to withſtand or ſtop him; and the reaſon yielded is, becauſe the fortes of England, for the moſt part, were buylte after the Normans poſſeſſed the realme. The words be theſe: Suen le roy des Danoys ala parmy Angleterre conquerant et ne lui contrediſoit lon nulle choſe quil vouluiſt faire car lors il n'avoit que peu ou nulles fortreſſes, et les y ont puys fait faire, celles qui y ſont les Normans quant & depuys quils conquiſtrent le pays." *Antiq. Diſcourſes, vol. 1. p.* 188. Of this opinion was alſo Sir William Dugdale, as appears by the following paſſage, in his Hiſtory of Warwickſhire: "In thoſe dayes (in the Saxons time I mean) were very few ſuch defenſible places as we now call caſtles, that being a French name; ſo that though the Engliſh were a bold and warlike people, yet for want of the like ſtrong holds, were they much the leſſe able to reſiſt their enemies."

(c) BORLASE's Hiſtory of Cornwall, p. 531.

This circumſtance was not overlooked by ſo good a general as the Conqueror; who, effectually to guard againſt invaſions from without, as well as to awe his newly-acquired ſubjects, immediately began to erect caſtles all over the kingdom; and likewiſe to repair and augment the old ones, with ſuch aſſiduity, that Rous ſays, "Nam Rex Will. Conqueſtor ad caſtella conſtruenda totam Angliam fatigabat." (d) Beſides, as he had parcelled out the lands of the Engliſh amongſt his followers, they, to protect themſelves from the reſentment of thoſe ſo deſpoiled, built ſtrong-holds and caſtles on their eſtates. This likewiſe cauſed a conſiderable encreaſe of theſe fortreſſes; and the turbulent and unſettled ſtate of the kingdom in the ſucceeding reigns, ſerved to multiply them prodigiouſly, every baron, or leader of a party, building caſtles; inſomuch that, towards the latter end of the reign of King Stephen, they amounted to the almoſt incredible number of eleven hundred and fifteen. (e)

As the feudal ſyſtem gathered ſtrength, theſe caſtles became the heads of baronies. (f) Each caſtle was a manor; and its caſtellain owner, or governor, the lord of that manor. (g) Markets and fairs were directed to be held there; not only to prevent frauds in the kings duties or cuſtoms, but alſo as they were eſteemed places where the laws of the land were obſerved, (h) and as ſuch had a very particular privilege. (i) But this good order did

(d) Rous Rot. 1.

(e) Registrum Prioratus de Dunſtaple.

(f) Madox's Baronia, pages 17, 18.

(g) Blount's Law Dictionary in Caſtel.

(h) Item nullum mercatum vel forum ſit, nec fieri permittatur, niſi in civitatibus regni noſtri, et in burgis, et muro vallatis, et in caſtellis, et in locis tutiſſimis, ubi conſuetudines regni noſtri, et jus noſtrorum commune et dignitates coronæ noſtræ, quæ conſtitutæ ſunt a bonis prædeceſſoribus noſtris deperiri non poſſent, nec defraudari, nec violari, ſed omnia ritè et in aperto, et per judicium et juſtitiam fieri debent. Et ideo caſtella, et burgi, et civitates, ſitæ ſunt et fundatæ et ædificate, ſcilicet, ad tuetionem gentium et populorum regni, et ad defenſionem regni, et idcirco obſervari debent, cum omni libertate, et integritate, et ratione. *Carta regis Willielmi Conquiſitoris. Tranſcribed from Wilkins, and the Red Book of the Exchequer, printed in the Appendix to Lord Lyttelton's Hiſtory of Henry II.*

(i) Item, ſi ſervi permanſerint ſine calumnia per annum et diem in civitatibus noſtris, vel in burgis muro vallatis, vel in caſtris noſtris, a die illa liberi officiuntur, et liberi a jugo ſervitutis ſuæ ſint in perpetuum.

not long laſt; (k) for the lords of caſtles began to arrogate to themſelves a royal power, not only within their caſtles, but likewiſe its environs; exerciſing judicature both civil and criminal, coining of money, and arbitrarily ſeizing forage and proviſion for the ſubſiſtence of their garriſons, (l) which they afterwards demanded as a right: at length, their inſolence and oppreſſion grew to ſuch a pitch, that, according to William of Newbury, "there were in England as many kings, or rather tyrants, as lords of caſtles;" and Matthew Paris ſtiles them, very neſts of devils, and dens of thieves. Caſtles were not ſolely in the poſſeſſion of the crown and the lay barons, but even biſhops had theſe fortreſſes; though it ſeems to have been contrary to the canons, from a plea made uſe of in a general council, (m) in favour of King Stephen, who had ſeized upon the ſtrong caſtles of the biſhops of Lincoln and Saliſbury. This prohibition (if ſuch exiſted) was however very little regarded; as, in the following reigns, many ſtrong places were held, and even defended, by eccleſiaſticks; neither was more obedience afterwards paid to a decree made by the Pope at Viterbo, (n) the fifth of the calends of June, 1220, wherein it was ordained, that no perſon in England ſhould keep in his hands more than two of the king's caſtles.

THE licentious behaviour of the garriſons of theſe places becoming intolerable, in the treaty between King Sephen and Henry II. when only duke of Normandy, it was agreed, that all the caſtles built within a certain period ſhould be demoliſhed; in conſequence of which, many were actually razed, but not the number ſtipulated. On the acceſſion of Henry to the throne, diverſe others were deſtroyed; and all perſons prohibited from erecting new ones, without the king's eſpecial licence, called licentia kernellare, (o) or crenellare. Few, if any, of theſe licences are of older date than the reign of Edward III. A copy

(k) ANTIQ. *Diſcourſes*, *p.* 190, 191.
(l) MADOX's Baronia, page 20.
(m) LYTTELTON's Hiſtory of Henry II. vol. 1. p. 219.
(n) ACTA Regia, page 46.
(o) FROM crena, a notch.

of

of one, granted by Richard II. to the Lord Scrope, for the erection of the caſtle of Bolton in Yorkſhire, is inſerted in the note below. (p) Licences to crenellate were alſo granted by the biſhops of Durham, and probably by other dukes and princes pallatine.

It does not however, ſeem as if the demolition of theſe caſtles put a ſtop to the depredations complained of; as to prevent like extortions, diverſe acts of parliament were paſſed in the reigns of Henry III. and Edward I. directing in what manner, and of whom purveyance for a caſtle ſhould be made, wherein it was ordained that no conſtable nor his bailiff ſhould take corn or other chattels of any man, not being of the town where the caſtle ſtood, without immediate payment for the ſame, unleſs the owner conſented to truſt for his money, and if he was of the ſame town, the value was to be paid to him within forty days.

Another ſpecies of tyranny exerciſed by the conſtables or governors of theſe caſtles, as late as the reign of Henry IV. is pointed out by the Rolls of Parliament, in a petition from the Commons, ſetting forth, that many of the conſtables of caſtles who were appointed juſtices of the peace, made uſe of their authority under different pretences to ſeize and impriſon perſons againſt whom they had any ill will, and to keep them till they had paid a fine or ranſom for their deliverance, wherefore the petitioners humbly prayed his majeſty to ordain for the future, that no conſtable of a caſtle ſhould be a juſtice of the peace in that county wherein his caſtle was ſituated, and that no one ſhould be impriſoned, except in the common gaol of the county,

(p) Richardus Dei gracia rex Angliæ et Francia et dominus Hibernie, omnibus ad quos preſentes litteræ prevenerint ſalutem, ſciatis quod de gracia noſtra ſpeciali conceſſimus & licentiam dedimus pro nobis & heredibus noſtris dilecto & fideli noſtro Ricardo Leſcrop, cancellario noſtro, quod ipſe manerium ſuum de Bolton in Wencelow Dale, ſeu unam placeam infra idem manerium muro de petra & calce firmare & kernellare & manerium illud ceu placeam, illam ſic firmatum & kernellatum vel firmatam & kernellatam, tenere poſſit ſibi & heredibus ſuis imperpetuum ſine occaſione vel impedimento noſtri vel heredum noſtrorum juſticiorum eſcaetorum vicecomitum aut aliorum baliorum ſeu miniſtrorum noſtrorum vel heredum noſtrorum quorumcunque. In cujus rei teſtimonium has literas noſtras fieri fecimus patentes. Teſte meipſo apud Weſtmonaſterium quarto die Julij anno regni noſtri tertio. Per breve de privato ſigillo. *Waltham.*

under

under a penalty to be ſettled by that parliament, reſerving to the lords their ancient franchiſes. This petition the king was pleaſed to grant.

ROYAL caſtles, for the defence of the country, were however erected, when deemed neceſſary, at the public expence.

THE few caſtles in being under the Saxon government, were probably on occaſion of war or invaſions, garriſoned by the national militia, and at other times ſlightly guarded by the domeſtics of the princes or great perſonages who reſided therein; but after the conqueſt, when all the eſtates were converted into baronies, held by knights ſervice, caſtle guard coming under that denomination, was among the duties to which particular tenants were liable. (q) From theſe ſervices the biſhops and abbots, who till the time of the Normans had held their lands in frank almoign, (r) or free alms, were, by this new regulation, not exempted; they were not indeed, like the laity, obliged to perſonal ſervice, it being ſufficient that they provided fit and able perſons to officiate in their ſtead. This was however at firſt ſtoutly oppoſed by Anſelm, archbiſhop of Canterbury; who being obliged to find ſome knights to attend King William Rufus in his wars in Wales, complained of it as an innovation and infringement of the rights and immunities of the church.

IT was no uncommon thing for the Conqueror and the kings of thoſe days, to grant eſtates to men of approved fidelity and valour, on condition that they ſhould perform caſtle-guard, in the royal caſtles with a certain number of men, for ſome ſpecified time; and ſometimes they were likewiſe bound by their tenures

(q) BY a ſtatute 9 Henry III. chap. 20. there is the following regulation reſpecting perſons bound to do caſtle guard, who may be called to ſerve in the king's army. "No conſtable ſhall diſtrain any knight for to give him money for the keeping of his caſtle, if he himſelf ſhall do it in his proper perſon, or cauſe it to be done by another ſufficient man, if he may not do it for a reaſonable cauſe, and if we do lead or ſend him in an army, he ſhall be free from caſtle ward for the time that he ſhall be with us in fee in our hoſt, for the which he hath done ſervice in our wars.

(r) As tenants in frank almoigne, their eſtates were only liable to the trinoda neceſſitas, building of bridges, caſtles for the defence of the country, and repelling invaſions; whereas, by the new eſtabliſhment and tenures, they were obliged to perform military ſervice in foreign countries, and in time of peace.

 to

to keep in repair and guard ſome particular tower or bulwark, as was the caſe at Dover caſtle.

In proceſs of time theſe ſervices were commuted for annual rents, ſometimes ſtiled ward-penny, and wayt-fee, (s) but commonly caſtle-guard rents, payable on fixed days, under prodigious penalties, called ſurſizes. At Rocheſter, (t) if a man failed in the payment of his rent of caſtle guard, on the feaſt of St. Andrew, his debt was doubled every tide, during the time for which the payment was delayed. Theſe were afterwards reſtrained by an act of parliament made in the reign of King Henry VIII. (u) and finally annihilated, with the tenures by knights ſervice, in the time of Charles II. (w) Such caſtles as were private property, were guarded either by mercenary ſoldiers, or the tenants of the lord or owner.

Castles which belonged to the crown, or fell to it either by forfeiture or eſcheat (circumſtances that frequently happened in the diſtracted reigns of the feudal times), were generally committed to the cuſtody of ſome truſty perſon, who ſeems to have been indifferently ſtiled governor and conſtable. Sometimes alſo they were put into the poſſeſſion of the ſheriff of the county, who often converted them into priſons: inſtances of this occur in many caſtles deſcribed in this work. (x) That officer was then accountable at the Exchequer, for the farm or produce of the lands belonging to the places entruſted to his care, as well as all other profits: he was likewiſe, in caſe of war or invaſion, obliged to victual and furniſh them with munition, out of the iſſues of his county: to which he was directed by writ of privy ſeal. Variety

(s) Blount's Law Dictionary.

(t) History of Rocheſter, page 40; and Antiq. Diſcourſes, page 190.

(u) Vide Dover Caſtle, plate I. in this work.

(w) 12 Charles II. cap. 24.

(x) Some of them ſeem to have been particularly appropriated to that uſe, for in 10 Richard II. anno 1389, the commons preſented a petition to the king in parliament, complaining that diverſe caſtles, which had at all times appertained to and been joined to the office of ſheriff, had of late been granted to other perſons, whereby the ſheriffs were deprived of their priſons to the great hurt and diſorder of the country, and praying that the ſaid caſtles may be rejoined to the offices of ſheriffs, as a work of charity and a benefit to the counties. Rolls of Parliament.

of

of theſe writs, temp. Edward III. are to be ſeen in Madox's Hiſtory of the Exchequer, one of which is given in the notes; (y) and it appears, from the ſame authority, that the barons of the Exchequer were ſometimes appointed to ſurvey theſe caſtles, (z) and the ſtate of the buildings and works carrying on therein.

THE materials of which caſtles were built, varied, according to the places of their erection; but the manner of their conſtruction ſeems to have been pretty uniform. The outſides of the walls were generally built with the ſtones neareſt at hand, laid as regularly as their ſhapes would admit; the inſides were filled up with the like materials, mixed with a great quantity of fluid mortar, which was called, by the workmen, grout work: a very ancient method of building, uſed by the Romans, and quoted by Palladio, and all the writers on architecture. The angles were always coigned, and the arches turned with ſquared ſtone, brought from Caen in Normandy, with which the whole outſide was now and then caſed. Sometimes, inſtead of ſtone, the inſides of the walls were formed with ſquared chalk, as is the caſtle of Guildford; and even the pillars and arches of a groined vault in that town, ſuppoſed formerly to have belonged to the caſtle. When the Normans found the ruins of an ancient building on the ſite of their intended ſtructure, which very frequently happened, they either endeavoured to incorporate it into their work, or made uſe of the materials; as may be ſeen by many buildings of known

(y) REX volens certis ex cauſis caſtrum ſuum Norwyce, quod eſt in cuſtodia vicecomitis ex commiſſione regis, competenter muniri & ſalvo & ſecure cuſtodiri: preceptum eſt vicecomiti in fide qua regi tenetur, quod caſtrum prædictum victualibus & rebus aliis neceſſariis, pro cuſtodia & municione ejuſdem congruentibus, de exitibus ballivæ ſuæ muniri faciat competenter, abſq; dilacionis incommodo aliquali; ne pro defectu munitionis aut ſufficientis cuſtodiæ, periculum regi, inde immineat quovis modo. Et hoc, ſicut ſe & ſua diligit, ac indignationem & forisfacturam regis graviſſimam vitare voluerit, non omittat. Cuſtos vero rationabilis, quos circa munitionem prædictam per ipſum vicecomitem apponi continget, cum rex illos rite ſciverit, eidem vicecomiti in compoto ſuo ad ſcaccarium debite allocari faciet. De hijs etiam quæ vicecomes circa municionem prædictam appoſuerit & eorum precio, (de quibus omnibus & ſingulis, niſi ex cauſa neceſſaria ea circa ſalvationem ejuſdem caſtri apponi & expendi opporteat, rex per ipſum vult reſponderi) theſaurio & baronibus di ſcaccario apud Weſtm. in Octabis, S. Hillarij, diſtincte & aperte per ſingula ſingillatim conſtare faciat. Et habebat ibi tunc hoc breve. T. W. de Norwico xxix die Decembris. Per breve de privato ſigillo directum prædicti W. tunc cuſtodi theſaurariæ regis, vol. 1. page 382.

(z) VOL. 2. page 67.

Norman

Norman conſtruction, wherein are fragments of Saxon architecture, or large quantities of Roman bricks; which has cauſed them often to be miſtaken for Roman or Saxon edifices.

THE general ſhape or plan of theſe caſtles depended entirely on the caprice of the architects, or the form of the ground intended to be occupied: neither do they ſeem to have confined themſelves to any particular figure in their towers; ſquare, round, and poligonal, oftentimes occuring in the original parts of the ſame building.

THE ſituations commonly choſen, were, ſteep rocks, cliffs, eminences, or the banks of rivers, but the engineers of thoſe days ſeem to have too much diſregarded the circumſtance of their works being commanded by neighbouring heights, within the range aſſigned to their battering engines, the ſituation of the caſtles of Corfe and Dover, have thoſe imperfections, notwithſtanding they were conſidered as two of the ſtrongeſt and moſt important caſtles in the kingdom.

THE names and uſes of the different works of ancient fortifications, can only be aſcertained by an attention to minute hiſtorical relations of ſieges in thoſe times; ancient records, relative to their repairs; and the labours of our gloſſographers. From theſe I ſhall endeavour to illuſtrate them.

To begin then from without:—The firſt member of an ancient caſtle was the barbican. (a) The etymology of this word, as explained by diverſe authors, is given in the notes below; and

(a) BARBICAN, barbacane, antemurale, ſpecula, turris ſpeculatoria, propugnaculi genus. *Vox Arabicæ originis.* Spelman autem ab A. S. Buigekenning (i.e.) urbs ſeu propugnaculi ſpecula deflectit *Junius Annon.* Burgh-beacon. Urbis ſpecula prœtenturis idonea. *Skinner.* Barbacana propugnaculum exterius, quo oppidum aut caſtrum; præſertim vero eorum portæ aut muri muniuntur. *Du Cange.* The caſtle, it ſeems, for the more ſecurity was forefenced with a barbican, or barbacan; which exotic word Sir Henry Spelman thus interprets: A barbacan is a fort or hold; a munition placed in the front of a caſtle, or an outwork; alſo a hole in the wall of a city or caſtle, through which arrows and darts were caſt out; alſo a watch tower; it is an Arabic word. So he. Minſhew thus: A barbican (ſaith he) or outnook in a wall, with holes to ſhoot out at the enemy: ſome take it for a centinel-houſe or ſcout-houſe. Chaucer uſeth the word barbican for a watch-tower, of the Saxon ber-ic-ken, i. e. I ken, or ſee, the borough: had he ſaid burgh-be-can, he had gone pretty nigh; for thence I would derive it, were I not convinced of its Arabic original. *Somner's Canterbury, page* 20.

although

although in this they fomewhat differ, yet all agree that it was a watch-tower, for the purpofe of defcrying an enemy at a greater diftance. It feems to have had no pofitive place, except that it was always an outwork, and frequently advanced beyond the ditch; to which it was then joined by a draw-bridge, (b) and formed the entrance into the caftle. Barbicans are mentioned in Framlingham and Canterbury caftles. For the repairing of this work, a tax, called barbacanage, (c) was levied on certain lands.

THE work next in order was the ditch (d), moat, graff, or fofs; for by all thefe different names it was called. This was either wet or dry, according to the circumftances of the fituation; though, when it could be had, our anceftors generally chofe the former: but they do not feem to have had any particular rule for either its depth or breadth. When it was dry, there were fometimes fubterranean paffages, through which the cavalry could fally. Ditches of royal caftles were cleanfed at the public expence; or that perhaps of the tenants of the lands adjoining, by an impofition, or tax; as appears from feveral charters in the Monafticon, whereby the monks are exempted from that charge. This ditch was fometimes called the ditch del bayle, or of the ballium; a diftinction from the ditches of the interior works. Over it was either a ftanding, or draw-bridge, leading to the ballium. Within the ditch were the walls of the ballium, or outworks. In towns, the appellation of ballium (e) was given to any work

(b) BARBICANUM, a watch-tower, bulwark, or breaft-work. Mandatum eft Johanni de Kitmyngton, cuftodi caftri regis, & honori de Pickering, quoddam barbacanum ante portam caftri regis prædicti muro lapideo, & in eodem barbicano quondam portam cum ponte verfatili, &c. De novo facere, &c. T. rege 10 Auguft. clauf. 17th Edw. II. m. 39. *Blount's Law Dictionary.*

(c) BARBICANAGE (barbicanagium), money given to the maintenance of a barbican, or watch-tower; carta 17 Edward III. m. 6. n. 14. *Blount.*

(d) MOTE, or moat, generally means a ditch, as in this place; yet it fometimes fignifies a caftle, on the fite of fome antient fortrefs. Mota de Windfor is ufed for Windfor caftle, in the agreement between King Stephen, and Henry duke of Normandy.

(e) DANS la fuite on fit une efpece de fortification a quelque diftance de la ville a la tete des Faux Bourgs, de la quelle, Froiffart fait très-fouvent mention, & qu'il apelle du nom de Bailles. Ce mot vient de battaglia mot Latin de la baffe Latinité qui fignifie une fortification, un retranchement ou l'onbattailloit. C'étoit la en effet que les partis ennemis qui couroient la campagne, venorent

 quelque

work fenced with pallisades, and sometimes masonry, covering the suburbs; but in castles was the space immediately within the outer wall. When there was a double enceinte of walls, the areas next each wall were stiled the outer and inner ballia. The manner in which these are mentioned below, (f) in the siege of Bedford Castle, sufficiently justify this position, which receives farther confirmation, from the enumeration of the lands belonging to Colchester Castle; wherein are specified, "The upper bayley, in which the castle stands, and the nether bayley, &c."

THE wall of the ballium in castles was commonly high, flanked with towers; and had a parapet, embattled, crenellated, or garretted: for the mounting of it, there were flights of steps at convenient distances, and the parapet often had the merlons pierced with long chinks, ending in round holes, called oillets.

FATHER DANIEL mentions a work, called a bray, (g) which he thinks somewhat similar to the ballium.

WITHIN

quelquefois fair le coup de lance avec ceux de la garnison. C'étoit par là que l'on commencoit l'attaque d'une ville.

SI se retrahit l'ost, dit Froissart en parlant de l'attaque que le comte de Hainaut fit a la ville de St. Amand en Flandre si tôt qu'l fut venu & sa campagnie á lassaut, qui fut moult grand & dur & conquirent de premiere venue les bailles & vindrent jusqu' á la porte qui ouvre devers Mortagne. Ce retranchement étoit quelquefois de bois ou de palissades, quelquefois il étoit de maconnerie. C'étoit un post avancé ou l'on faisoit la garde, pour empêcher la surprise de la place par les portes. . . . Je ne scai si ces bailles étoient differentes d'un espece de fortification que nos anciens auteurs appelloient du nom de barbacane. Les murailles ausi hautes que solides, dit le Moine d'Auxerre sous l'an 1201, outre les avant-murs qu'ils appellent barbacannes, furent renversées. Or les bailles quand elles étoient faites de maconnerie; étoient des especes d'avant-murs. Ainsi il y a de lapparence que cetoit la meme chose. *Pere Daniel. Hist. de la Milice Francoise*, tom. I. p. 604.

(f) BALLIUM, propugnaculi species, *Du Cange*. Et coururent plusieurs fois jusques a la baille, & la mirent en feu. *Chronicon Flandr. cap.* 113. La feirent l'un á lautre moult grant honneur, & mangerent seant sur les bailles ensemble. *Ibidem.*—The castle was taken by four assaults: in the first was taken the barbican, in the second, the outer ballia; at the third attack the wall by the old tower was thrown down by the miners, where, with great danger, they possessed themselves of the inner ballia, through a chink; at the fourth assault, the miners set fire to the tower, so that the smoke burst out, and the tower itself was cloven to that degree, as to shew visibly some broad chinks; whereupon the enemy surrendered. *Camden's Britannia. Bedford.*

(g) LES braies paroissent avoir eté encore une fortification comme les bailles, & la barbacane. Quelques auteurs l'apellent en Latin brachiale. Les braies étoient donc, ce me semble, une espece d'avant-mur elevé devant la porte; ou peut etre une saillie de tour, & apparement de la est venu le nom de fausse-braie dans les fortifications modernes, qui est comme l'avant-mur du bastion qu' elle entoure. *P. Daniel, tom.* 1. p. 604. Herse, est un grillage compose de plusieurs piéces de bois

qu'on

WITHIN the ballium were the lodgings and barracks for the garriſon and artificers, wells, chapels, and even ſometimes a monaſtery. Large mounts were alſo often thrown up in this place: theſe ſerved, like modern cavaliers, to command the adjacent country.

THE entrance into the ballium was commonly through a ſtrong machicolated and embattled gate, between two towers, ſecured by a herſe, or portcullis. Over this gate were rooms, originally intended for the porter of the caſtle: the towers ſerved for the corps de garde.

ON an eminence, in the center, commonly (h), though not always, ſtood the keep (i), or dungeon (k); ſometimes, as in the relation of the ſiege of Bedford Caſtle, emphatically called the tower; it was the citadel, or laſt retreat of the garriſon, often ſurrounded by a ditch, with a draw-bridge, and machicolated gate (l); and occaſionally with an outer wall, garniſhed with ſmall towers. In large caſtles it was generally a high ſquare tower, of four or five ſtories, having turrets at each angle: in theſe turrets were the ſtair-caſes: and frequently, as in Dover and Rocheſter Caſtles, a well. If, inſtead of a ſquare, the keep

qu'on met au deſſus de la porte d'une fortreſſe en dedans & qu'on ſuſpend avec une ou pluſieurs cordes, qui tiennent á un moulinent pour len laiſſer tomber ſur le paſſage & boucher, l'entree d'une porte, en cas de ſurpriſe. *Dict. d'Ingenieur.* The ſame as portcullis; which is ſo called from porta clauſa, or port-cloſe, a ſort of machine like a harrow.

(h) THE keeps at Portcheſter, Cambridge, and Oxford Caſtles, were in the exterior walls.

(i) THE keep, or (as the Frenchmen term a ſtrong tower or platform, as this is, in the middle of a caſtle or fort, wherein the beſieged make their laſt efforts of defence, when the reſt is forced) dungeon. *Somner's Roman Forts, page* 93.

(k) Cotgrove gives, verbatim, the ſame explanation of dungeon. Donjon. En fortification, eſt une reduit dans une place ou dans une citadelle, ou l'on ſe retire quelque fois pour capituler, *Dictionaire portatif de l' Ingenieur.* Dunjo. Caſtellullum, minus propugnaculum, in duno ſeu colle edificatum, unde nomen donjon. *Du Cange.*

(l) MACHECOLLARE vel machecoulare (from the French máchecoulis, to make a warlike device; eſpecially over the gate of a caſtle) reſembling a grate, through which ſcalding water, or offenſive things, may be thrown upon pioneers or aſſailants. 1 *Inſt..ſol.* 5, 8. *Blount's Law Dictionary.* Machlcolations over gates are ſmall projections, ſupported by brackets, having open intervals at the bottom, through which melted lead and ſtones were thrown down on the heads of the aſſailants; and likewiſe large weights faſtened to ropes or chains, by which after they had taken effect, they were retracted by the beſieged. *See a plan and ſection in the plate.*

or

or dungeon happened to be round, it was called a Julliet (m) from a vulgar opinion, that large round towers were built by Julius Cæſar.

THE walls of this edifice were always of an extraordinary thickneſs; which has enabled them to outlive the other buildings, and to withſtand the united injuries of time and weather: the keeps, or dungeons, being almoſt the only part now remaining of our ancient caſtles.

HERE, commonly on the ſecond ſtory, were the ſtate rooms for the governor, if that title may be given to ſuch gloomy cells; whoſe darkſome appearance induced Mr. Borlaſe to form a conjecture, more ingenious than well grounded; namely, that theſe buildings were ſtiled dungeons, from their want of light; becauſe the builders, to ſtrengthen their ramparts, denied themſelves the pleaſure of windows: not but moſt of them had ſmall chinks, which anſwered the double purpoſe of admitting the light, and ſerved for embraſures, from whence they might ſhoot with long and croſs bows: theſe chinks, though without they have ſome breadth, and carry the appearance of windows, are very narrow next the chambers, diminiſhing conſiderably inward. Some of the ſmaller keeps had not even theſe conveniences, but were ſolely lighted by a ſmall perforation in the top, or ſkylight, called courts. It was from this ſort, Mr. Borlaſe formed his ſuppoſition.

THE different ſtories were frequently vaulted, and divided by ſtrong arches; ſometimes indeed they were only ſeparated by joiſts: on the top was generally a platform, with an embattled parapet, from whence the garriſon could ſee and command the exterior works.

THE total change of the art of war, brought about by the invention of gunpowder and artillery, the more ſettled ſtate of the nation, Scotland becoming part of the dominions of the kings of England, the reſpectable footing of our navy, whoſe wooden

(m) ANTIQ. Diſcourſes, page 187.

walls

walls ſecure us from invaſions, and the abolition of the feudal ſyſtem, all conſpired to render caſtles of little uſe or conſequence, as fortreſſes: ſo the great improvements in arts and ſciences, and their conſtant attendant, the encreaſe of luxury, made our nobility and gentry build themſelves more pleaſant and airy dwellings; relinquiſhing theſe ancient, dreary manſions of their forefathers, where the enjoyment of light and air was ſacrificed to the conſideration of ſtrength; and whoſe beſt rooms, according to our modern refined notions, have more the appearance of gaols and dungeons for priſoners, than apartments for the reception of a rich and powerful baron.

HOWEVER, in the reign of Charles I. a little before the breaking out of the civil war, ſome enquiry into the ſtate of theſe buildings ſeems to have taken place; for, on the 22d of January, 1636 (n), a commiſſion was iſſued, appointing Lieutenant Colonel Francis Coningſby, commiſſary-general of and for all the caſtles and fortifications in England and Wales, with an allowance of 13s. 4d. a day to be paid out of the cheques and defalcations that ſhould be made by him from time to time; or, in default thereof, out of the treaſury. Whether this office was really inſtituted for the purpoſe of ſcrutinizing into the ſtate of theſe fortreſſes, as foreſeeing the events which afterwards happened; or whether it was only formed to gratify ſome favourite, does not appear. During the troubles of that reign, ſome ancient caſtles were garriſoned and defended; ſeveral of which were afterwards deſtroyed, by order of the parliament: ſince that period, they have been abandoned to the mercy of time, weather, and the more unſparing hands of avaricious men. The laſt have proved the moſt deſtructive; many of theſe monuments of ancient magnificence having been by them torn down, for the ſake of the materials; by which the country has been deprived of thoſe remains of antiquity, ſo eſſential, in the eyes of foreigners,

(n) ACTA Regia.

to the dignity of a nation; and which, if rightly confidered, tended to infpire the beholder with a love for the now happy eftablifhment; by leading him to compare the prefent with thofe times when fuch buildings were erected, times when this unhappy kingdom was torn by inteftine wars; when the fon was armed againft the father, and brother flaughtered brother; when the lives, honour, and properties of the wretched inhabitants depended on the nod of an arbitrary king, or were fubject to the more tyrannical and capricious wills of lawlefs and foreign barons.

THE method of attack and defence of fortified places, practifed by our anceftors, before, and even fome time after the invention of gunpowder; (o) was much after the manner of the Romans; moft of the fame machines being made ufe of, though fome of them under different names.

THEY had their engines for throwing ftones and darts, of different weights and fizes; the greater anfwering to our battering cannon and mortars; the fmaller, to our field-pieces. Thefe were diftinguifhed by the appellations of balifta, catapulta, efpringals, terbuchets, mangonas, mangonels, bricolles, the petrary, the matafunda and the warwolf. Father Daniel alfo mentions a machine, called engine-a-verge, ufed by the Englifh, in France, as late as the reign of Charles VII. but acknowledges, he did not know what fort of machine it was.

FOR approaching the walls, they had their moveable towers; by which the befiegers were not only covered, but their height, commanding the ramparts, enabled them to fee the garrifon, who were otherwife hid by the parapet: for paffing the ditch, the cattus and fow, machines anfwering to the pluteus and vinea, or teftudo and mufculus, of the Romans: the ram was fometimes, but not commonly, ufed.

(o) MANGONELS were ufed fifty years after the invention of cannon. *P. Daniel Hiftoire de la Milice Francois, p.* 562, & *ibid.* 563. Indeed, the art of war was pretty fimilar all over Europe, at leaft after the firft crufade: where fo many generals meeting, each undoubtedly adopted what he faw excellent in any of the confederated nations.

Mines too were frequently practiſed. Theſe were either ſubterraneous paſſages into ſome unfrequented part of the fortreſs; or elſe made with an intent, as at preſent, to throw down the wall. Countermines were alſo in uſe, and the engineers of thoſe days were not unacquainted with artificial fireworks.

Few of theſe machines, except the baliſta and catapulta, are ſo deſcribed as to give any tolerable idea of their conſtruction; concerning even them, authors conſiderably differ: for the remainder, of ſome we have only the name and uſe, and of others, barely the name; probably owing to moſt of the hiſtorians of thoſe times being monks, who knew them only by hearſay; or from an account of their effects: nevertheleſs, in order to obtain ſuch knowledge of them as theſe ſcanty materials will furniſh, it will be neceſſary to collect what thoſe writers relate concerning them, tending to elucidate either their form, uſe or powers.

Of baliſtas and catapultas writers deſcribe various ſorts, and frequently confound thoſe two machines together. Indeed, though the baliſta moſtly threw darts, it was ſometimes uſed for caſting ſtones, (p) as was alſo the catapulta, (q) which, from its name, ſhould ſeem to be appropriated for darts. Theſe have been deſcribed by Vitruvius, Ammianus Marcellinus, Iſidorus, Lipſius, Follard, Perrault and others; and from all their accounts, it is evident, that the force or moving power, depended on the elaſticity of twiſted cords, made with women's hair, that of horſes, or the bowels of animals; (r) the thicker this cordage, the greater was the force of the engine.

Another

(p) Balistam verbere nervorum torqueri, magnâ vi jacere aut haſtas aut ſaxa. *Iſidorus.*

(q) Catapulta, ſignifying a dart. Accidit interea commiſſo contra Anglo prælio per regem præfatum, eundem ſagitta ferrea & hamata, quæ vulgo catapulta dici ſolet lethaliter vulnerari. *Vita S. Monani to 1 S S, Martin, p. 88.* Plautus uſus eſt etiam pro telo; alii pro baliſta. *Du Cange.*

(r) Vegetius ſays, Onager, autem dirigit lapides, ſed pro nervorum craſſitudine, & magnitudine ſaxorum, pondera jaculatur; nam quanto amplior fuerit, tanto majora ſaxa fulminis more contorquet. On this principle the catapulta M was conſtructed. The cords, like a ſkein of thread, were wound evenly over the iron pieces, croſſing the two holes, D and E, called capitals, till they were full. In the center of theſe cords, the arm of the catapulta W is fixed, having a cavity, or ſpoon at its extremity, for holding ſtones, which were encloſed in a ſmall baſket. The cords were then twiſted, by means of the wheels and pinions marked X; the arm which before ſtood perpendicular, was now brought down to the poſition repreſented, and kept faſt by a catch; the ſtones were then put into the ſpoon,

and

Another kind, ſometimes alſo called oniger, or ſcorpio, acted by the fall of a great weight, fixed to the ſhorteſt arm of a ſuſpended lever; this raiſing the other arm, to which a ſling was fixed, threw a ſtone with great velocity. A repreſentation of this is given in the plate, marked O.

From an ancient record it appears that one Edmund Willoughby, (s) held lands in England, by the ſervice of finding a catapulta every year; but it is doubtful whether by this is meant the engine here treated of, or only a ſling which was ſometimes called by that name.

The bricolle, (t) petrary, (u) mangana and mangonel, (v) matafunda, (w) tirbuchet and warwolf, (x) were all engines for throwing

and the arm being ſuddenly let go, ſtruck againſt the upright piece Z, and projected the contents of the ſpoon with amazing force. When a dart was uſed, the contrivance K was annexed.——The baliſta depended on the ſame principles: its form was more that of a croſs-bow. It is delineated in the plate: ſee N.——Mr. Follard conſtructed a catapulta, according to this model; which, though only ten inches long, and thirteen broad, threw a leaden ball of a pound weight, 230 French toiſes, or fathoms; and ſhot ten darts the diſtance of one hundred paces.

(s) Catapulta, a warlike engine to ſhoot darts; a ſling. Edmundus Willoughby tenet unum meſſuagium & ſex bovatas terræ in Carleton, ut de maniero de Shelford, per ſervicium unius catapultæ per annum pro omino ſervicio. Lib. Schedul. de term. Mich. 14. Hen. IV. Not. fol. 210. *Blount's Law Dictionary.*

(t) Pour ce jour ils ne menſtrerent autre defenſe que de bricolles, qui geſtoient gros carreaux. *Froiſſart, 4th vol. c. 18.*——Baliſtam majores dixere priſci trabem validam, ita libratam, ut cum pars denſior ponderibus, attracta deſcenderet, elevata proceritas ſua funiculis, quos haberet alligatos, funda ſaxum maximi ponderis longe emitteret. Eique maxime nunc machinæ bricholllæ eſt appellatio. Blondius, lib. 3. *Roma Triumphant.*——Trabuchi, machinæ litholbolæ (ejuſdem fere generis ſunt & bricolæ vocatæ) quibus avorum noſtrorum memoria vaſti molares in hoſtes jaculabantur. *Hieronymus Magius, lib. 1. Miſcell. c. 1.*——Bricole is a term uſed in tennis, and ſignifies a rebound.

(u) Petrariæ Gall. Pierieres. Tormentum quod vulgo dicitur petraria, vel mangonum. *Ugutio.*—Machinas jaculatorias quas mangana vel petrarias vocant. *Willelm. Tyrius, lib. 8. cap. 6.*

(v) Alii vero minoribus tormenti, quæ mangana vocantur minores immitando lapides. *Will. Tyrius, lib. 8. cap. 6.* Mangonellus diminutivum, a mangana hoc eſt, minor machina jaculatoria. *Du Cange.*—Interia groſſor petraria, mittit ab intus aſſidue lapides, mangonelluſque minores. *Will. Britto. 7 Philip.* De Mezeray, in his Treatiſe on Ancient Sieges, ſays, the greateſt range of a mangonel did not exceed five ſtadia, each ſtadia conſiſting of 125 geometrical paces of five feet, making in the whole 1041 yards and 2 feet. He ſuppoſes mangona to be a generical word for an engine uſed for throwing ſtones or darts.

(w) Matafunda. Machina bellica, qua lapides in hoſtes ejaculabantur. *Du Cange.*—Jaciebant ſi quidem hoſtes ſuper noſtros creberrimos lapides cum duobus trabuchetis, mangonello & pluribus matafundi. *Monachus Valis Sarnai in Hiſt. Albigenſ, c. 86.*—Some derive its name from funda & mactare, ſometimes written matare; i. e. a murdering ſling.

(x) Trebuchetum, trabuchetum. Catapultæ ſpecies, ſeu machina grandior ad projiciendos lapides, & concutiendos urbium obſeſſarum muros. *Du Cange.*——Per ſeptem trebucheta ordinata, quæ

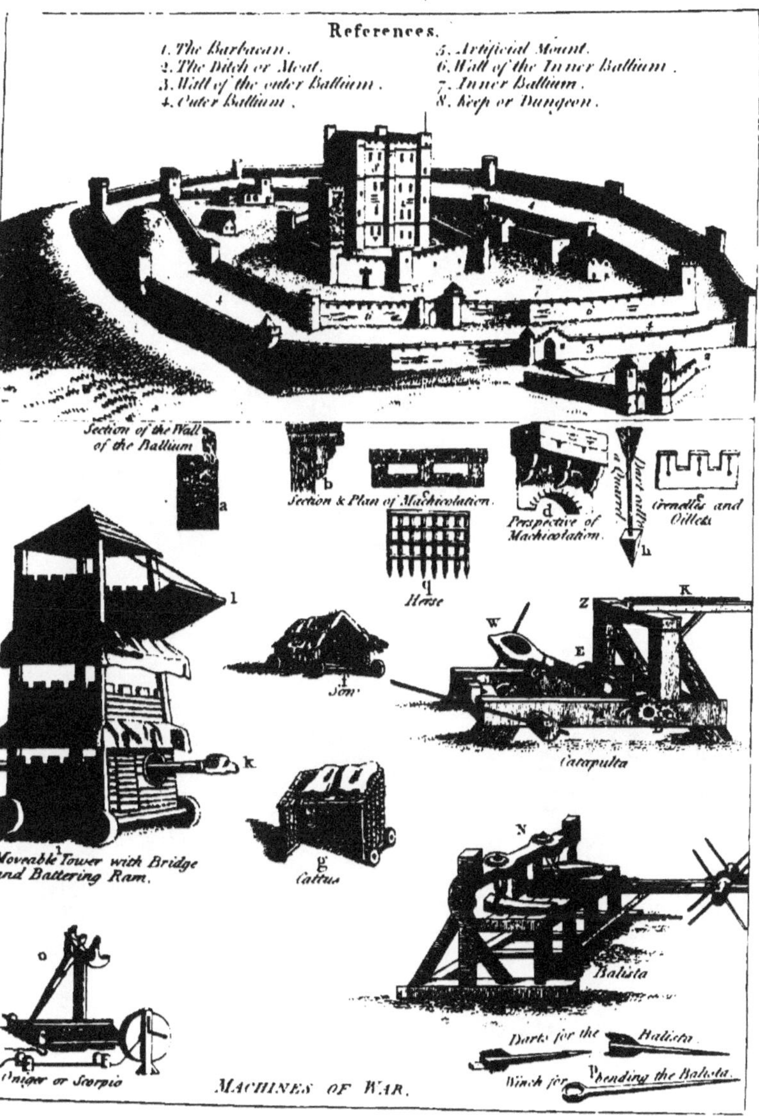

MACHINES OF WAR.

throwing ſtones, and other great maſſes, and probably of the ſame mechaniſm, but differently called, according to the magnitude of the weights they projected, as was the caſe in our ancient artillery, where, according to their caliber, the pieces were ſtiled, cannon, demicannon, culverin, ſaker, robinet, falcon and baſe. The eſpringal (y) threw large darts, called muchettæ, ſometimes, inſtead of feathers, winged with braſs.

Of the vaſt force of theſe machines, (z) ſurpriſing ſtories are related. No wall, however thick, was able to reſiſt their ſtroke; and in the field, they ſwept away the deepeſt files of armed men. With them were thrown not only large millſtones, but ſometimes the carcaſes of dead horſes, and even living men. The former, according to Froiſſart, (a) was practiſed by John duke of Nor-

quæ tam de die, quam de nocte, in caſtrum capacii projicere non ceſſabant. *Matt. Paris, an.* 1246. ——D'un trabukiet fit trabukier, mult grant partie de lor murs. *Philippus Mouſbes in Phil. Auguſto.* ——Otto imp. ab Apulia & Italia reverſus obſedit oppidum Viſenſe, quod ſimiliter expugnavit uſque ad arcam.——Ibi tunc primam cæſſit haberi uſus inſtrumenti bellici quod vulgo tribock appellari ſolet. *Fragmentum Hiſt. poſt. Albert. Argentim. an.* 1212.——Withouten ſtroke it mote be take of trepeget, or mangonell. *Chaucer Roman. of the Roſe*, 6278.——This machine took its name from the word trebuchare, to throw down, according to the Latin of thoſe times; or from trabucher, to outweigh, as its manner of working might be by means of great weights.

The warwolf is thus mentioned from Mat. Weſtm. by Camden, in his Remains, ſpeaking of king Edward the firſt: "At the ſiege of Stivelen, where he, with another engine, named the warwolfe, pierced with one ſtone, and cut as even as a thread, two vauntmures; as he did before at the ſiege of Brehin, where Thomas Maule, the Scotſman, ſcoffed at the Engliſh artillerie, with wiping the walle with his handkerchief, until both he and the walle were wiped away with a ſhot." Again, in his Britannia, relating the ſiege of Bedford: "Concerning theſe mangonels, petraries, trabucces, bricoles, eſpringolds, and what our anceſtors called the warwolf, out of which, before the invention of bombs, they threw great ſtones, with ſo much force as to break open ſtrong gates; concerning theſe (I ſay) I have ſeveral things to add, if they were not foreign to my purpoſe."——Juſſit rex arietem fabricari, quem Greci Nicontam vocant, quaſi vincentem omnia, & lupum belli. Verum aries indecens & incompoſitus parum aut nihil profuit: lupus autem belli, minus ſumptuoſus incluſis plus nocuit. *Matt. Weſtminſter, ann.* 1304.

(y) Espringal baliſta validior que telum emittitur. *Du Cange.*——Muſchetta telum quod baliſta validiori emittitur. *Du Cange.*—Poteſt preterea fieri quod hæc eadem baliſtæ tela poſſent trahere quæ muſchettæ vulgaritur appellantur. *Apud Senatum, lib.* 2. *part* 4. *c.* 22——Et font getter leur ſpringales.

Ca' & la ſonnent li clarain
Li garrot empené d'arain. *Guiart l'an.* 1304.

(z) Compositis autem ab ingenioſis piſanorum artificibus manganis, gattio atque lignus caſtellis, urbem fortitur expugnabant; et cum his machinis urbis mœnia & mœnium turres potentiſſimæ rumpebant.

(a) Froissart vol. 1. chap. 50.

mandy, ſon of King Philip de Valois, when he beſieged the count de Hainault, in Thyn-Leveque, in the Low Countries, and whom he thereby obliged to capitulate, on account of the infection cauſed in the town; and as Camden ſays, (b) it was alſo done by the Turks at Negroponte.

THE other, namely throwing a living man, is alſo mentioned by Froiſſart.(c) It happened at the ſiege of Auberoche, in Gaſcoigne; where the Engliſh, being cloſely preſſed by the count de Laille, lieutenant general to Philip de Valois, they ſent out an eſquire, with a letter, which he was to endeavour to deliver to the earl of Derby, their general; but, being taken, his letter was read, and afterwards tied round his neck; and he, being put into an engine, was thrown back into the caſtle, where he fell dead among his companions.

THEY were alſo ſometimes uſed for the execution of perſons condemned to die: (d) perhaps ſomewhat like the method practiſed in the Eaſt Indies; where military criminals are tied faſt to, and fired from the mouth of a cannon: though, in the caſe mentioned by the note here alluded to, probably the unhappy ſufferer was only fixed to this machine, in order to be more conveniently tortured.

MOVEABLE towers are repeatedly mentioned, (e) as much in uſe, particularly by the Engliſh. Froiſſart is very circumſtantial in his account of one, (f) uſed at the ſiege of Reole, by the earl of Derby; who having laid before that place nine weeks, cauſed two towers, three ſtories high, to be built with large beams. Each tower was placed on four ſmall wheels, or trucks, and towards the town covered with boiled leather, to guard it from fire, and to reſiſt the darts: on every ſtory were placed an hundred

(b) CAMDEN's Remains. *Vide Artillery.*

(c) FROISSART, vol. 1. chap. 107.

(d) PRIMITUS eum ligaverat, proh dolor, ad machinam inſtructam, quam vulgo mangonam appellant. *In Paſſione. S. Thyomonis Archiepiſcopi Juvenenſis.*

(e) VIDE Pere Daniel Hiſt. Milice, Fr. tom. 1. p. 558.

(f) FROISSART vol. 1. chap. 18, 19.

archers.

archers. Theſe towers were puſhed, by the force of men, to the city wall; the ditch having been filled up, whilſt they were building. From theſe the ſoldiers, placed in the different ſtages, made ſuch vigorous diſcharges, that none of the garriſon, except ſuch as were extremely well armed, or covered with large ſhields, dared to ſhew themſelves on the rampart. He likewiſe mentions another of theſe machines, (g) with which the Engliſh, (h) under John de Holland, and Thomas de Percy, took the town of Ribadana, in Gallicia; and ſo terrified the garriſon of Maures, (i) that

(g) ENVIRON quatre jours aprés ce que meſſire Jehan de Hollande et meſſire Thomas de Percy furent venuz en loſt du mareſchal eurent chevaliers et eſcuyers et toutes géns ordonné ung grant appairellement d'eſſault & eurent fait faire ouvrer & charpenter ung grant engin de boys ſans roes que on pouvoit bien mener & bouter a force de gens la ou on vouloit & dedans pouvoit bien aſéement cent chevaliers et cent archers, mais par aſſault archiers y entrerent. Et avoit on remply aux foſſez a l' endroit ou l' engin devoit eſtre mené. Lors commenca l' aſſault et approcherent les engins a force de boutemens ſur roes et lá eſtoient archiers bien pourveauz de Saiettes qui tiroient a ceulx de dedans de grant facon, et ceux de dedans gettoient a eux dardes de telle maniere qui c'eſtoit grant merveille. Deſſoubz avoit manteaulx couvers de fors cuirs de beufz & de vaches pour le geſt des pierres & pour le traiſt des dardes. Et deſſoubz ces manteaulx a la couverture ſe tenoient gens d'arms qui approchient le mur, leſquelz eſtoient bien paveſchez et picquoient de piez, et de hoyaulx au mur, et tant firent quilz empirerent grandement le mur, car les defendans ny pouvoient entendre pour les archiers qui vivement tyroient et qui fort les enſoignoient. La fiſt on reverſer ung pang du mur et cheoir es foſſez. Quand les galiciens qui dedans eſtoient virent le grant meſchief ſi furent tous eſbahiz et crierent tout hault, nous nous rendons, nous nous rendons, mais nul ne leur reſpondit, et avoient les Anglois bon ris de ce quilz veoient & diſoient. Ces villains nons ont battuz et fait moult de paine et encores ſe mocquent ils de nous quant ilz veulent que nous les recuillons a mercy et ſi eſt la ville noſtre. Nenny reſponderent aucuns des Angloys, nous ne ſcavons parler Eſpaignol, parlez bon Francois ou Anglois ſi vous voulez que nous vous entendons. Et toujours alloient ilz et paſſoient avant et chaſſoient ces villains qui fuyoient devant eulx et les occioient a monceaulx, et ye eut ce jour mors que dungs et dautres parmy les Juifz dons il y avoit aſſez pluz de xv cens. Ainſi fut la ville de Ribadane gagnée a force. Et y eurent ceulx qui premier y entrerent grant pillage, et par eſpecial ils trovverent plus d'or et dargent es maiſons des Juifz que autre part. *Vol.* 3. *feu*. 12.

(h) TEMP. Richard II.

(i) OR ſe deſlogerent de ribadane & cheminerent vers la ville de maures en galici & faiſoient mener par membres le grant engin quilz avoient fait charpenter aprés eux, car ilz veorent bien que ceſtoit ung grant eſpouentail de gens et des villes. Quant ceulx de maures entendirent que les Anglois venoient vers eulx pour avoir leur ville en obeyſance & que ribadane avoit eſté prinſe a force & les gens mors dedans et faiſoient les Anglois amenas après eulx ung dyable dengin ſi grant & ſi merveilleux que on ne le pouoit deſtruire. Si ſe doubterent grandement de loſt et de ce grand engin. Et ſe trayrent en conſeil pour ſavoir comment ilz ſe maintiendroient, ou ſi ilz ſe defendroient. Eux conſeillez ilz ne pouvoient veoir que le rendre ne leur vaulſiſt mieulx aſſez que ſe deffendre, car ſe ils eſtoient prins par force ilz perdroient corps & avoir: et au deffendre, il ne leur apparoiſſoit conforte de nul coſté. Regardez diſoient les ſaiges comment, il eſt prins de leur defenſe á ceulx de ribadane, qui eſtoient bien auſſi fors ou plus que nous ſommes. Ilz ont eu le ſiege prés d'un mois & ne les a nulz renfortes ni ſecourus. Le roy de caſtille, a ce que nous entendons comte pour ceſte ſaiſon tout ſe pays de galice, a perdu

that they did not wait to be ſummoned, but ſent a deputation to offer their ſubmiſſion: ſee the account, in his own words. Here it appears, that whilſt the archers in the tower, by their aſſaults, employed the attention of the garriſon on the ramparts, the armed men, with pickaxes and other inſtruments, deſtroyed the wall. Theſe towers had alſo ſometimes bridges from the upper ſtories; which, being let down upon the parapet, made a paſſage into the town. When the ram was in uſe, it frequently was placed in the ground-floor of this machine; where the men worked it, under the cover and protection of the archers and croſs-bow men above them.

THE cattus, (k) cathouſe, or gattus, was a covered ſhed, occaſionally fixed on wheels, and ſimilar to the vinea and pluteus of the ancients. Under it the beſiegers filled up and paſſed the

a perdu juſque a la riviere de dorne, ne vous verrez ia de ceſte aneé entrer francoys. Si nous rendons donc debonnairement ſans dommage, & ſans riote en la forme & maniere, que les autres villes ont fait c'eſt bon dirent ilz. Tous furent de ceſte opinion, et comment ferons nous dirent aucuns, en nom de Dieu dirent les plus ſages nous irons ſur le chemin, a l' encontre deux et ſi porterons les clefs de la ville avecques nous etl es leur preſenterons, car Anglois ſont courtoiſes gens. Ilz ne nous feront nul mal, mas ilz nous recueilleront douleement, & nous en ſcauront trop grant gré. A ce propos ſe tindrent tous. Adonc iſſirent hors cinquante hommes de la ville deſſus nommée, tous de plus nobtables de la ville, ſi toſt quilz ſceurent que les Anglois approchoient, et ſe mirent ſur le chemin entre la ville et les Anglois, et portoient les clefs de la ville avecques eulx. Et la ainſi comme au quarte dunelieue ils attendirent, les Anglois qui approchoient. *Vol.* 3, *fol.* 13.

(k) VINEAS dixerunt veteres, quos nunc militari barbaricoque uſu cattos vocant. *Vegetius, lib.* 4, *cap.* 15.——Catti ergo ſunt vineæ, ſive plutes, ſub quibus miles in morem felis: quam cattum vulgo dicimus, in ſubſeſſis aut inſidiis latet. *Du Cange.*——Hic faciunt reptare catum, tectique ſub illo ſuffodiunt murum. *Willielmus Brito, lib.* 7, *Phillipid.*

Devant boves fu l'oſt de France,
Qui contre les flamans contance;
Li mineur pas ne ſoumeillent,
Un chat bon et fort appareillent;
Tant euvrent deſſous & tant cavent,
Qu' une grant part du mur diſtravent. *Guillelmus Guiart in Phillippo Auguſto.*

Interim rem in deſperato ponentes Leodini, quoddam inſtrumentum ligneum ex trabibus immenſae magnitudinis conſtruentes, quod cattum nuncupant, ſubſtratis artificioſe rotis ligneis ad diruendos muros, trajecti & oppidi wick minare caeperunt. *Zantfliet in Chronico apud Marten, to* 5 *col.* 389. Gatus, quippe viam per medium foſſatum faciens jam antea prope murum ipſius caſtri præceſſerat; in ipſo enim gato quædam trabs ferrata, quam bercellum appellabant, conſtabat, quam ipſi, qui infra ipſum gatum fuerant foras plus de viginti brachiis projicientes, in murum ipſius caſtri mirabiliter feriebant, ac tandem tantum jam ferierant, quod de ipſo muro plus de viginti brachiis in terram projecerant. *Murator, to* 6 *col.* 1041.

ditch,

ditch, ſapped or mined the wall, and ſometimes worked a kind of ram. It is probable, this machine, in different countries, might vary a little in its ſize and form; but its eſſential properties and uſes were the ſame. Some of theſe catts were crenellated, that is, had crenelles and chinks, from whence the archers and croſs-bow men might ſhoot their arrows and quarrells, theſe were then called, chatz-chaſtillez or caſtellated catts, and are mentioned in Joinville's Hiſtory of St. Louis. Sometimes theſe were made with a ſalient angle, by which the arrows and ſtones thrown againſt them, ſtriking obliquely, glanced off, or had leſs effect.

The ſow was alſo a covered machine for the ſame purpoſe, (l) and of much the ſame conſtruction, but probably leſs. It was called, in Latin, ſus, ſcropha and truja; from its being uſed for rooting up the earth, like a ſwine; or becauſe the ſoldiers contained therein, were like pigs under a ſow. This was alluded to by the counteſs, who defended the caſtle of Dunbar againſt Edward III. when ſhe threatened, that unleſs the Engliſhmen kept their ſow better, ſhe would make her caſt her pigs. Camden, who mentions this circumſtance in his remains, ſays, "The ſow is yet uſed in Ireland." Two machines of this kind, one called the boar and the other the ſow, were employed by the parliamentary forces, in the ſiege of Corfe caſtle, in Dorſetſhire.

The ram is ſo well known, (m) that a deſcription of it would be unneceſſary. It was ſometimes, though not frequently, in the later

(l) Sus, machina bellica, quæ & ſcropha, gallis truis. *Du Cange.*——Unum fuit machinamentum, quod noſtri ſuem, veteres vineam vocanti, quod machina levibus lignis colligata, tecto, tabulis, cratibuſque contexto, lateribus crudis coriis communitis, protegit in ſe ſubſidentes, qui quaſi more ſuis ad murorum ſuffodienda penetrant fundamenta. *Willel. Malmſbur. lib.* 4. *Hiſt.*——Dum quidam nobiles, ligneis obumbrati, machinis, quæ, quia verrere videbantur in antra; ſues appellari non videtur inconſonum. *Elmham in viata Hen. V. Reg. Angl. cap.* 59, *p.* 153. Quandam machinam, quæ ſus appellatur, per quam & plures armati defendi, & foſſata tellure repleri poſſent, fabricari fecit. *Ibidem. cap.* 122, *p.* 317.——Machinas ad ſufficiendum murum habiles & neceſſarias quas vulgo ſcrophas appellant. Truja machina bellica. Gallis truie ita dicta, quod humum, ut ſus, ſubvertat. *Du Cange.*

(m) Arietes, vulgo carcamuſas, reſonatos dimeſere duos. *Abbo de Obſid. Paris, lib.* 2.——Dr. Deſagaliers has demonſtrated, in the Annotations on his ſecond Lecture on Experimental Philoſophy, that the momentum of a battering ram, twenty-eight inches in diameter, one hundred and eighty feet long, with a head of caſt iron, of one tun and a half; the whole ram, with its iron hoops,

weighing

later times, uſed. We find it mentioned in the ſiege of Paris, which happened about the year 886: it is there called aries carcamuſus. It alſo occurs in the notes relative to the warwolf and cattus. Father Daniel ſays, (n) the uſe of it was left off in France, long before the invention of cannon. It is however mentioned, in a paſſage of Froiſſart, as employed in the time of Philip de Valois, cotemporary of Edward III. at the attack of St. Amand in Flanders, by the count of Hainault: but this he thinks rather the extemporaneous idea of the engineer, than the application of a machine then in faſhion. It is however certain, the Venetians uſed it at the ſiege of Zara, which happened about the ſame time i. e. anno 1345.

Mines, before the uſe of gunpowder, were, as has been before obſerved, of two ſorts: one, where the aſſailants ſimply dug themſelves a paſſage under the walls of the place beſieged; the other, where a breach was intended. In both caſes, by degrees, as the earth was removed, the top of the gallery, or paſſage of the mine, was ſupported by planks, propped up with ſtrong poſts; and, in the latter, the work being carried under the wall or tower propoſed to be thrown down, theſe props were ſmeared over with pitch, roſin, or other combuſtible matters; and likewiſe faggots of dry underwood thrown looſely about; which being ſet on fire, ſoon conſumed the props; when the incumbent earth, wanting their ſupport, fell in, and overthrew the building. Where the mine was of no great depth, theſe poſts

weighing 41112 pounds, and moved by the united ſtrength of 1000 men, will be only equal to that of a ball thirty-ſix pounds weight ſhot point blank from a cannon.

(n) Pour ce qui eſt du belier, je crois que même longtems avant le canon on ne s'en ſervoit guéres en France, j'en trove cependant un example dans Froiſſart ſous Phillipe de Valois, lorſque le Comte de Hainhault attaqua la petite place de ſaint Amand en Flandres: et donc fut la un, dit cet hiſtorien, qui dit, ſire, en celuy endroit ne les aurions jamais; car la porte eſt forte et la voye etroite. Si couſteroit trop des voſtres a conquerre: mais faites apporter de gros merriens ouvrés en manieres de pilots & heurtes aux murs de l' abbaye, nous vous certifions que de force on les pertuiſera en pluſieurs lieux, & ſe nous ſommes en l'abbaye la ville eſt notre. . . . Donc commanda le comte, qu'on fit ainſi; car pour li mieux on li conſeilloit pour le toſt prendre. Si quiſt grans merriens de cheſne, qui furent tantoit ouvrez & agniſez devant, & s'évertuoient; & puis boutoient de grand randon contre le mur & tant verteuſement, quils pertuiſereut & rompirent le mur de l'abbaye en pluſieurs lieux. *P. Daniel, tom. 1, p.*

might be pulled away with cords, or chains. This kind of mine was uſed by Philip Auguſtus, (o) at the ſiege of the caſtle of Boves, near Amiens, the firſt at which that prince was preſent. Father Daniel ſays, (p) he had always in his ſervice a number of ſkilful miners; mines being one of his moſt ſucceſsful methods of attack practiſed againſt the Engliſh.

THE galleries of theſe mines were both higher and broader than thoſe of the preſent times; being ſo large, as to admit of engagements hand to hand; (q) when the beſieged, by counter-mines,

(o) P. Daniel, tom. 1, page 575.——(p) Ibidem.

(q) AT the ſiege of Melun, by Henry V. King of England, and the Duke of Burgundy, anno 1420, when the mine was pierced almoſt to the walls.——"Les aſſiéges (dit Monſtrelet l. 1. p. 244.) contreminerent á l'oppoſite & les Anglois firent une barriere, ou combattirent le Roi et le Duc contre deux Dauphinois á coup de lances, & vindrent pluſieurs Chevaliers & Ecuyers combattre á la dite mine." Comme ces combattans étoient armés de pied-en-cap, il falloit qui les galeries euſſent au moins ſept pieds de hauteur & autant de largeur pour que deux hommes poſſent y agir de front avec aiſance. Il arrivoit ſouvent qu'on s'ydonnoit des defis, & que l'on convenoit de la maniere du combat. A ce même ſiege de Melun, que Barbaſan defendoit "on met un gros chevron en travers d'une mine & hauteur de la poitrine, & il étoit defendu que nul ne poſſat par deſſus ni, pardeſſous." pluſieurs Compions des deux partis s'y preſenterent ſucceſſivement & combatterent avec l'epee " ou la hache. Quand on faiſoit un Chevalier pendant une ſiege & que l'on travailliot pour miner la muraille de la Ville, le Recipiendaire, au lieu de faire a veille d'armes dans une Chapelle, ſelon la coutume, la faiſoit dans la mine, ou il poſſoit la nuit avec une ancien Chevalier." *De Maizray ſur l'Art des Sieges, p. 229.*——La ſiege tenant devant reims eſtoient ſes ſeigneurs, les contes & les barons, es pays de la marche de reims, ſicomme vous avez oui compter cy deſſus pour mieulx eſtre a leur ayſe et pour garder les chemins que nulles pourveances n'entraſſent en la dicte cité dequoy, ce chevalier meſſire Barthelemy de bonnes a grant barronie d'Angleterre eſtoit a tout ſa charge & ſa route, de gens d'armes & d'archiers, loges a comercy ung moult bel chaſtel qui eſt a l'archeveſque de reims, lequel archeveſque y miſt en garniſon le chevalier deſſus nommé, et auſſi pluſieurs bons compagnions pour le garder et deffendre contre leurs enemys. Ce chaſtel ne doubtoit nul aſſault, car il y avoit une tour carèe mallement groſſe et eſpeſſe de mur et bien garnie d'armes de deffence. Quant meſſire Barthelemy qui le chaſtel avoit aſſiegé l'eut bien advisé et conſideré ſa force, et la maniere que par aſſault, il ne le pourroit avoir il fiſt appareiller une quantité de mineurs quil avoit avec luy & a ſes gages & leur commanda, quilz fiſſent leur devoir de la fortreſſe miner & que bien il les payeroit, leſquelz reſpondirent quils le feroient tres volontiers. Adonc entrerent les ouvriers en leur myne et mineren, continuellement nuit et jour en firent, tant quils vindrent moult avant ſoubz la groſſe tour, et a la meſure quilz minoient ilz eſtanconnoient et nen ſcavoient riens ceulx dedans. Quant ilz furent au deſſus de leur mine tant que pour faire renverſer la tour quant ilz voldroient, ilz vindrent a meſſire Barthelemy de bonnez & ly dirent. Sire nous avons tellement appareiller noſtre ouvrage, que ceſte groſſe tour treſbuchera quand il vous plaira. Or bien reſpondit le chevalier, n'en faictes plus ſans mon commandement, & ceulx dirent volontiers. Adonc monta le dit chevalier, et emmena ichan de guiſtelle avecques luy qui eſtoit de ces compaignons, et ſe vindrent juſques au chatel. Meſſire Barthelemy feiſt ſigne quil vouloit parlementer a ceulx de dedans. Tantoſt meſſire Henry ſe tira avant & ſen vint aulx creneaulx et demanda quil vouloit. Je veuil diſt meſſire Barthelemy, que vous vous rendez

mines, as was then the practice, attempted to drive out the assailants. Mines of this sort remained in use till the reign of Louis XII. Froissart gives a very curious and circumstantial account of one of them.

Of artificial fireworks, used both by the besieged and besiegers, history relates many instances: but what these fireworks were, is not clearly expressed. The historians of the Crusades speak of a composition, called Greek wildfire, used by the Turks. One of these historians, Geoffry de Vinesauf, who accompanied King Richard I. to those wars, says of it, "With a pernicious stench and livid flame it consumes even flint and iron; nor could it be extinguished by water; but by sprinkling sand upon it, the violence of it may be abated; and vinegar poured upon it, will put it out.

Joinville in his history of St. Louis, describes the appearance and effect of this fire, (r) of which he was an eye witness, when

dez ou vous estez tous mors sans remede. Et comment dist le chevalier Francoys qui se print a rire, nous sommes bien pourveus de toutes choses & vous voulez que nous rendons si simplement. Ce ne sera ia dist messire Henry. Certes si vous est ces informez, en quel party vous estes dit le chevalier Anglois, vous vous rendiz tantost a peu de parolles. En quel party sommes nous sire respondit le chevalier Francois. Vous ystrez hors respondit messire Barthelemy, & ic le vous monstreray par condicions et par asseurance. Messire Henry entra en ce traicte & creut le chevalier Anglois, & yssit hors du fort luy iveme tant seulement, et vint la ou messire Barthelemy, et Jehan de Guistelles estoient. Si tost comme ils furent la venuz, ilz le menerent, a leur mine et luy monstrerent, comme la grosse tour ne tenoit plus que sar estancons de boys. Quant le chevalier Francoys veit le peril il dist a messire Barthelemy, certainement vous avez bonne cause ce que fait en avez, vient de grant gentilesse. Si nous rendons a vostre volonté. La les print messire Barthelemy, comme ses prisonniers & lest fist tous hors de la tour partir & ungz & autres & leurs biens aussi. Et puis fist bouter le feu en la myne. Si ardirent les estancons, et puis quant ilz furent tous hors la tour qui estoit mallement grosse ouvrit, et se partit en deux & renversa d'autre part. Or regardez dist messire Barthelemy, a messire Henry de Vaulx, et a celui de la fortresse, si je vous disoye verité. Sire ouy nous demeurzons voz prisonniers a vostre volonté, et vous remercions de vostre courtoysie. Car si Jacques bons homs eussent ainsi de nous, eu laudessus que vous avez or aine ilz, ne nous eussent mye faict la cause pareille, que vous avez. Ainsi furent prins ses compaignons, de la garnison, de commercy, et le ohastel effondie. *Vol.* 1, *fouilliet*, 106.

(r) On croit communement que la poudre a eté trouvé par Berthold Schwartz, moine Allemand, dans le commencement du quatorzieme siecle, mais les effets du melange donc elle est composée etoient connus depuis long-temps. Le Moine Bacon, qui vivoit plus d'un siecle avant Berthold, en a parlé sans equivoque. Il est certain que les Chinois s'en servent depuis plus de deux mille ans; & que le feu grégeois de Coïllinque, donné á l'Empereur Constantin Pogonat, n'etoit qu'une composition oú dominoient le soufre et le salpêtre. On peut voir lâ dessus une dissertation qui est a la fin de la dieuxieme portie de ma Traduction de l'Empereur Léon. *De Maizeray sur l'Art des Sieges*, *p.* 203. *Note.*

made uſe of by the Turks, againſt the French cruſades under that king. He ſays it was thrown from the bottom of a machine called a petrary, and that it came forwards as large as a barrel of verjuice, with a tail of fire iſſuing from it as big as a great ſword, making a noiſe in its paſſage like thunder, and ſeeming like a dragon flying through the air, and from the great quantity of fire it threw out, giving ſuch a light that one might ſee in the army, as if it had been day. Such was the terror it occaſioned among the commanders, that Gautier de Cariel a valiant knight gave it as his advice, that as often as it was thrown they ſhould all proſtrate themſelves on their elbows and knees, and beeſech the Lord to deliver them from that danger, againſt which he alone could protect them: this council was adopted and practiſed; beſides which, the king being in bed in his tent, as often as he was informed that the Greek fire had been thrown, raiſed himſelf in his bed and with uplifted hands, thus beſought the Lord, "Good Lord God, preſerve my people!" The effects of this fire does not ſeem to juſtify the great terrors it here occaſioned. Some of their caſtellated cats were ſet on fire, but extinguiſhed. This fire was thrown three times in the night from the petrary, and four times from a large croſs bowe.

FATHER DANIEL ſays, this wildfire was not only uſed in ſieges, but even in battles; and that Philip Auguſtus, king of France, having found a quantity of it ready prepared in Acre, brought it with him to France, and uſed it at the ſiege of Dieppe, for burning the Engliſh veſſels then in the harbour. The ſame author tells the following marvellous ſtory, of another compoſition of this ſort. An engineer, named Gaubet, native of Mante, found the ſecret of preſerving, even under water, a ſort of burning compoſition, ſhut up in earthen pots, without openings: he was beſides ſo excellent a diver, as to be able to paſs a river under water. He availed himſelf uſefully of this ſecret, to ſet fire to ſome thick palliſades that ſtopped up the entrance into the iſle of Andely, which the army of Philip Auguſtus was then beſieging, and which he took before he attacked Chateau Gaillard; for, whilst the enemy made an attack on the bridge, that prince had built over the Seine, and as all the attention of the besieged was directed that way, Gaubert dived with his pots of firework, and, being arrived at the pallisades, he in an instant set them on fire. As boats were ready for the passage of the soldiers into the isle, it was surprised on that side, and the garrison of the castle obliged to surrender. (s)

In the reign of King John of France, the castle of Remorantin was also taken by the prince of Wales, through the means of artificial fireworks: (t) and, in 1447, the Count de Dunois, besieging Pont Audemer in Normandy, which was defended by the English with great valour, set fire to the city by artificial fireworks, and then took it by assault.

The manner of using these fireworks was, by throwing them from petraries, or cross bows, or fixing them to the great darts and arrows, and shooting them into the towns: a method frequently practised, both by the ancients, with darts and arrows, called falarica and malleoli; and used with good success by the English, the last war, in a naval engagement in the East Indies, between the squadrons of Monsieur D'Ache and Admiral Watson.

The progressive steps taken in attacking fortified places, and the methods opposed thereto, as anciently practised, were, allowing for the difference of engines, much the same as at present. In small towns or castles, the assailants threw up no works, but, having hurdles or large shields called pavais borne before them, advanced to the counterscarp; here some with arrows, slings and cross-bows, attempted to drive the besieged from the ramparts; and others brought fascines to form a passage over the ditch, if wet, and scaling-ladders to mount the walls: the besieged, on their part, attempted to keep the enemy at a distance, by a superior discharge of their missive weapons, to burn the fascines brought to fill up the ditch, or to break, or overturn the scaling ladders. In larger places, or strong castles, lines of circumvalla-

(s) P. Daniel Hist. de Milice Fr. tom 1, p. 276.
(t) P. Daniel, ibid.

tion and contravallation were conſtructed; the former to prevent any attack or ſuccour from without, and the latter to ſecure them from the ſallies of the beſieged. In both theſe, ſmall wooden towers were often erected, at proper diſtances, called Briſtegia, or rather Triſtegia, (u) from their having three floors, or ſtages.

When the garriſon of the place was numerous, and a vigorous reſiſtance expected, they often formed a blockade, by encloſing it with lines, ſtrengthened by large forts, and ſometimes even a kind of town. Of the firſt, there is an inſtance in the reign of Stephen; when that king, being unable to take by force the ſtrong caſtle of Wallingford, ſurrounded it with a line, ſtrengthened by forts, the principal of which he called the caſtle of Craumer; he alſo cut off the paſſage of the garriſon over the Thames, by erecting a ſtrong fort at the head of the bridge. It was however held by Brier Fitz Comte, till relieved by Henry II. then duke of Normandy; who, on notice of the danger of this important place, ſet out from France, encamped before it, and encompaſſing theſe works with a line of circumvallation, to prevent Stephen from ſuccouring them, beſieged the beſiegers: this brought on the conference and peace between thoſe two princes. The latter is mentioned by Froiſſart, (v) as practiſed by King Edward III. at the ſiege of Calais; where, not content with blocking it up by ſea, and making lines on the Downs, and at the bridge of Nieulay, he alſo built a kind of city of timber about the place beſieged; where, ſays that author, there were palaces and houſes, laid out in regular ſtreets: it had its markets on Wedneſdays and Fridays, merceries, ſhambles and cloth-warehouſes, and all ſorts of neceſſaries, which were brought from England and Flanders: in fine, every convenience was there to be had for money. Such was alſo the blockade made by the Turks, at the ſiege of Candia.

(u) Dein vallo munire ſtudent, foſſiſque profundis
Omnem circuitum caſtrorum, nec minus altè
Per loca briſtega, caſtellaque lignea ſurgunt
Ne ſubitò Saladinus eos invadere poſſit. *Guillaume le Breton, lib.* 4, *p.* 272.

(v) Froissart, vol. 1, chap. 133.

It

It ſeems doubtful whether any thing like approaches were carried on. It is more probable, that the beſiegers took the opportunity of the night, to bring their engines and machines as near the walls as poſſible: batteries were then formed, and covered with an epaulement.

The mangonels and petraries began now to batter the walls, and the working parties to make the paſſage into the ditch, carrying hurdles and faſcines, which, with their bucklers, ſerved to ſhield them in their approach: they were ſuported by a number of archers, covered with large targets, arrow-proof, held by men particularly appointed for that ſervice: theſe archers, by ſhooting into the crenelles, and other openings, ſcoured the parapet and protected the workmen in their retreat for freſh faſcines.

An eaſy deſcent being formed into the ditch, the cattus, or ſow, was puſhed forwards, where the men, under cover, filled up and levelled a paſſage for the moveable tower; which being thruſt cloſe to the walls, the archers, on the different ſtages, kept a conſtant diſcharge of darts, arrows and ſtones; the miners began to ſap the wall, or it was battered with the ram. When the mine was finiſhed, the props were ſet on fire: during the confuſion occaſioned by the falling of the part mined, which was commonly a tower, the aſſault was given, and the breach ſtormed. If there were more works, theſe operations were repeated. Where no moveable tower was uſed, both mines were made, and the ram worked under the cattus and ſow.

On the other hand, the beſieged oppoſed, for their defence, flights of darts and large ſtones, ſhot from their engines, with arrows and quarrels from their croſs-bows; ſallies, wherein they attempted to burn or demoliſh the machines of their enemies; and mines under their moveable towers, in order to overthrow them. Upon the cattus and ſow they threw monſtrous weights to break, and wildfire to burn them.

Upon the front attacked, they placed ſacks, filled with wool, which were looſely ſuſpended from the wall; and to break the ſtroke of the ram, beſides this, divers other contrivances were invented;

vented; ſuch as nippers, worked by a crane, for ſeizing it; and ſometimes they let fall upon it a huge beam, faſtened with chains, to two ſtrong leavers.

The heavy cavalry, knights, or men at arms were compoſed of the chief nobility and gentry who held their lands by military ſervice, they were completely caſed in armour from head to foot, ſo as to be rendered, in a manner invulnerable. The armour of a man at arms, till near the middle of the fourteenth century, (w) conſiſted of the following particulars; a looſe garment ſtuffed with cotton or wool, called a gambeſon, over which was worn a coat of mail, formed of double rings or maſcles of iron, interwoven like the meſhes of a net; this was called a hawberk, to it were fixed a hood, ſleeves and hoſe alſo of mail; the head was defended with a helmet, and by a leather thong round the neck, hung a ſhield; the heels of the knight were equipped with ſpurs having rowels near three inches in length: over all theſe, men of conſiderable families wore rich ſurcoats like thoſe of the heralds, charged with their armorial bearings. Men thus harneſſed could have but ſmall powers of action, and a knight overthrown was as incapable of eſcaping as a turtle turned on his back. The difficulty of ſupporting theſe heavy trappings, eſpecially after the introduction of plate armour, is ſtrongly marked by the regulations made at tournaments, where it was deemed reprehenſible for a knight to diſarm himſelf till the buſineſs of the day was over: this was calculated to accuſtom our youths by degrees, to ſuſtain the weight and incumbrance of armour in the day of battle. The offenſive arms were, lances, battle-axes, maces, and cutting ſwords; alſo a ſmall dagger called a miſericorde, (x) but in their charges, as is indeed the caſe with all cavalry, the ſucceſs depended more on the ſtrength of the horſe, than the efforts of the rider. Their

(w) Fauchet from, Froiſſart ſays, armour made of plates of iron was not in common uſe till the year 1330.

(x) Encore avoit le chevalier un petit courteau nommé miſericorde: pour ce que de ce ferrement, volontiers eſtoient occis les chevaliers abbatus: et leſquels voyant telles armes en la main de leurs ennemis demandoient miſericordè s'ils deſiroient etre repitez de la mort. *Faucbet Orig. Mil. Francois, p.* 34.

horſes were therefore of the ſtrongeſt kind, and barded or armed with iron or jacked leather, on the head, neck, cheſt and flanks. There were beſides theſe a kind of dragoons, called hobelers; theſe were infantry, generally archers or croſs bow men, mounted on hobbies or light horſes; they never charged with the cavalry, but were occaſionally uſed to reconnoitre, or to attack convoys; but in engagements, generally acted on foot; they were compoſed of the yeomanry of the country. The infantry conſiſted of archers, croſs bow men, and ſuch as uſed bills, morris pikes, or halberts. The Engliſh archers were at all times conſidered, as at leaſt equal to any in the world, the long bow having ever been a favourite weapon with the Engliſh, and ſuch was their attachment to it, that it kept its footing in our armies long after the introduction of fire arms. In the 13th year of the reign of Q. Elizabeth, an act paſſed enforcing a ſtatute of the 12th of Edward IV. by which foreign merchants were obliged, under diverſe penalties and forfeitures to bring in a certain number of bow ſtaves, in proportion to the quantity of their other goods imported; the preamble to the act of Elizabeth recites "that whereas the uſe of archery not only hath ever been, but alſo yet is, by God's eſpecial gift, to the Engliſh nation a ſingular defence of the realm;" and ſo late as the reign of Charles I. two different commiſſions were granted by that king for enforcing the practice of archery, alſo according to Ruſhworth, on the parliamentary ſide, a precept was iſſued by the Earl of Eſſex, November 1ſt, 1643, to ſtir up the benevolence of well-affected people towards raiſing a company of archers for the ſervice of the king and parliament; it was directed to Mr. Thomas Taylor, citizen of London, who was thereby authoriſed to raiſe the ſaid company.

The Engliſh archers, beſides their bow and arrows, were ſometimes armed with a mall of lead with a handle five feet long, their defenſive armour was a head-piece, with a kind of looſe garment of linen ſtuffed with wool, under which they wore a ſhirt of mail, and to protect them from the horſe, every one carried a ſtake or two, pointed at both ends, which they ſtuck in the ground before them,

them, the point ſloping and preſenting itſelf to the horſes breaſts. In ſieges they were directed to make themſelves large ſhields or rather portable mantlets, which covered them from head to foot, called pavoys or pavaces; theſe were held before them by one of their comrades, whilſt they ſhot their arrows at the enemy on the walls.

THE croſs bow, called in law Latin baliſta or manubaliſta, is by Verſtegan ſaid to be of Saxon original. Croſs bows were however either diſuſed or forgot, till again introduced by the Conqueror, at the battle of Haſtings, they were afterwards forbidden (y) by the ſecond lateran council held anno 1139, under pain of an anathema, as hateful to God, and unfit to be uſed among Chriſtians, in conſequence of which they were laid aſide during the reigns of Stephen and Henry II. but revived in France by Richard I. who was himſelf killed by an arrow diſcharged from that engine, at the ſiege of the caſtle of Chaluz (z): theſe bows ſhot darts called quarreaux, or quarrels; from their heads, which were ſolid ſquare pyramids of iron, theſe were alſo ſometimes trimmed with braſs inſtead of feathers.

IT appears from a record, that our kings had an officer, (a) ſtiled baliſtrarius regis; and that lands were held in capite, of the king, by the ſervice of preſenting annually a croſs bow, (b) and of finding thread, (c) to make a croſs bow-ſtring, as often

(y) ARTEM illam mortiferam & Deo odibilem balliſtariorum et ſagittarium adverſus Chriſtianos & Catholicos exerceri de cætero ſub anathemate prohibemus. *Can.* 29

(z) WILLIAM Brito, in the Life of Philip Auguſtus, ſpeaking of the death of Richard, puts the foll owing words in the mouth of Atropos, one of the deſtinies:

Hac volo, non alia Richardum morte perire,
Ut qui Francigenis balliſtæ primus uſum
Tradidit, ipſe ſui rem primitus experiatur
Quamque alios docuit, in ſe vim ſentiat artis.

(a) BALISTRARIUS. Gerard de la warr, is recorded to have been baliſtrarius donimi regis, &c. 18 & 29 *Hen.* III.

(b) WALTERUS Gatelin tenet manierum de Weſtcourt, in villa de Bedinton in com. Surrey, in capite de domino rege reddendo inde domino regi per annum unam baliſtam precii xii. *Blount's Ancient Tenures.*

(c) QUÆDAM terræ & tenementa in ſuburbia ciceſtriæ in parochia ſancti Pancratii tenentur de rege in capite per ſervitium reddendi regi quandacunque venerit, per quandam venellam vocatam Goddeſtrete ſuper mari auſtrali, unum fucillum plenum fili crudi ad falſam cordam pro baliſta ſua facienda. *Blount's Ancient Tenures.*

as

as he paſſed through a certain diſtrict. Croſs bows according to Father Daniel were uſed by the Engliſh at the Iſle of Rheé in 1627.

The dreſs and defenſive armour of the croſs bow men, were much the ſame as was uſed by the archers.

In the earlier period of the Britiſh monarchy the infantry not being archers were held in the loweſt eſtimation, they were generally compoſed of the peaſantry, ſervants, or the loweſt order of the common people; their defenſive arms were open helmets, called bacinets, (perhaps from their reſemblance to baſons,) a ſhort linen or leathern doublet ſtuffed with wool or cotton, called a hoqueton or acqueton, and ſometimes they carried a roundel or a target; their offenſive arms were a ſword, dagger, halbert, (d) Giſarmes, Black bill, Morris pike or two handed ſword, and occaſionally in common with the archers, the leaden mallet, theſe arms, drawings of which are given in the plate, were uſed at the battle of Floddon Field, as appears from the following ſtanza in the old poem, deſcribing that engagement, publiſhed by the Reverend Mr. Lamb.

Then on the Engliſh part with ſpeed,
The bills ſtept forth, and bows went back,
The mooriſh pikes, and malls of lead,
Did deal there many a dreadful thwack.

Besides the feudal troops, who were bound in conſequence of their tenures to ſerve for a certain number of days, in caſe of invaſion or an inſurrection, every man, as well eccleſiaſtic as lay-

LXXII.

(d) Some made a mell of maſſey lead,
With iron all about did bind,
Some made ſtrong helmets for the head,
And ſome their griſly giſarings grind.

LXXIII.

Some made their battle-axes bright,
Some from their bills did rub the ruſt,
Some made long pikes and lances bright,
Some pitchforks for to join and thruſt. *Floddon Field.*

man

man between the age of ſixteen and ſixty was liable to be called forth to arms; and ſeveral inſtances occur in the reigns of Edward III. and Richard II. (e) wherein mandates were iſſued to the archbiſhops directing them to aſſemble the clergy of all denominations within their provinces, between the ages above mentioned, to arm, array and regiment them, and hold them in readineſs for ſervice: added to the forces here mentioned, from the time of Harrold downwards, mercenary troops have been entertained by almoſt every one of our monarchs.

THE moſt ancient code of military laws for the government of the Engliſh army, which has been handed down to us, is that of King Henry V. enacted at Mance, this with ſome additional articles made by the earl of Saliſbury, are preſerved in the Library of the Inner Temple. (f) As matters of great curioſity, they are here inſerted at large, in the words, ſpelling and abbreviations of the originals, there is another copy in the Britiſh Muſeum. Theſe laws do not differ ſo greatly from thoſe now in force, as might on a ſlight conſideration be ſuppoſed, but ſubordination, good order in camp and quarters, the preventing of deſertion and falſe muſters, with ſafety for perſons bringing proviſions to the army, being immutably neceſſary to the very exiſtence of every army, muſt therefore always be ſtrongly enforced, both by rewards and puniſhments, and will ever give a ſtriking ſimilarity to the chief articles in the military code of every age and every nation.

NICHOLAS UPTON firſt a ſoldier in France under the earl of Saliſbury, and afterwards about the year 1452, a canon of Saliſbury, has in his book entitled, " De Studio Militari, printed a Latin copy of this code, (g) which though in ſubſtance the ſame as the Engliſh, contains ſome articles not there mentioned and ſlightly differing in others, theſe differences and additions will be taken notice of in the notes.

(e) SEE Rymer, ann. 1369, 43 Ed. III. alſo 46th and 47th of the ſame reign and 1ſt Richard II.

(f) A MS. of Mr. Petyt's entitled Collectanea, vol. 1. folio, p. 509. & ſeq.

(g) IN the exordium to this code it is ſaid to have been made with the advice of " our peers, lords and nobles," in order that every one might be ſhewn the proper path, and alſo that the conſtable and mareſchal of the army might be enabled the more prudently to determine in the cauſes daily brought before them.

ORDINANCES for WARRE, &c.

AT THE
TREATE AND COUNCIL OF MANUCE.

Obeysance.

FIRST, That all manner of men, of what soever nacon, estate, or condicon soever he be, be obeysant to our soveraigne lord the king, and to his constable and marshall, upon payne of as much as he may forfeite in bodie and goodes. (h)

For Holy Churche.

ALSOE, That no man be soe hardy, unlesse he be a priest, to touch the sacrament of Godes body, upon the payne to be hanged and drawen therefore, nor that noe man, be soe hardy to touch the bode or vessell in which the sacrament is in, upon the same payne; alsoe that noe manner of man be soe hardie to robbe or pill holy church of noe good, nor ornament longinge to the churche; nor to sley any man of holye church, religeous nor none other, but if he be armed, upon payne of death; nor that any man be soe hardie to sley or enforce any woman upon lyke payne, and that noe man take noe man nor woman of holy church, prisoner, nor other religeous pson, except they be armed, upon payne of imprisonment, and his bodie at the kings will.

For Herbergage.

ALSOE, That noe man be soe hardy to goe before, in the battayle under the banner or penon of his lord or maihter, except herbeges,

(h) ALSO all soldiers and other persons receiving wages to be obedient to their immediate captains or masters, in all things legal and honest. All merchants travelling with the army or buying or selling in the markets thereof, to obey the constable and marefchal and even the clerk of the market as they would the king. And all offences and suits whatsoever, respecting the followers of the army, to be tried and determined by the judgment of the constable, or in his absence by the marefchal. These followers are specified under the following whimsical arrangement: " Whether soldiers or merchants, or handy crafts, such as shoemakers, taylors, barbers, physicians or washerwomen, and also our scouts especially appointed.

herberges, (i) the names of whome ſhall be delyvered, and take to the conſtable and marſhall, by their ſaid Lord and Mrs. upon his payne, (viz) he that otherwiſe offendeth ſhall be put from his horſe and harneſſe, both unto the warder of the cunſtable and marſhall, unto the tyme that he that offendeth have made his fyne with the ſaid cunſtable and marſhall, and found ſuretie that he ſhall noe more offend.

Alsoe, That noe man take noe herberges, but if it be by the diſignment of the cunſtable and marſhall or of the herberger; and that after tyme that the herbergage is aſſigned and delyvered, that noe man be ſoe hardie himſelf to remove, or to diſaray for any thing that may fall, without commandment of him that hath power, upon payne of horſe and harneſſe to be put in areſte of the cunſtable and marſhall, to the tyme they have made fine with them, and moreover his bodie at the kings will.

For keeping of Watch and Warde.

Alsoe, That every man be obeyſante to his captayne to keep his watch and his warde, and to doe all that longeth a ſouldier to doe, upon payne his horſe and harneſſe to be put in the warde of the marſhall, unto the tyme that he that thus offendeth hath agreed with his captayne, after the warde of the courte.

For takinge of Priſoners.

Alsoe, be it at the battayle or other deedes of armes, where that priſoners ben taken, he that firſt may have his fay ſhall have him for his priſoner, and ſhall not neede to abyde upon him until the end of the journey, and none other ſhall take him for priſoner, but if that it be that the ſaid priſoner be found from his defendaunt.

For robinge of Marchaunts.

Alsoe, That noe man be ſoe hardy to pill ne robbe none other of victual, ne of none other livelode the which they have

(i) Herbergage, quarters. Herberger, a harbinger or quarter-maſter.

by

by lyvinge, upon payne of death; and that noe man robbe noe vitaller, marchaunt, ne none other pſon cominge to the markett with victalls or other marchandize for ye refreſhment of the hoſte, upon the ſame payne; ne that noe man robbe from other, horſe meate or mans meate, ne none other thinge that is gotten of enemyes goodes, upone payne his bodie to be arreſt at the kings will.

For Barrettors.

Alsoe, That noe man debate for armes, priſoners, lodginge, ne for none other thinge, ſoe yat no ryot can teke nor waſt be in the hoſte; ne yat noe man make him ptie in aſſemble of ye hoſte nor none otherwiſe, and yat as well of principall as of oyer prties, upon payne of leeſinge yeir horſe and harneſſe, till yey have made fyne with the cunſtable, and their bodies to be arreſt at the kinges will, and yf he be groom or page, he ſhall leeſe his left eare therefore; and if any man find him grieved, let him ſhewe his greivance to the conſtable or marſhall, and right ſhall be done.

For Debate.

Alsoe, That noe man make noe debate nor conteſt for any hate of tyme paſt, ne for tyme to come, for ye wich hate, if any man be dead for ſuch conteke or debate, he or yey that be pteners or encheſon of ye death ſhall be hanged therefore; or if it happe yat any man eſcreye his owne name, or his captayne, lord or maiſter, to make a reyſeinge of ye people, by ye wich affray might fall in ye hoſte, he yat in ſuch caſe a ſtreith ſhall be drawen and hanged for his labour.

For them that crye Havoke.

Alsoe, That noe man be ſoe hardy to cry havoke, upon payne that he that is found beginner ſhall die therefore, and ye remnannte, yeir horſe and harneſes to be put in the warde of ye conſtable and marſhall, unto ye tyme yey have made fyne with them,

them, and yeir bodies in prifon at the kinges will, till yey have found furety yat yey fhall noe more offend. (k)

For unlawful Efcries.

Alsoe, That none efcreye be wich is called mounte, ne none oyer unreafonable efcrey be in ye hofte, upon payne that he yat is founde beginner of fuch unreafonable efcry be put from his horfe and harneffe, and his bodie in arreft of ye conftable and marfhall to the tyme he make his fyne with them, and his bodie at the kinges will and pleafure; and he yat certifieth who is the beginner, fhall have a ------ for his labour of ye conftable and marfhall. (l)

For Mufters.

Alsoe, When it liketh the kinge to take mufters of his hofte, that noe man be foe hardy to have other men at his mufters yen thofe yat be with himfelf witholden for the fame voyadge wyout fraud, upon payne to be holden falfe and reproved, and alfoe to loofe his waiges and penemt that fhould longe to him. (m)

For Prifoners.

Alsoe, if any manner deede of armes be, and any man be born to the earth, he yat firft foe hath born him to the earth, fhall have him to be prifoner; but if foe be yat another cometh

(k) Havoke or Havock was probably a word fignifying that no quarter fhould be given, or elfe implying a permiffion to plunder a town or camp; that it was fomething of this kind feems likely from the following exception in Upton's tranfcript of this article, "without fpecial licence from the king," which implies that fuch licence was fometimes granted.

(l) Mounte, the vulgar Englifh pronunciation of the French word montez, mount or to horfe poffibly a falfe or feditious alarm to the cavalry. In Upton this word is written mountee, and a reward of an hundred fhillings of Tours, to wit ten fhillings Englifh, is to be paid by the conftable or marfhall to any one who fhall difcover the beginner of this cry.

(m) Every captain when duly required by the king, or his commiffary to mufter his men before them, and all commiffaries in the faid mufter were commanded diligently to enquire after and fee that the foldiers had their proper armes, which was particularly to be obferved refpecting bows and arrows, and the commiffary, if he thought it neceffary, might compel the captain to anfwer upon oath. *Upton.*

after that, and taketh the fey of ye ſaid priſoner, then the (n) ſunter down ſhall have the one half and ye taker of ye faith tho-ther half: but he yat taketh the faith ſhall have the warde of ye priſoners, makinge ſufficient ſurety to his ptner for ye other half.

AND if any man take a priſoner, and eny other man come upon him aſkinge pte, meaning ells yat he would ſley the ſaid priſoner, he ſhall have noe pte though ſoe be that pte hath bin graunted him; and yf he ſley the priſoner, he ſhall be arreſted by the marſhall and putt in warde till he have a fyne, after the awarde of ye conſtable.

For the payinge of Thirds.

ALSOE, That every man pay his thirdes to his captayne, lord and maiſter, of all manner wynninge by ware; and yat as well thoſe yat be not in ſould but lodginge, under ye banner or penon of yeir captain, upon payne to looſe his part of his fore ſaid wynninge to his captayne, and his bodye to be in ward of the marſhall unto ye have agreed with his fore ſaid maiſter. (o)

For them that make themſelves Captaynes to withdrawe Men from the Hoſte.

ALSOE, That noe man be ſoe hardy to rayſe banner or penon of St. George, ne of none other to drawe together the people, and to withdrawe them out of the hoſte to goe to one other pte, upon paynne of yem that in ſuch wiſe make themſelves captens to be drawen and hanged, and they that follow him to have yeir heades ſmytten of, and yeir goods and heretages for-fayted to the kinge.

(n) SUNTER down, the perſon by whom the priſoner was thrown down. The perſon that had the keeping of the priſoner was bound to give ſufficient ſecurity to his partner, for his ſhare of the ranſom. *Upton.*

(o) ONE third of theſe thirds belonged to the king, for which each captain was accountable at the exchequer, the captains who had indented to ſerve King Henry V. after his deceaſe, 1 Henry 5, cap. 5, petitioned parliament that this might be deducted out of the arrears of pay due to them. All perſons following the army, to pay the thirds of their gains in war to the chief captain. *Upton.*

A Statute

A Statute for them that beare not a Banne of St. George.

ALSOE, That every man of what eſtate, condicon or nacon he be of our pty, bere a band of St. George ſuffiſaunt large upon ye pyle, that he be wounded or dead in ye fault yereof, he yat him woundeth or ſleyeth ſhall beare noe paine for him; and yat noe enemy beare ye ſaid ſeigne but yt he be priſoner and in ye warde of his maiſter, upon payne of death therefore. (p)

For them that aſſault without Leave of his Maiſter.

ALSOE, That noe aſſault be made, ne to ſtrength by archer, ne by none other of the comons wthout ye preſence of a man of eſtate. And if any aſſault be, and ye kinge, conſtable, or marſhall, or any lord of the hoſte ſend for to diſturbe the ſaid aſſault, that noe man be ſoe hardy to aſſault after, upon payne to be priſoned and looſe all his other profitt that he hath wonne by the ſaid aſſault, and his horſe and harneis in the warde of ye conſtable and marſhall.

For to bringe in Priſoners into the Kinges Knowledge, Conſtable, or Marſhall.

ALSOE, If any man take any priſoners a none right as he is commen into the hoſte, that he bring his priſoner unto his captayne or maiſter, upon payne of looſeing his pte to his ſaid captain or maiſter, and yen that his ſaid captaine or maiſter bringe him within eight dayes to the kinge, conſtable, or marſhall, or as ſoone as he may ſoe yat he be not ladde noe oyer waye, upon payne to looſe his pte to him yat ſhall enforme ye conſtable or marſhall firſt of yt. And yt every doe keepe his priſoner yat he byde not or goe at large in ye hoſte, ne in lodginge; but if ward be had upon him upon payne of looſinge ye ſaid priſoner, reſervinge to his lord or maiſter his thirds of the whole, that he be not

(p) THIS was for a diſtinction, the ſoldiers of thoſe days not being dreſſed in uniform.

ptie

ptie of ye default, and ye ſecond pte to him that firſt ſhall accuſe him, and ye third part to the conſtable and marſhall, and alſoe moreover his bodie in arreſt at the kinges will. Alſoe yat no man ſuffer his priſoner to goe out of ye hoſte for his ranſome, ne for none other cauſe without ſaffe conduct upon the payne aforeſaid. (q)

For keepinge the Watche.

ALSOE, That every man keepe dulie his watche in ye hoſte, and yat with as manne men of armes and archers as to him ſhall be aſſigned, but yat he have a cauſe reaſonable and to abide upon his watche and warde the term to him lymitted, not deptinge from his watch no waye, but it be by the aſſignment or lycence of him by the wich the ſaid watch is made, upon payne of ſmytinge of his head that otherwiſe depteth.

For givinge of ſaffe Conductes or Congrs, and for to breake them.

ALSOE, That noe man give ſafe conducts to priſoner, ne to none other, nor lycence noe enymie to come nor to goe out of the hoſte ne into the hoſte, upon payne to forfeit all his goods to the kinge, and his body in arreſt at ye kinges will, except our liege l. ye kinge, conſtable or marſhall. And yt noe man be ſoe hardy to breake our liege lord the kinges comanndment and ſaffe conduct, upon payne to be drawen and hanged, and his goods and heritages forfeat to the kinge; nor yet ye conſtable or marſhall ſaffe conducte, upon payne of death.

(q) THE intent of this article was to prevent the king and general from being defrauded of their ſhare of ranſome. Priſoners of a certain rank were the property of the general. In Upton there is the following clauſe reſpecting this regulation. "And if the priſoner ſo taken ſhall be his ſuperior in one part of the army, and ſhall have from his ſovereign permiſſion to diſplay his ſtandard, or if the priſoner ſhall be of the blood royal, a duke, marquis, earl, or chief captain, then the ſaid captain be he whom he may, ſhall be the priſoner of the chief captain of that part of our ſaid army, unleſs the taker of ſuch priſoner ſhall be his equal or ſuperior in armes or dignity, or ſuch baron or notable ſoldier, who ſhall have before diſplayed his banner, the chief captain in that caſe ſhall agree with the taker, giving him a ſufficient reward for his capture." Selden ſays that by the law of armes, thoſe captains whoſe ranſom come to above 10000 crowns, belonged to the king.

For the withdrawinge mens Servants fro' their Masters.

Alsoe, That noe man be soe hardye to take noe servannt of other mens ye wich is in covenant with him for ye voyage, as well soldier, man of armes, archer, groome or page, after tyme he is -------- or challenged by his maister, upon payne his bodie to be arreste to the tyme he have agreed with the ptie complaynant after ye warde of ye court, and his horse and harnesse to the constable and marshall to the tyme he have made his fyne.

For departing from the Hoste without leave.

Alsoe, That noe man depte from the state without leave or lycence of his lord and maister, upon payne to be arrest and in ye ward of ye marshall, and at ye kings will of his life, and alsoe to loose all his wynninge of that daye, reserved to his lord or maister ye thirds of his wynninge, and to the lord of ye estate surplus of ye same wynninges wonne by him that same day, and soe fromday to day till ye ordinance be kept.

For Scries made by the Enimyes in the Hoste.

Alsoe, if any escryes fall in the hoste when they be lodged, that every man drawe him to the kinge or his chieftaine of ye battaille where he is lodged, leaving his lodginge sufficiently kept. But if ye enemies fall on that syde whereas he is lodged, and in his case he said capen shall abide here and all his men.

For keepinge of the Countrye.

Alsoe, if any countrey or lordshippe be wourd other by free will offered unto ye kinge obeysance, that noe man be soe hardy to robbe ne pill yerein after the peace is proclaymed, upon payne of death. And that any man of what degree soever he be come unto our said soveraigne lord obeisance, that noe man take him, robbe him, ne pille him, upon ye same payne, soe that he or they that his wolle obey beare a token of our soveraigne lord the kinge.

For they that ransome their Prisoners, or sell them without Leave of their Captaine or Lordes.

Alsoe, That noe man be soe hardy to ransome or sell his prisoner without especiall lycence of his captayne, the wch indenteth with the kinge under his letter and seale; and yat upon payne that he that doth the contrary thereof to forfeite his part in the prisoner unto his captayne, and he to be under arrest of the marshall to the tyme he have agreed wth his captayne, and yat noe man bye no such prisoner upon payne to loose the gold and silver that he payeth for him, and ye prisoner to be arrested to the captayne aforesaid.

A Statute for the Children within the Aige of fourteen.

Alsoe, That noe man be soe hardy to take noe children within the age of 14 years, but if he be a lordes son, or else a worshipfull gentlemans sonne, or a captayne; and that as soon as he hath brought unto the hoste, or into the garrison where he is abidinge, that he bringe him to his lord, mr, or captayne, upon payne of loosing his horse, harness, and his pte of ye same child, reserving unto his lord, mr, or captayne his dutye, soe yat they be not consentant unto his said default: and alsoe that ye said lord, mr, or captayne bringe him unto the kinge or constable within eight days uppon.

For Women that lie in Gesom. (r)

Alsoe, That noe man be soe hardy to goe into noe chamber or lodginge where that eny woeman lyeth in gesem, her to robbe ne pille of any goods wch longeth to her refreshinge, nor for to make noe defray where yrough she or her child might be in any disease or mispiere, upon payne that he in such wise offendeth shall loose all his goods, half to him that accuseth him, and half to the

(r) Women in child bed, or lying in.

constable

conſtable and marſhall, and himſelf to dye, except the kinge give him his grace.

For the reſiſtinge of Juſtice.

Alsoe, if any man be judged to the death by the kinge, conſtable, marſhall, or any other judge ordinary, or any oyer office lawfull, that noe man be ſoe hardy to ſett hand upon the condemyned, to reſiſt the kinges judge, upon payne that if ye ſaid condemyned be traytor, he yat is the chief to have ye ſame death that the condemyned is judged unto; and althoe that be pticipannte or conſentinge to have their heades ſmitten of: and if it be any other cauſe cryminall the cauſe of the reſiſting, to have the ſame death that ye ſame man being judged ſhould have had, ye remnant at ye kings will.

For them that fortifie Places without Leave of the Kinge.

Alsoe, That noe man be ſoe hardie to edifie or ſtrengthen any manner of place dyſepered by the kinge or his councell, without epeciall lycence or comandment of yem yat have power: and alſoe yat noe man compell the country, the wich is in ye obeyſañce or appatized unto our ſoveraigne lord the kinge, to come unto the donage, repacon, watch or warde of the ſaid place, upon payne of looſeinge horſe and harneiſs, and to reſtore again and make ſatiſfaction unto the countrey where yat he hath offended, ye coſts and damages, and moreover his bodie at the kings will.

For them that robbe and pill Lodginges.

Alsoe, That noe man be ſoe hardy to robbe ne pill one others lodginge, after tyme it is appointed by ye herberges ne to lodge yerein, without leave of him the wich the lodginge is aſſigned to, upon payne of impriſonment, after the warde of ye conſtable and marſhall.

A Statute

A Statute for them that let (s) *Labourers and Men goinge to the Ploughe.*

Alsoe, That noe man be ſoe hardy to take from any man goinge to the plouge, harrowe, or carte, horſe, mare, nor oxe, nor any other beſt longinge to labour within the kings obeiſance, without leave and agreement with the ptie, upon payne of and alſo that noe man give noe impedyment unto noe man of labour, payne of impriſonment until ſuch tyme he have made a fyne after the award of ye conſtable and marſhall.

For them that give Men Reproaches.

Alsoe, That noe man give none reproch to none other becauſe of the countrey that he is of (viz.) be he French, Engliſh, Welch, or Iriſh, or of any other countrey whence that ever be: that noe man ſey noe villane to none other, through ye wch villane ſayinge may fall ſodayne manſlaughter, or reſeinge of people, all ſuch barrators ſhall ſtand at ye kings will what death they ſhall have for ſuch noyſe making.

For them that take Traytors and put them to Ranſome.

Alsoe, if any man take any enemye the wch hath been ſworn and had billet, or any man which oweth leigance to our leige lord ye kinge, thatt is to wit, Engliſh, Walſh, Iriſh, or any other, that aſſoone as he is come to the hoſte or ellſwhere, that he be brought to the warde of the conſtable and marſhall, upon payne to have the ſame death yat the ſaid traytors or enymie ſhould have; and he yat any ſuch bringeth in ſhall have tenne ſhillings of the kinge, conſtable or marſhall for his travayle.

For them that breake the Kinges Arreſte.

Alsoe, That every man obey unto the kings ſerveants, porters of places, or any other officers made by conſtables, marſhalls, or

(s) To let, to obſtruct, or moleſt.

by

by any officers comyssed; that noe man be soe hardy to breake ye kings arrest, upon payne to loose horse and harness, and his bodie at the kings will; and if ye mayme them or hurt them to die therefore.

For Brenninge.

Alsoe, without cómandment special of the kinge, that noe man brenne upon payne of death.

For Watche within Lodginge.

Alsoe, both day and night, that every captain have watch within his lodginge, upon payne his bodie to be arrest till he made fyne or ransome with the kinge, and at the kings will.

For them that shall be Wasters of Victuall.

Alsoe, if any man fynd wyne or any other victuall, that he take himself thereof as much as him needes, and yat he save the remnant to other of the hoste without any destruction, upon payne his horse and harnesse to be arrest till he have made fyne with the constable and marshall.

For a Copie to be had of the Premises in the Hoste.

Alsoe, That theis articles afore written the which that thinketh needful to be cryed in the hoste, he woole, that ye copy be given to every lorde and governor of mene in the aforesaid hoste, soe that yey may have playne knowledge, and informe their men of their foresaid ordinances and articles.

For makinge of Roodes. (t)

Alsoe, that noe man make noe roodes by day nor night, but by lycence and knowledge of the captens of the hoste and warde, soe that ye captens may know what way yey drawe them, that

(t) Roodes, inroads, or expeditions to plunder.

they may have ſuccour and helpe and neede be, upon payne of them yat offendeth their bodies and goodes at ye kings will.

For Roodes.

Alsoe, That noe captayne of noe warde graunt noe roods without lycence of our ſoveraigne lord the king.

That noe Man diſaraye him in the Battayle for no Scrie that cometh in the Hoſte.

Alsoe, That for noe tydings ne for noe manner of ſcrie that may come in the hoſte, that noe man in diſaraye out of ye battayle if the ryde, but by leave of ye chieftayne of ye battayle, upon payne that he yat offendeth ſhall be put from his horſe and harneſs to ye warde of ye conſtable and marſhall, unto the tyme he have made his fyne with them and found ſurety that he ſhall noe more offend, and moreover his bodie to ſtand at the kings will.

OTHER ORDINAUNCES

Made by the EARL of SALISBURYE with others, &c.

For the Country appatized. (u)

First, That noe man of armes, ne archer of what eſtate condicon or nacon, that ever he be, that they abide not, nor hold them under the colour of our ſaid lord the earle, but that their captene be in this preſent aſſembly and company, and they be muſtered and muſter at all tymes that they be required, and alſoe, that they lodge them under the ſtanderd of their captene,

(u) The countrye appatiſed, diſtricts which have paid compoſition or contribution, in order to ranſom their towns from military execution.

and

and in ſuch lodginge as is delyvered them by the herbergers, upon payne of looſinge horſe and harneis, and their goods, moreover their bodies at the kinges will.

For ſoreinge the ſaid Country appatized.

ALSOE, That noe man forrage in the country appatized, but if it be hey, ots, rye, and other neceſſary vitaylls, nor that noe man give unto his horſe, noe wheate, nor to gether none, but if it be, only to make bread of, and if the ſaid fforrayers take any beſtaill for their ſuſtenaunce, that he take reaſonable, and to make noe waſt, nor for to devoure nor deſtroy noe vittayles upon payne of looſinge horſe and harneſſe and goods, and their bodies at the kinges will, and alſoe that the ſaid forrayners, take nor ſley noe great oxen, ne none milche kyen, but ſmall beſtiall, and that they accord with the ptie upon the payne aforeſaid.

For them that bye or ſell Pillage in the ſaid Country, or take.

ALSOE, That noe man, ſouldier, marchaunt or man uſinge the warre, bye noe pillage, nor take none within the ground appatized upon payne of death, and if ſoe be, that any man have any of the enimyes goodes, the which he woolle ſell that he bringe it into the comon markett, and proclaymed it by a officer of the marſhalcie, or ells of the markett, upon payne the buyer to be in arreſt of the marſhall to the tyme he have made a ffyne, with the conſtable and marſhall, and to looſe all his money and gold that he hath payed for the ſame pillage, and the ſeller to looſe horſe and harneis, and his bodie at the kinges will.

For them that deſtroye Vines and other Trees bearinge Fruite.

ALSOE, That noe man beate downe hows'rs to brenne, ne none apple trees, peare trees, noote trees, ne none other trees bearinge

bearinge fruite, nor that noe man putt noe beaſtes into noe vynes nor drawe up the ſtakes of the ſame vynes, for to deſtroye them, upon payne to leeſe their ſaid beaſtes and themſelf in warde, unto the tyme they have made a fyne with the conſtable and marſhall for the default.

For to berry Caren and other Corruption in Seginge. (v)

ALSOE, That every Lo: captene, or governor of people doe compell their ſervants and ------ to be berry their carren and bowells about their lodgings and within the earth, that noe ſtinche be in their ſaid lodginge, where thorowe that any peſtilence or mortalitie might fall within the hoſte, upon payne to make amendes at the king's will.

For the takinge of Priſoners of Men Bulleted. (w)

ALSOE, That noe man take noe priſoner of men bulleted of that ſaid ground patized, nor noe man, nor childe having bullet upon him, in payne to looſe horſe and armes and their bodies at the kings will.

For drawinge awaye beaſtiall out of the hoſte. (x)

ALSOE,. That noe ſouldiour goe fro' the hoſte with noe beſtiall upon payne that is found in default, ſhalbe priſoned and looſe the ſaid beſtaill, notwithſtandinge in what place ſoever he take them, and he that them taketh or arreſted ſhall have the half of the ſaid beaſts and the king the other halfe, but if ſoe be he have leave of the conſtable and marſhall, of the which leave he ſhall have a billett under the conſtables ſignett, and alſoe that he preſent up the nomber of the beaſts, the which he dryveth.

(v) PROBABLY loginge, a camp or poſt being frequently ſtiled the loginge of the hoſt.

(w) PERSONS having paſſes, certificates, or ſome badge or mark, worn round their necks like the Roman Bulla.

(x) BESTIALL, cattle.

For

For to make ſtakes againſt a Battayle or Ioyrney.

Alsoe, That every captayne doe compell their yeomen every man in all haſte to make him a good ſubſtantiall ſtake of a xi feete (y) in length, for certain (z) tieings that lords have heard, and in payne to be puniſhed as hereto belongeth.

For makinge of Fagottes at Seiges for Bolworkes and Ditches.

Alsoe, That every man make a good ſubſtantiall fagott of thirteen foot of length, without leaves againſt (N) day next cominge upon payne of looſinge a monthes waiges, and that as well the marchaunts, the which cometh unto the markett, as other ſouldiers, and alſo that every captene doe ley his fagotts apart, to that yntent that it may be ſcene whether he have his number of ffagotts after the company the which he leadeth.

For Hoolye Churche.

Alsoe, That noe man take from noe houſe of religeon, ne none other place havinge ſaufgondit noe manner of goodes, ne vitaill without accordinge and will of the wardens of the ſame place upon payne to be arreſt, and at the kings will of his life.

That noe man ſpeake with them in the Caſtle or in the Town after that they be charged.

Alsoe, That noe man be ſoe hardy to ſpeake with them of the towne or of the caſtle from henceforth, upon payne to be chaſticed at my lo: will.

(y) These ſtakes were planted before them like paliſades to keep off the cavalry.

(z) So in both copies perhaps tydings, as an account of a large body of the enemy's cavalry ordered to attack them, on their march: indeed ſeveral articles in theſe ordinances made by the earl of Saliſbury ſeem temporary orders.

Ordinannces for Forragers in Places danngerous.

Alsoe, that noe manner of mann goe for noe forrage, but it be with a ſtale, the which ſhall fourth twyce a week, that is to meet N day at N upon payne to be chaſticed at my lo: will.

For Ladders.

Alsoe, That every ſeaven gentlemen or men of armes, make them a good ſufficient ladder and a ſtronge of xv rouges, and that it be ready betwixt this and N day upon payne to be chaſticed at my lo: will.

For Pauiſes. (a)

Alsoe, That every twoo yeomen make them a good paviſe of bordes and of XX in the beſt manner that they can deviſe, that one may hold that whiles the other doth ſhete upon the payne.

For them that ſault or renners to make them bootie.

Alsoe, That all men make them boty vii or v together, and that three of the vii or twoo of the v be deſeigned to waite and not to departe from the ſtandards, upon payne to looſe all the wynninges that may be wonne by him as that day, or by the ffellowſhip of him, halfe to the kinge, and halfe to him that accuſeth him, and his bodie in pryſon at the kings will, and that every captayne give me by N. day all the names of his men as they be made in their botie, certifienge by name which be they ſhall abyde with the ſtandards, and which ſhall doe there advantage.

For them that uſe Bordell, the which lodge in the Hoſte.

Alsoe, That noe man have, ne hold any commen weomen within his lodginge, upon payne of looſinge a months wages, and

(a) Pavises were large ſhields or rather portable mantlets, covering a man from head to foot.

if

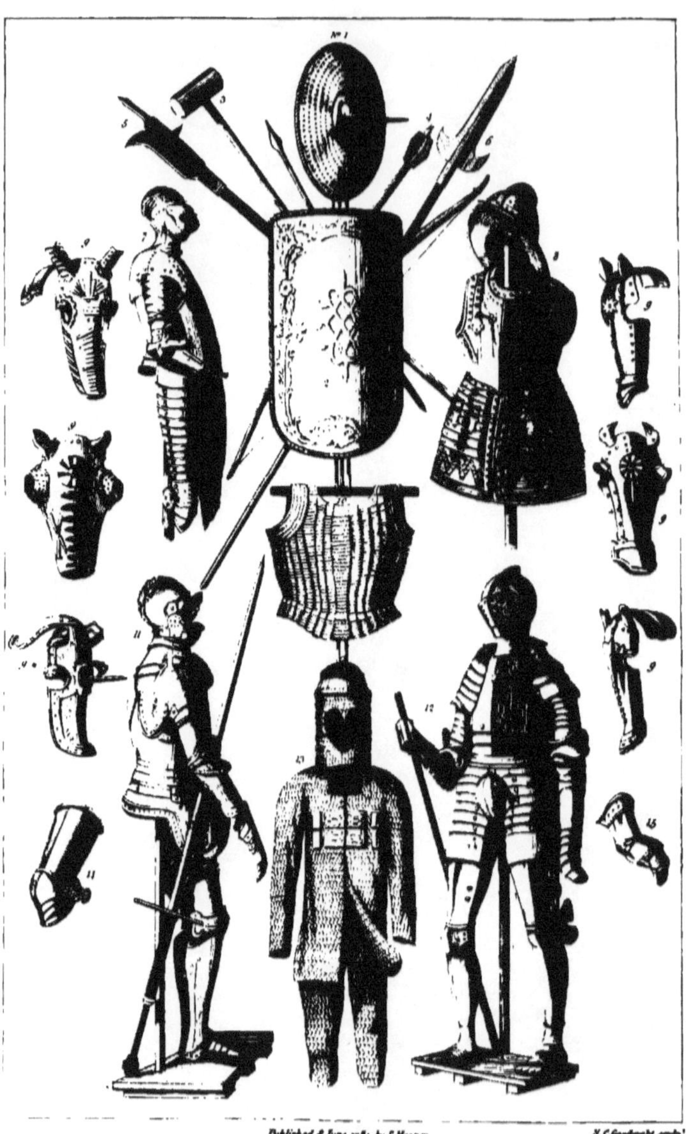

Published 8 June, 1784, by S. Hooper. *N. C. Goodnight sculp.*

if any man fynd or can fynde any commen woman lodginge, my ſaid lord comanndeth him to take from her or them, all the money that maye be found upon her or them, and to take a ſtaff and dryve her out of the hoſte and breake her arme. (b)

(b) By this article in Upton which occurs among thoſe made by King Henry it is ordered, that public and common whores be by no means permitted to remain with the army, eſpecially during ſieges of towns, caſtles and fortreſſes of any ſort; but that they ſhall be ſtationed together, within a diſtance not leſs than a league, this is to be obſerved in all cities hereafter taken and yielded to the king, any one found with the army after admonition, to be puniſhed with the fracture of her left arm.

EXPLANATION
OF THE
PLATE OF ARMOUR.

No. 1. A Shield called a Roundel.

No. 2. A Target.

No. 3. A Leaden Mallet, uſed by the archers, mentioned in the military part of the preface.

No. 4. An Iron Mace uſed by the cavalry, the original is in the Tower.

No. 5. A Black Bill in the Armory of the Town Hall, Canterbury.

No. 6. A Pertuiſan in the Muſeum of Mr. Green of Lichfield.

No. 7. A Suit of Armour in the Tower of London, which it is pretended belonged to John de Curcy, earl of Ulſter, confined there anno 1204, but probably is not ſo ancient, plate armour, as it is generally conceived, not being in uſe at that period.

No. 8.

No. 8. A Suit of bright Morion Armour, worn by the Infantry in the reign of Queen Elizabeth; it derives its name from the head piece ſtiled a Morion.

No. 9. Different Chanfrins or Cheiffronts, being maſks of iron for defending the heads of horſes, from the horſe armory in the Tower of London.

No. 10. A Cuiraſs of Plate Mail, compoſed of ſmall iron plates faſtened one over the other, ſo as to yield to every motion of the body, the original is in the collection of curioſities at Don Saltero's Coffee Houſe, Chelſea.

No. 11. A Complete Suit of Armour ſhewn in the Tower of London, and ſaid to have belonged to John of Gaunt, Duke of Lancaſter, fourth ſon of Edward III. He died 1399.

No. 12. A Complete Suit of Armour in the Tower of London, made for Henry VIII. when he was but eighteen years of age. It is rough from the hammer.

No. 13. A Hawberk or ſuit of chain mail armour, compoſed of iron rings. It conſiſts of a helmet, coat and breeches, the original is in the Muſeum of Mr. Green of Lichfield.

No. 14. Knee Piece called a Genouillere.

No. 15. A Gauntlet.

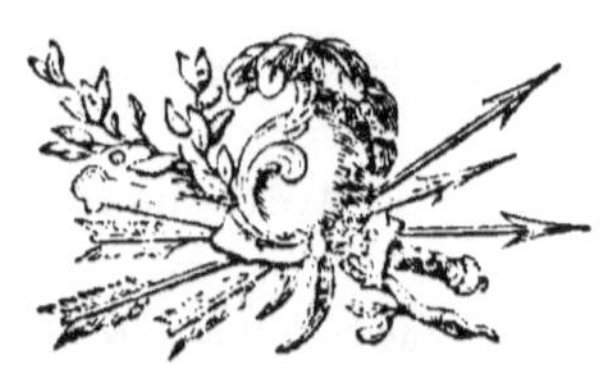

MONAS-

MONASTERIES.

THE era of the firſt inſtitution of monaſteries in England, is by no means aſcertained: nothing can be more diſcordant than the accounts and opinions of our hiſtorians and antiquaries on this ſubject; ſome making them coeval with the introduction of Chriſtianity into this iſland; which, it is pretended, was preached A. D. 31, by Joſeph of Arimathea, and certain diſciples of Philip the apoſtle. A very learned writer ſurmiſes, (a) that ſome converted druids became our firſt monks: others ſay, (b) there was a college or monaſtery at Bangor in Flintſhire, as early as the year 182; though this, with greater probability, is generally placed later by almoſt three hundred years.

THE learned Biſhop Stillingfleet, (c) and others, ſuppoſe the firſt Engliſh monaſtery was founded at Glaſtonbury, by St. Patrick, about the year 425; whilſt, on the other hand, it has been doubted, (d) whether St. Patrick was ever at Glaſtonbury, any more than Joſeph of Arimathea.

ABOUT the year 512, the Britiſh hiſtorians report, that St. Dubritius, archbiſhop of St. David's, founded twelve monaſteries, and taught his monks to live, after the manner of the Aſians and Africans, by the work of their hands. Camden thinks, that Congellus firſt brought the monaſtic life into England, towards the year 530; but Mr. John Tanner, editor of the Notitia Monaſtica, ſays, "It was certainly here before that time." Theſe inſtances are ſufficient to ſhew, that the exact period is not known.

THE date of the firſt foundation of nunneries, or houſes of religious women, in this country, is enveloped in the ſame ob-

(a) SIR George Macartney, in his Defence of the Royal Line of Scotland, p. 13.
(b) ARCHBISHOP Uſher's Antiq. Eccl. Britan. folio, p. 69.
(c) STILLINGFLEET's Original of the Britiſh Churches, p. 184, 185.
(d) VIDE Wharton, in his notes to Angl. Sacr. vol. ii. p. 92.

ſcurity. Some think them nearly of equal antiquity with thoſe for monks. Leland ſays, Merlin's mother, who is reported to have lived about the year 440, was a nun at Caermarthen; and it is ſaid, St. David's mother was a nun alſo. But the firſt Engliſh nunnery ſeems to have been that erected at Folkſtone in Kent, by King Eadbald, A. D. 630: ſoon after which ſeveral others were founded; particularly that of Barking in Eſſex, anno 675; and, about the ſame time, another by St. Mildred, in the iſle of Thanet, A. D. 694. Abbeſſes were then in ſuch great eſteem for their ſanctity and prudence, that they were ſummoned to the council of Beconsfield: the names of five are ſubſcribed to the conſtitutions there enacted, without that of one abbot. Biſhop Adian made Hien (afterwards foundreſs and abbeſs of Hartlepool) the firſt nun amongſt the Northumbrians, A. D. 640. It was anciently a cuſtom in Northumberland and Scotland, for monks and nuns to live together in the ſame monaſtery, but ſubjected to the immediate government of the abbeſs. This was the caſe at Whitby, Repiadon, Beverley, and Ely.

On the converſion of the Saxons and Northumbrians, a great number of monaſteries were founded and richly endowed, particularly in the north, where many of the nobles, and even ſome kings and queens retired from the world, and put on religious habits: but after the devaſtations made by the Danes, in 832, 866, and the three following years, theſe religious communities were almoſt eradicated. In the ſouth there were but few monaſteries remaining, and thoſe chiefly poſſeſſed by the married clergy: Glaſtonbury and Abingdon ſtill retained their monks, but at Wincheſter and Canterbury, in the reign of King Alfred, there were not monks ſufficient to perform the offices; for which they were obliged to have recourſe to the aſſiſtance of the ſecular clergy: (e) and, according to Gervaſius, the name of an abbot was

(e) J. Tanner, in his Preface to the Notitia Monaſtica, ſays, "To give ſome account of the ſecular clergy, who are ſo much ſpoken of in the eccleſiaſtical hiſtory of the Saxon times, and for the moſt part diſadvantageouſly, becauſe we have no account of them, but what is tranſmitted to us by their bittereſt enemies the monks, and ſuch as favoured the monks; but who, if we knew the truth, might

was then ſcarce known; and few then living had ever ſeen a convent of monks. Of the north, Simon Dunelmenſis ſays, "After the devaſtation of that country, A. D. 867, by the Danes, who reduced the churches and monaſteries to aſhes, Chriſtianity was almoſt extinct; very few churches (and thoſe only built with hurdles and ſtraw) were rebuilt: but no monaſteries were refounded, for almoſt two hundred years after; the country people never heard the name of a monk, and were frighted at their very habit, till ſome monks from Winchelcomb brought again the monaſtic way of living to Durham, York, and Whitby."

IN

might perhaps have lived as much to the glory of God, and the good of mankind, as thoſe who ſpoke ſo much againſt them; and yet 'tis uncertain what the difference between the old ſecular canons and the monks was; for hiſtorians, by calling the houſes of the monks, Collegia, and the houſes of the ſecular canons, Monaſteria, confound theſe two ſorts of religious perſons, and make the opinion of Wharton not unlikely, viz. that before the reformation by King Edgar and St. Dunſtan, our monaſteries were nothing but convents of ſecular married clergy. Nor is the marriage of monks and nuns, in thoſe ages, unlikely; for Bede tells us, that in John of Beverley's time, the abbeſs of a monaſtery, then called Vetadun (ſince Watton) had a carnal daughter, who was a nun of that houſe. On the other hand, ſome of the ſeculars obliged themſelves to the vows of chaſtity; and many of them obſerved ſome regular conſtitution: for the canons of Durham read the Pſalms in the ſame order as was required by the rule of St. Benedict.

AT Peykirk they obſerved the canonical hours of the monks, and took the vows of chaſtity and obedience: at Canterbury (as Gervaſius obſerves) they wore the habit of the monks, and partly conformed to their rule: ſo that in all likelihood, the terms of monks and ſecular canons were indifferently uſed, or with very little diſtinction, till King Edgar's time; when St. Dunſtan enforcing a ſtricter obſervation of St. Benedict's rule, thoſe that were willing to retain their wives and parochial cures, were termed ſecular clerks; and thoſe were called monks or regulars, who quitted both, according to the conſtitution of that order."

A FRUITLESS attempt was made, about the begining of the eleventh century, to force theſe canons, and the clergy in general, to celibacy, by Aelfrick, archbiſhop of Canterbury. In the year 1076, the council of Wincheſter, aſſembled under Lanfranc, decreed, that no canon ſhould have a wife; that ſuch prieſts as lived in caſtles and villages ſhould not be forced to put away their wives, if they had them: but ſuch as had not, were forbidden to marry; and biſhops were exhorted, for the future, not to ordain either prieſt or deacon, unleſs he firſt profeſſed that he had no wife. In the year 1102, Archbiſhop Anſelm held a council at Weſtminſter, by which it was decreed, that no archdeacon, prieſt, or deacon, or canon, marry a wife, or retain her if married; that every ſubdeacon be under the ſame law, though he be not a canon, if he hath married a wife after he had made profeſſion of chaſtity. Anſelm, according to William of Malmſbury, deſired of the king, that the chief men of the kingdom might be preſent in council, to the end that the decrees might be enforced by the joint conſent and care of both the clergy and laity; to which they aſſented. Thus the king, and the whole realm, gave their ſanction to theſe canons; yet it appears, that the clergy of the province of York remonſtrated againſt them; and thoſe who were married, refuſed to part with their wives; and the unmarried to make profeſſion of celibacy: nor were the clergy of Canterbury more obedient. Anſelm, therefore, in the year 1108, held a new council at London, in the preſence of the king and barons, partly on this matter, where ſtill ſeverer canons were enacted. Thoſe who had kept

or

In the reign of King Edgar, about the year 960, St. Dunſtan was promoted to the ſee of Canterbury. He was a great reſtorer of monaſtic foundations, and repaired many of the ruined churches and religious houſes, diſplaced the ſeculars, and prevailed on that king to make a reformation of the Engliſh monks, in the council of Wincheſter, A. D. 965; when rules and conſtitutions were formed for their government; partly taken from the rule of St. Benedict, and partly out of the ancient cuſtoms of our Engliſh devotees: this was called Regularis Concordia Anglicæ Nationis, and it is publiſhed, in Saxon and Latin, by the learned Selden, in

or taken women ſince the former prohibition, and had ſaid maſs, were enjoined to diſmiſs them ſo entirely, as not to be knowingly with them in any houſe: any eccleſiaſtic accuſed of this tranſgreſſion, by two or three lawful witneſſes, was, if a prieſt, to purge himſelf by ſix witneſſes; if a deacon by four; if a ſubdeacon by two; otherwiſe to be deemed guilty. Such prieſts, archdeacons, or canons, as refuſed to part with their women, here ſtiled adulterous concubines, were to be deprived not only of their offices and benefices, and put out of the choir, being firſt pronounced infamous, but the biſhop had authority to take away all their moveable goods, and thoſe of their wives.

But all theſe rigorous conſtitutions were ſo inſufficient, that in the year 1125, the cardinal legate, John de Crema, preſiding in a council held at Weſtminſter, thought it neceſſary to enforce them by the papal authority. In his exhortation, he is ſaid to have made uſe of theſe remarkable words: "That it was the higheſt degree of wickedneſs to riſe from the ſide of an harlot to make the body of Chriſt;" nevertheleſs, this very man, as Henry, archdeacon of Huntingdon, a cotemporary writer, relates, after having that day made the body of Chriſt, was caught at night with a real harlot: he adds, that a fact ſo public and notorious could not be denied, and ought not to be concealed; and that the ſhame of this diſcovery drove the legate out of England.

In the year 1129, William Corboyl, archbiſhop of Canterbury and then legate, obtained the king's leave to hold another council at London, to which all the clergy of England were ſummoned; and by the authority of which all thoſe who had wives were requeſted to put them away before the next feaſt of St. Andrew, under pain of deprivation; and the more to enforce it, the archbiſhop and council granted to the king a power of executing their canons, and doing juſtice on thoſe who ſhould offend againſt them; which Henry of Huntingdon ſays, had a moſt ſhameful concluſion; for the king received from the married clergy a vaſt ſum of money, by way of compoſition, and exemption from obedience to theſe conſtitutions of the council. This account is alſo confirmed by Hoveden and Brompton. The Saxon Chronicle ſays, that the conſtitutions of this ſynod had no effect; for all the clergy retained their wives, with the permiſſion of the king, as they had done before; but no notice is taken there of this permiſſion being purchaſed.

It is worthy of obſervation, that whereas, by one of the canons of the council held at Weſtminſter, under Archbiſhop Anſelm, in the year 1102, it had been decreed, that the ſons of prieſts ſhould not be the heirs to the churches of their fathers; Pope Paſchal ordered, that ſuch of them as were perſons of good character ſhould be continued in their benefices; and, in a letter to Anſelm, gave this reaſon for the favour ſhewed them, viz. that the greateſt and beſt part of the clergy in England were the ſons of the clergy. But in Stephen's reign, the power of the papacy acquiring more ſtrength, the celibacy of the clergy was generally eſtabliſhed in England.

Notes to Lord Littleton's Hiſtory of Henry II.

his Spicilegium, after Eadmerus. By this rule all the monaſteries of the ſouth were governed. Edgar, during his reign, is ſaid to have erected, or refounded, forty-ſeven monaſteries; and alſo, at the inſtances of Dunſtan, Ethelwold and Wulſton, biſhops of Wincheſter and Worceſter, to have cauſed reſtitution to be made of all the lands formerly belonging to, and taken from, the religious houſes.

AT the conqueſt, the monks and nuns were conſiderable ſufferers; not only in their lands and poſſeſſions, but alſo by the infringements on their rights and immunities; for no ſooner was the Conqueror quietly ſeated on the throne, than he began to rifle their treaſures, to depoſe their abbots, and ſeize their beſt eſtates, beſtowing them on his Norman followers: he alſo obliged them to alter their miſſals; forcing them to exchange the ancient Gregorian ſervice for a new form, compoſed by William Fiſcam. This innovation was, however, ſtopped by the interpoſition of Oſmund, biſhop of Saliſbury; who, to compromiſe matters, compoſed a new ritual, afterwards called Miſſale in Uſum Sarum, and generally uſed in England, Scotland, and Ireland.

BUT a more material injury was that of making the ſecular clergy, biſhops of the churches of cathedral convents; contrary, as it is ſaid, to a canon made in the time of archbiſhop Theodore, and confirmed by King Edgar. This cauſed that diſtinction then firſt made between the lands belonging to the biſhop, and thoſe the property of the convent; which, before this period, were in common; all donations being made Deo et Eccleſiæ. Beſides, after this diſtinction, the biſhops aſſigned what part they thought proper for the ſupport of the prior and convent; reſerving the beſt eſtates for themſelves and ſucceſſors. This led benefactors to nominate the particular uſes to which they choſe their donations ſhould be applied; either to the maintenance or cloathing of the monks, for lights, hoſpitality, building or repairing the church and its ornaments; and afterwards opened the way for the appropriation of diſtinct portions to the ſeveral great officers of the houſe.

ANOTHER grievance, and which affected the clergy in general, was the alteration made in the nature of the tenure whereby they held their lands; which, from frank almoin ſubject to no duties or impoſitions but the trinoda neceſſitas, (or ſuch as they laid upon themſelves in eccleſiaſtical aſſemblies) was changed into tenure, in baronage, by knights ſervice.

ANNO 1075, the third and laſt regulation of monks was made by Archbiſhop Lanfranc; which brought thoſe of the ancient foundations nearer the Benedictine order than ever. (f) During this reign, the Cluniacs were brought into England; of whom five houſes were founded: as were alſo four houſes of black canons, two or three hoſpitals, thirteen Benedictine abbies and priories, with ſix cells depending upon them, and about fourteen alien priories; whereof the great abbies of Battle and Selby, with the priory of Hinchinbrook, and four or five alien priories, were built and endowed by the king.

WILLIAM RUFUS, ſucceeding to his father, greatly oppreſſed the monks; ſeizing upon the revenues of vacant abbies and biſhopricks, and ſelling them to the beſt bidders. It is even by ſome aſſerted, that he meditated a ſeizure of all their lands. (g) Efforts were made by ſeveral biſhops of this reign, particularly Walkeline, biſhop of Wincheſter, to expel the monks out of the cathedral churches, and to place ſecular canons in their room.

(f) IT is to be noted, that the monks of this iſland were never under one rule, before the ſecond reformation; for, not to mention the difference between the Britiſh, Scotiſh, and Roman monks, we may obſerve, that almoſt every abbot laid down particular rules of living for thoſe under his juriſdiction; ſo that we meet with the rules of St. Patrick, St. Congal, St. Columb, St. Molva, St. Columban, St. Carthavid, St. Aſaph, St. Cuthbert, St. Adhelm, &c. amongſt the Britons and Saxons. Neither did Archbiſhop Cuthbert's regulation make an uniformity in theſe matters; for in King Alfred's time, there were "diverſi generis monachi;" and even after the Conqueſt, at a general viſitation of religious houſes, A. D. 1232, amongſt the Benedictines there were not two monaſteries that lived after the ſame manner.

Preface to Tanner's Notitia Monaſtica.

(g) A MANUSCRIPT in the Cotton library, written by Geraldus Cambrenſis, affirms, that William Rufus had conceived a deſign of taking from all the monaſteries, or religious houſes in England, founded and endowed by the Engliſh, all their lands and poſſeſſions, or the greater part thereof, and converting them into knights fees; ſaying, that near one half of the kingdom had been beſtowed on the church; from all which little or nothing could be drawn by government, in any exigence whatſoever, for the defence of the ſtate.

This

This was prevented by Archbiſhop Lanfranc, who prevailed on the king to retract his conſent; and likewiſe procured a bull from Rome, prohibiting ſuch change. During the thirteen years which this king reigned, there were founded about thirteen houſes of Benedictines; five of the Cluniac order, two of black canons, two colleges, two hoſpitals, and five alien priories; whereof the priories of Armethwayte in Cumberland, and St. Nicholas in Exeter, and the hoſpital of St. Leonard in York, were built and endowed by the king.

King Henry I. is recorded to have been a pious prince, an encourager of learning, and one that had a great eſteem for the church, and all religious perſons. He founded nine or ten monaſteries: viz. the epiſcopal ſee, and priory of regular canons, at Carliſle; the abbies of Cirenceſter and Merton; the priories of Dunſtable, St. Dennis near Southampton, Southwike, and Welhove, of the ſame order; the ſtately Benedictine abbies of Reading and Hyde, and the alien priory at Steventon; as alſo the hoſpitals of St. John in Cirenceſter, Le Mallardry in Lincoln, and St. Mary Magdalene in Newcaſtle. Five new orders were brought into the kingdom in this reign: in the firſt year of it came the knights hoſpitalars; and, about five years after, the Auguſtine canons; towards the year 1128, the Ciſtertians, the canons of the holy ſepulchre, and the monks of Grandmont. In the thirty-five years which this king reigned, there were founded above one hundred and fifty religious houſes; viz. about twenty alien priories, twenty Benedictine monaſteries, and fifteen cells; near fifty houſes of Auguſtine canons, thirteen Ciſtertian, and ſix Cluniac monaſteries, three of knights hoſpitalars, one for canons of the holy ſepulchre, one for Grandmotenſians, one college, and thirteen hoſpitals.

The troubles in which this kingdom was involved, during the greateſt part of the reign of Stephen, did not prevent either that king, or his people, from founding religious houſes; for, in the eighteen years and nine months which he governed this nation, there were founded twenty-two Benedictine abbies and priories, with

with three dependant cells, five alien priories, thirty-two Ciſtertian abbies, twenty-three houſes, and four cells of Auguſtine canons; five Præmonſtratenſian, two Cluniac, and eleven Gilbertine houſes; thirteen preceptories of knights templars, one houſe for ſiſters of the hoſpitalars, one of canons of the holy ſepulchre, four colleges, and twelve hoſpitals: of which the houſes of Benedictines at Carhow in Norfolk, and Heyham in Kent, the black canons at Thornholme in Lincolnſhire, the Cluniacs at Feverſham in Kent, and the commanderies of the knights templars at Creſſing Temple in Eſſex, and Egle in Lincolnſhire, were royal foundations. In the beginning of this reign, the knights templars were introduced into England; as were the Præmonſtratenſians, in the year 1146: and ſhortly after, the Gilbertine order was inſtituted, at Sempringham in Lincolnſhire.

HENRY THE SECOND, after the death of Thomas Becket, affected to be a great friend to monaſtic inſtitutions: himſelf founding a Carthuſian monaſtery at Witham in Somerſetſhire, the firſt of that order in England; houſes at Newſtade in Nottinghamſhire, Ivychurch in Wiltſhire, and Morton in Yorkſhire, for Auguſtines; for whom he likewiſe refounded and augmented the monaſtery of Waltham in Eſſex: he alſo founded Newſtede in Lincolnſhire, for Gilbertine canons; Stonely in Warwickſhire, for Ciſtertian monks; and the alien priory of Hagh in Lincolnſhire. In his reign were founded twenty-eight houſes of Benedictines, whereof twenty were nunneries, as were moſt of the Benedictine convents founded after this time; twenty-ſeven Auguſtine, ſixteen Præmonſtratenſian, one Carthuſian, two Gilbertine, and five Cluniac monaſteries; two collegiate churches, twenty-nine hoſpitals, ten preceptories (Buckland was made a general houſe for all the ſiſters of the hoſpitalars,) twenty-ſix alien priories; and, though contrary to a canon made at a general chapter held A. D. 1151, nineteen Ciſtertian abbies. This canon prohibited the erection of any more houſes of that rule, on account of their great number; which perhaps the other monks were fearful would give them too much weight at councils

and

and general chapters. It is ſaid, there were then in Chriſtendom upwards of five hundred; and they afterwards increaſed ſo much, that, in the year 1250, they amounted to eighteen hundred.

DURING the reign of Richard I. which did not extend to quite ten years, notwithſtanding the vaſt expences of the Cruſade, and the money paid for the ranſom of that king, there were founded fourteen houſes of Benedictines, thirteen of Auguſtine canons, eight of Præmonſtratenſians, three of the Gilbertines, four preceptories of Templars, two alien priories, one college, and ſeven hoſpitals. It does not appear that this king founded any monaſtery; indeed, he is ſaid to have diſliked monks in general, and to have entertained a mortal hatred to the black monks, Ciſtertians and Templars.

KING JOHN, notwithſtanding he was no great friend to eccleſiaſtics, founded a ſtately abbey of Ciſtertians, at Boileau in Hampſhire; to which he made Farendon in Berkſhire a cell; he likewiſe built the Benedictine nunnery of Lambley in Northumberland, made Otterington in Devonſhire an alien priory, and is ſaid, whilſt earl of Moreton, to have founded a Benedictine priory at Waterford, and another at Corke, in Ireland; both which he made cells to the abbey at Bath. In this reign, of upwards of ſeventeen years, were founded eight houſes of Benedictines, eight of Ciſtertians, three of Præmonſtratenſians, nineteen houſes of Auguſtine canons, ſix of Gilbertines, one ſmall Cluniac houſe, and ten alien priories; three preceptories of Templars, four of Hoſpitalers, one college, and eighteen hoſpitals.

IN the reign of King Henry III. the riches, and conſequently the power of the eccleſiaſtics, increaſed to ſuch an alarming pitch, that an act of parliament was made in the ninth year of that reign, to reſtrain the ſuperſtitious prodigality of the people, in beſtowing lands upon religious foundations; particularly in a manner which deprived the king, and the lords of the manors, of their reſpective rights. This was called the ſtatute of Mortmain, (h) wherein it was enacted, "that it ſhall not be lawful, from henceforth, to any to give his lands to any religious houſe, and to take the ſame land again to hold of the ſame houſe; nor ſhall it be lawful to any houſe of religion to take lands of any, and to leaſe the ſame to him of whom he received it: if any, from henceforth, give his lands to any religious houſe, and thereupon be convict, the gift ſhall be utterly void, and the land ſhall accrue to the lord of the fee." (i) The neceſſity of this ſtatute ſee in the notes. (k) Succeeding kings ſometimes diſpenſed with this

(h) MORTMAIN, in mortua manu. Hottoman, in his Commentaries de Verbis Feudal. verbo manus mortua: "Manus mortua locutio eſt, quæ uſurpatur de iis quorum poſſeſſio, ut ita dicam, immortalis eſt, qui nunquam hæredem habere deſinunt. Qua de cauſa res nunquam ad priorem dominum revertitur: nam manus pro poſſeſſione dicitur, mortua pro immortali," &c. And Skene ſays, "That dimittere terras ad manum mortuam eſt idem atque dimitterre ad multitudinem ſive univerſatim, quæ nunquam moritur."

(i) KEEBLE's Statutes.

(k) BY the common law, any man might diſpoſe of his lands to any other private man, at his own diſcretion; eſpecially when the feudal reſtraints of alienation were worn away: yet, in conſequence of theſe, it was always, and is ſtill, neceſſary for corporations to have a licence of mortmain from the crown, to enable them to purchaſe lands: for as the king is the ultimate lord of every fee, he ought not, unleſs by his own conſent to loſe his privilege of eſcheats, and other feudal profits, by the veſting of land in tenants that can never be attainted or die: and ſuch licences of mortmain ſeem to have been neceſſary among the Saxons, about ſixty years before the Norman conqueſt. But, beſides this general licence from the king, as lord paramount of the kingdom, it was alſo requiſite, whenever there was a meſne, or intermediate lord between the king and the alienor, to obtain his licence alſo (upon the ſame feudal principles) for the alienation of the ſpecific land: and if no ſuch licence was obtained, the king or other lord might reſpectively enter on the lands ſo alienated in mortmain, as a forfeiture. The neceſſity of this licence from the crown was acknowledged by the conſtitutions of Clarendon, in reſpect to advowſons, which the monks always greatly coveted, as being the groundwork of ſubſequent appropriations; yet ſuch were the influence and ingenuity of the clergy, that (notwithſtanding this fundamental principle) we find that the largeſt and moſt conſiderable donations of religious houſes happened within leſs than two centuries after the conqueſt: and (when a licence could not be obtained) their contrivance ſeems to have been this: that as the forfeiture for ſuch alienations accrued, in the firſt place, to the immediate lord of the fee, the tenant who meant to alienate, firſt conveyed his lands to the religious houſe, and inſtantly took them back again, to hold as tenant to the monaſtery; which kind of inſtantaneous ſeiſin was probably held, not to occaſion any forfeiture: and then, by pretext of ſome other forfeiture, ſurrender or eſcheat, the ſociety entered into theſe lands, in right of their newly acquired ſigniory, as immediate lords of the fee. But when theſe donations began to grow numerous, it was obſerved, that the feudal ſervices ordained for the defence of the kingdom were every day viſibly withdrawn; that the circulation of landed property, from man to man, began to ſtagnate; and that the lords were curtailed of the fruits of their ſigniories, their eſcheats, wardſhips, reliefs, and the like: and therefore, in order to prevent this, it was ordained by the ſecond of King Henry the Third's great charters, and afterwards by that printed in our common ſtatute books, that all ſuch attempts ſhould be void, and the land forfeited to the lord of the fee. *Blackſtone's Commentaries.*

law,

law, by their ſpecial licence; previous to which, there was an inquiſition of Ad quod dampnum, and a return, upon oath, that it would not prejudice either the dignity or the revenues of the crown. For this licence, fees, and perhaps a fine, were paid.

In the beginning of this reign alſo, the friars, preachers, and friars minors came into England; and, before the end of it, eight ſorts of friars more came amongſt us; and many of them, for the pretended ſeverity of their lives, and their frequent preaching, were at firſt admired by the people, to the great loſs of the pariſh prieſts, as well as the regulars. However, in this long reign of fifty-ſix years, there were founded nine monaſteries of Benedictines, twenty-ſeven of Auguſtine canons, eight of Ciſtertians, three of Præmonſtratenſians, two ſmall houſes of Cluniacs, of Carthuſians and Gilbertines one each, three preceptories of knights templars, and two of hoſpitalars, twelve alien priories, ſeven colleges, and forty-ſeven hoſpitals; beſides twenty-eight houſes of grey friars, twenty-five of black friars, ſeventeen of white friars, four of Auguſtine friars, two of Maturine, or Trinitarian friars; of Croſſed, and Bethleemite friars, friars de Pica and de Areno, one each; ſix houſes of friars de Sacco, two of brethren of St. Anthony de Vienna, and one of brethren of St. Lazarus: of theſe, the king founded the Ciſtertian abbey of Netteley, the ſmall Gilbertine priory of Fordham, the hoſpitals of St. Bartholomew's in Glouceſter, Baſingſtoke, and Oſpring, and ſeveral of the friaries.

In the reign of Edward I. (l) the reverence which the people had hitherto entertained for the monks, began greatly to abate; owing to the writings, preaching, and artful inſinuations of the friars: and, on account of their ſuppoſed riches, the former ſtatute, intended to prevent an increaſe in their poſſeſſions, was

(l) Bishop Kennet, in his Gloſſary, at the end of the Parochial Antiquities, under the word Religioſi, ſaith, Before the ſtatute of Mortmain, the nation was ſo ſenſible of the extravagant donations to the religious, that in the grant and conveyance of eſtates, it was often made an expreſs condition, that no ſale, gift, or aſſignation of the premiſes, ſhould be made to the religious: "Tenenda ſibi et hæredibus ſuis vel cuicunque vendere vel aſſignare voluerint exceptis Religioſis et Judæis."

ſtrengthened

ſtrengthened by additional acts. In this reign, the ſtately abbey of Vale Royal was founded by the king; and, by divers of his ſubjects, three Ciſtertian abbeys, five Auguſtine priories, one Gilbertine, and one Cluniac monaſtery; two preceptories, three alien priories, twelve colleges, and eighteen hoſpitals; beſides thirteen houſes of black, and eleven of grey friars; two of minoreſſes, or nuns of Clare; thirteen of white, and thirteen of Auguſtine friars; two of Trinitarians, four of Croſſed friars, two of friars de Sacco, and one of Bonhommes. About this time, or a little after, a number of chantries were founded, by which the ſecular clergy were ſomewhat benefited.

EDWARD, in the twenty-fourth year of his reign, during his war with France, ſeized all the alien priories, and removed their monks twenty miles from the ſea-ſide, to prevent their giving aſſiſtance or intelligence to his enemies.

IN the nineteen years reign of King Edward II. the religious foundations were, one Benedictine and one Auguſtine monaſtery, five houſes of white friars, three of black friars, ſix of grey friars, four of Auguſtine friars, one of Trinitarians, and one of Croſſed friars; two of the preſent colleges in Oxford, and ſix others; alſo fourteen hoſpitals; of theſe, the white friars at Scardeburgh, the Auguſtine friars in Boſton, and the black friars in Winchelſa, were founded by the king.

IN this reign, anno 1312, the knights templars were ſeized, their order diſolved, and their goods confiſcated.

THE pretence was, their vicious lives, and too great riches and power; though ſome have attributed their downfal to the intrigues of the king of France. Indeed, though they were greatly accuſed, but little was proved againſt them. Their eſtates were at firſt ſeized by the king, and other lords, as fees or eſcheats, and the judges affirmed, that by the laws of the land they might warrantably hold them. But becauſe they had been given for pious uſes, it ſeemed good to the king, the nobility and others, aſſembled in parliament, for the health of their ſouls, and the diſcharge of their conſciences, that the eſtates, &c. according to the

the wills of the donors, ſhould be appropriated to religious uſes; wherefore they were accordingly, by an act of parliament paſſed anno 1323, given to the Hoſpitalars; nevertheleſs, divers of their lands which had been granted to the laity, continued in their poſſeſſions, and ſome tythes were recovered by the parochial clergy.

KING EDWARD III. though, according to the monks, a pious as well as valiant prince, on account of his wars with France, was not only prevented from making many religious foundations, but alſo forced to exerciſe ſeverities on the alien priories: (m) nevertheleſs, he founded and liberally endowed the Auguſtine nunnery at Dartford in Kent; the two large colleges of St. George at Windſor, and St. Stephen at Weſtminſter; and gave to the abbey of St. Mary Graces, by the Tower, the revenues of twelve chantries, ſeized for not having licence of mortmain.

IN this reign of fifty-one years, were founded four houſes of Auguſtine canons, one of Gilbertines, two of Carthuſian monks, ſeventeen hoſpitals, one of the preſent colleges at Oxford, and twenty-five others; two houſes of black friars, eight of grey friars, five of white friars, eight of Auguſtine friars, and one of Bonhommes.

IN the reign of Richard II. the doctrine of Wickliffe began greatly to prevail, and the mendicant friars to loſe their reputation. (n) Although the alien priories were ſequeſtered during the wars, yet many of the principal houſes abroad now obtained the king's licence to ſell their lands to the religious here; and ſometimes to particular perſons, who intended to endow religious foundations.

(m) SEE in Rymer, vol. ii. page 778, his directions about ſeizing alien priories; the lands of which, or large penſions out of them, were granted to noblemen, during the war. *As Dugd. Baron. vol. ii. p.* 74.

(n) THIS evidently appears from the ludicrous ſtories told of them by Chaucer. And that it was then the caſe with them in other kingdoms, appears from the Decameron of Boccace, written much about that time, wherein the friars make a very conſpicuous figure: had they been in much eſteem or authority, neither Boccace nor Chaucer would have ventured thus to ſatyrize them; or at leaſt have done it with impunity: the more juſt their ſatire, the more likely to be ſeverely reſented.

In this reign, which lasted twenty-two years, were founded only four chartreuse houses, six hospitals, six colleges, besides the two founded by Bishop Wickham, at Oxford and Winchester; one house of grey friars, and three of Augustine friars; for after the restraint laid upon endowing houses for the regular orders, the secular priests were more regarded; licences of mortmain being perhaps obtained with greater facility for them, who had not so many privileges as the regulars; or else they were maintained by appropriations, which were then no lay fees, and so not within the reach of the statute; or lastly, it was no hard matter to enfeoff a proper number of persons with lands, for the payment of certain annual stipends to the deans and prebendaries.

The erection of so many chantries and hospitals in the two centuries before the Reformation, may also be ascribed to the same reason. This king founded no monastery or college, but gave to several; particularly the Carthusians at Montgrace in Yorkshire, and St. Ann's near Coventry, the estates of several alien priories seized by his grandfather.

King Henry IV. in the first year of his reign restored all the conventual alienal priories; reserving, in times of war, to the crown, the sums they paid in times of peace to the foreign abbies. In a parliament held A. D. 1404, at Coventry, called the lack-learning parliament, because no practising lawyers were permitted to sit therein, it was moved by the commons, that for raising of money for the carrying on of a foreign war, and the defence of the realm against the Welch and Scots, the clergy should be deprived of their temporal possessions: but Archbishop Arundel shewing to the king, that more of their tenants went to his wars than those of the lay fees; that the clergy were always ready to assist him with their prayers, councils, and purses; and desiring his majesty to recollect his coronation oath, wherein he had promised to advance the honour of the church, and to protect its ministers, the project was laid aside; the king declaring, that he was resolved to leave the church in as good, or a better state than he found it.

The

The archbiſhop then addreſſing himſelf to the commons, told them, that although ſeveral of the king's predeceſſors had, in purſuance of former advice, ſeized the alien priories, which were certainly of great value, yet was not the king half a mark the richer, theſe lands having been begged by his courtiers; and that their preſent motion proceeded from the ſame intereſted motives; their aim being to benefit themſelves, and not the king; who would not, the enſuing year, be the richer by a farthing.

Notwithstanding this rebuke, A. D. 1410, the commons exhibited a new bill againſt the biſhops, abbots, and priors; ſetting forth, that by the ſeizure of their eſtates, the king would be enabled to create and provide for fifteen earls, fifteen hundred knights, ſix thouſand two hundred eſquires, and to found one hundred new hoſpitals. But the king again rejected this propoſal, and commanded them for the future, never to revive that matter. This monarch built the college of Battlefield in Shropſhire, with five others, and about ſix hoſpitals, which were all the religious foundations in the thirteen years of his reign.

In the ſecond year of the ſucceeding reign of Henry V. another attempt, but with no better ſucceſs, was made againſt the revenues of the church; for Archbiſhop Chichely artfully diverted the ſtorm, by inciting the king to aſſert his title to the crown of France; promiſing him ſuch a benevolence from the clergy, for the carrying on of the war, as had never before been given. But in a parliament held the ſame year at Leiceſter, all the alien priories were given to the king, with all their lands and revenues; except ſuch as were conventual, or had the liberty of chooſing their own prior. Moſt of them were, however, beſtowed on other monaſteries or colleges; ſome were to remain in the king's fee; and a very ſmall number of them were granted, or ſold to the laity. (o) In this ſhort reign only two colleges were founded, beſides the Carthuſian abbey at Sheen, and the abbey at Sion for

(o) Scarce any in fee, and not many for life or years, and thoſe to whom ſuch alien priories were given, were obliged to find a maſs-prieſt, to officiate in ſuch alien priories, and pray for the king; ſometimes for the founder.

nuns

nuns of St. Bridget, which were built and munificently endowed by the king himſelf.

During the unhappy reign of Henry VI. there were founded three colleges and one hall at Oxford, three colleges at Cambridge, and eight elſewhere; fifteen hoſpitals, and one houſe of grey friars. Beſides theſe, the king himſelf founded Eaton College, in Buckinghamſhire, and King's College, Cambridge; which he chiefly endowed with the revenues of alien priories.

In the reign of Edward IV. were founded ſix colleges, beſides Katharine hall, in Cambridge, and Lincoln College, in Oxford; and ſeven hoſpitals, or alms-houſes.

King Henry VII. founded ſome few houſes of obſervant friars, and began the hoſpital at the Savoy, in London: his mother founded Chriſt's and St. John's Colleges, in Cambridge. Beſides theſe, there were founded in his reign three hoſpitals, and one ſmall college.

Soon after the acceſſion of King Henry VIII. the colleges of Brazen Noſe and Corpus Chriſti were founded at Oxford; and Magdalene College in Cambridge; as alſo, before the diſſolution, five hoſpitals.

From this account of the riſe and progreſs of monaſtic affairs, it is obſervable, that the richeſt monaſteries were founded before the conqueſt; at which period there were about one hundred: many of them were afterwards refounded.

Within an hundred and fifty years after the conqueſt, or before the firſt of Henry III. there were founded and refounded, four hundred and ſeventy-ſix abbies and priories; beſides eighty-one alien priories. (p)

After that time, there were many chantries, houſes of friars, hoſpitals, and colleges founded; but very few houſes of monks, nuns, or canons. "I think" (ſays Tanner, whom I have cloſely followed in this account) "but one Benedictine houſe, viz. that

(p) It is not clear that any alien priories were founded after the reign of Edward I. The whole number of them was about ninety-ſix; there being fifteen founded after the beginning of the reign of Henry III.

of

of Holand in Lancaſhire, after the death of Henry III. and after the death of King Edward III. (which was about an hundred and ſixty years before the diſſolution) no monaſtery for monks, or nuns, or canons, except Sion, and five chartreuſe houſes:" ſo that the nation in general ſeemed to have quite loſt its taſte for theſe kind of inſtitutions, a great while before the ſubverſion of them.

HAVING thus traced the monaſtic inſtitutions of this kingdom, from their riſe to their total ſuppreſſion, it remains to give ſome account of the different rules, or orders of religious, with their diſcipline, dreſs, and other particularities relative to them.

THE orders were either religious or military: of the former were all monks, nuns and canons.

OF the monks, the moſt ancient are the Benedictines; ſo called from their following a ſet of rules laid down by St. Benedict, a native of Nurſia, in the dukedom of Spoleto in Italy; who was born about the year 480, and died about the year 543: his rule was not confirmed till fifty-two years after his death; when it received the ſanction of Pope Gregory the Great.

ST. BENEDICT founded twelve monaſteries in his own country; the chief of which was at Monte Caſino. His rules are divided into ſeventy-three chapters. In them are many ordinances, inculcating every Chriſtian virtue: at the ſame time it muſt be allowed, that ſome which have been ſince added, are extremely ſingular. (q) All ſorts of perſons, without diſtinction, were, by the

(q) THE ſtatutes and ordinances of Lanfranc concerning the rules to be obſerved by the Benedictines, have one whole chapter or decree concerning the diminution of blood; where it is appointed, that leave muſt firſt be aſked: but this leave was not to be granted, at ſome certain ſolemn ſeaſons (unleſs upon unavoidable neceſſity) as when their abſence from officiating or aſſiſting in the public ſervice of their church was not to be diſpenſed with.

BUT leave being granted, the hour was to be notified to the cellerer of the convent: thoſe who were to have a vein opened, were to come to the place appointed for that purpoſe, where ſeveral ceremonies and formalities were ordered to be performed at that time, and upon that occaſion. Afterwards they were to appear before the prior and chapter; and it being openly ſaid, that ſuch and ſuch a brother had blood taken from him, the monk was to ſtand up (eſpecially if a vein in his arm had been opened) and to ſpeak for himſelf. Then it follows, if he had been guilty of a ſmall offence, it ſhould be forgiven him; but if the offence was ſuch as could not be forgiven, or paſſed over without bodily punishment,

the order of St. Benedict, to be received into this order: children, boys, youths, the poor and the rich, gentlemen and peasants, servants and freemen, the learned and unlearned, the laity and clergy.

THE form and colour of the habits of these monks, it is said, were at first left to the direction of the abbots, who varied them according to the season and climate. But it was afterwards ordained, that they should wear a loose gown, of black stuff, reaching down to the heels, with a cowl or hood of the same, and a scapulary; under this, another habit, of the same size, made of white flannel, and boots on their legs. From the colour of their outward habit, they were generally called black monks.

To the end that no man might have any particular property, the abbot found them in every thing that was necessary; which, besides their habit, was a knife, a needle, a steel pen, and tablets to write on. Their beds were a mat, some straw, and a pillow; their covering, a blanket, and a piece of serge.

THERE were nuns of this order, as well as monks; their habit was a black robe, with a scapulary of the same; under which was a tunic of white undyed wool; and, when they went to the choir, they had, over all, a black cowl, like that worn by the monks. (r)

THE

punishment, the punishment of him should be deferred till another time; namely, till he had recovered better health and strength, after the loss of blood.

THIS chapter is somewhat mystical; and perhaps designedly so, that the reputation of the members of the convent might be defended from being openly charged with irregularities and foul enormities: such things were like the rights of Ceres, religiously to be concealed. But it seems plain, that the want of having blood taken away, was frequently occasioned by irregularity and excess.

I MAY further observe, that when the lord high-steward, with his retinue, had, according to his office, attended at an enthronization feast of an archbishop, it was one branch of his accustomed right and fee, which he claimed at his going away, to stop three days at one of the nearest manors of the archbishop, to diminish his blood; that is, to have a vein opened, or properly to cool his blood, which had been heated by high feeding and drinking at the feast. *Battely's Additions to Somner's Canterbury, p.* 133.

(r) THIS order is said by many (among whom are Sir Henry Spelman, Camden, and Selden) to have been brought into England by St. Augustine, A. D. 596: but Sir John Masham, Bishop Patrick, Dr. Hickes, Dr. William Thomas, and Bishop Nicholson, think this rule was little known, till King Edgar's time; and never perfectly observed till after the Conquest.

SOME have said, that St. Wilfrid brought it into England, A. D. 666; and others, with greater probability, that he improved the English church by it. It is expressly mentioned in King Kenred's charter to the monks of Eversham, A. D. 709; and in the bull of Pope Constantine, granted in the

same

The great riches and power of the Benedictines causing a remissness in the observance of their rules, a reformation was set on foot by Bernon, abbot of Gigni, in Burgundy; which was compleated by Odo, abbot of Cluni, (s) anno 912, who added thereto some stricter ordinances. (t) This gave rise to a new order, called, from

same year to that monastery: But Bede, who hath given us a very accurate account of the state of religion in this island till the year 731, hath nothing of it; nor is there any mention of it in the first regulation of the monks in England by Archbishop Cuthbert, in the great synod at Cloveshoe, A. D. 747.

If Wilfrid really advanced this rule, it was not over all England, but in Kent only; and if the charter of King Kenred, and the bull of Pope Constantine be genuine, (for all the antient grants produced by the monks are not so) this rule, which is there prescribed to the monks of Eversham, is however said, in the bull, "to have been at that time but little used in those parts:" so that, instead of the Saxon monks being all Benedictines, there were probably but few such, till the restoration of monasteries under King Edgar; when St. Dunstan and St. Oswald (the latter of whom had been a Benedictine monk at Fleury in France) not only favoured the monks against the secular clergy, but so much advanced the Benedictines, that William of Malmsbury saith, "This order took its rise in England, from St. Oswald." Of this order were all our cathedral priories, except Carlisle; and most of the richest abbies in England. Reyner, vol. i. p. 217, saith, that the revenues of the Benedictines were almost equal to those of all the other orders. *Tanner's Notitia Monastica.*

(s) This abbey, which was situated at Cluny, in the Massonnois, a little province in France, was anciently so very spacious and magnificent, that in 1245, after holding of the first Council of Lyons, Pope Innocent II. went to Cluni, accompanied with the two patriarchs of Antioch and Constantinople, twelve cardinals, three archbishops, fifteen bishops, and a great number of abbots; who were all entertained, without one of the monks being put out of his place; though St. Louis, Queen Blanch his mother, the duke of Artois, his brother and his sister, the emperor of Constantinople, the sons of the kings of Arragon and Castile, the duke of Burgundy, six counts, and a great number of lords, with all their retinue, were there at the same time.

Cluni, at its first erection, was put under the immediate protection of the apostolic see; with express prohibition to all secular and ecclesiastical powers, not to disturb the monks in the possession of their effects, or the election of their abbot. By this they pretend to be exempted from the jurisdiction of bishops; which at length gave the hint to other abbies to insist on the same.

Cluni is the head of a very numerous and extensive congregation: in effect, it was the first congregation of divers monasteries, united under one chief, so as to constitute one body, or, as they call it, one order, that ever arose. *Chambers's Dictionary.*

(t) If we may believe their own abbot Peter, these ordinances were not much observed. His words are: "Our brethren despise God, and having past all shame, eat flesh now all days of the week except Friday, not only in secret but in public; also boasting of their sin, like those of Sodom: they run here and there, and, as kites and vultures, flie with great swiftness where the most smoke of the kitchen is, or where they smell the best roast and boiled.

Those that will not do as the rest, them they mock, and treat as hypocrites and profane. Bacon, cheese, eggs, and even fish itself, can no more please their nice palates: they only relish the flesh-pots of Egypt: pieces of boiled and roasted pork, good fat veal, otters and hares; the best geese and pullets; and, in a word, all sorts of flesh and fowl, do now cover the tables of our holy monks. But what do I talk? Those things are grown now too common; they are cloyed with them: they must have something more delicate: they would have got for them kids, harts, boars, and wild bears. One must for them beat the bushes with a great number of hunters; and, by help of birds of prey, must

from the place of its inſtitution, Cluniacs: they were the principal branch of the Benedictines; and, like them, they wore a black habit.

All the houſes of this order in England were governed by foreigners, and ſubordinate to foreign monaſteries, (v) by whom only they could be viſited: neither could they elect their own priors, profeſs novices, or determine their own differences; but, for all theſe, were obliged to refer to their ſuperiors beyond ſea; by which the greateſt part of their revenues were carried abroad; (u) and theſe convents contained more French than Engliſh monks.

On theſe accounts, during the wars with France, the priories of this order were generally ſeized by the king, as alien priories; but after the petition to the parliament of Wincheſter, the fourth of Edward III. theſe inconveniences were by degrees removed; ſome of their houſes were in that and the following reign made denizen; Bermondſey was made an abbey; and at length all the others diſcharged from their ſubjection to foreign abbies. (w) There were twenty-ſeven priories and cells of this order in England; and it was introduced here about the year 1077.

The order of Grandmont was alſo a branch of the Benedictines, inſtituted on the mountain of Muret, by one Stephen, a gentleman of Auvergne, in France, anno 1076; who compoſed a rule taken from that of St. Benedict, the regular canons, and the manner of living of the Hermits. It was confirmed by ſeveral Popes; and afterwards, by reaſon of its great auſterity, moderated

muſt one chaſe the pheaſants, and partridges, and ring-doves, for fear the ſervants of God (who are good monks) ſhould periſh with hunger."

Short Hiſtory of Monaſtical Orders, by Gabriel Emilliane, p. 92.

(v) The houſes of Cluni, la Charité ſur Loire, and St. Martin's de Champs, at Paris.

(u) The houſe of Cluni had a penſion out of every houſe of that order in England, called Apportus, which probably amounted in the whole to a great ſum; for Cotton, in his Abridgment, p. 51, ſaith, The abbot of Cluni had a penſion from England of 2000*l.* *per annum*: and, according to Rymer, vol. iii. p. 1009, and Prynne's Records, vol. iii. p. 386, 858, the foreigners ſometimes demanded occaſional ſupplies from their houſes here; and even run them into debt, as Prynne, vol. iii. p. 750. *Tanner.*

(w) But perhaps not till the thirty-fixth of Henry VI. or A. D. 1457; when three monks were ſent from Cluni, to deſire reſtitution of thoſe poſſeſſions which had long been detained from them, and leave to enter all places depending on their houſes; but, inſtead of obtaining any thing, were deprived of the ſubjection of all houſes of this order in England.

by

by Innocent IV. in the year 1247; and again, by Clement V. in the year 1309. This Stephen is ſaid to have worn, by way of mortification, an iron cuiraſs next his ſkin; to have ſlept in a wooden coffin, laid ſome feet deep in the ground, without either bed or ſtraw; and, by his frequent kneeling, to have made the ſkin of his knees like that of a camel; and moreover, to have ſo often kiſſed the earth, that his noſe was thereby turned up.

THIS order obtained the name of Grandmont, from the place of their reſidence, pointed out by a pretended miracle. One Peter, a native of Limoges, a diſciple and ſucceſſor of Stephen, having aſked a ſign from Heaven, informing him where he and his monks ſhould fix their abode, they having been chaſed from Muret; a voice in the air thrice diſtinctly pronounced Grandmount, which is a high mountain in the neighbourhood of Muret. Their dreſs is much like that of the Benedictines.

THERE were but three houſes of this order in England: viz. Abberbury in Shropſhire, in which they were placed, at their firſt introduction, by Henry I. Creſſewal, in Herefordſhire; and Groſmont, or Eſkdale, in Yorkſhire.

ANOTHER branch of the Benedictines were the Carthuſians, the ſtricteſt of all the religious orders. It was inſtituted about the year 1080, as is pretended, on the following occaſion. The body of a profeſſor of the univerſity of Paris, eſteemed a man of piety and exemplary life, being brought, according to the cuſtom of the country, upon a bier for interment, whilſt the funeral ſervice was performing, the corpſe raiſed itſelf upright, and with a lamentable voice cried, "I am accuſed by the juſt judgment of God;" which putting the congregation into a great fright, the ceremony ſtopped, and the interment was defered till the next day; when on beginning again, the body cried, "I am judged by the juſt judgement of God;" whereupon the obſequies were put off yet one day longer: at laſt, on the third day, in the preſence of a number of ſpectators, aſſembled by the report of this prodigy, the dead man cried, with a terrible voice, "By the juſt judgment of God am I condemned."

ONE Bruno being preſent, was ſo ſtruck, that he addreſſed himſelf to the aſſembly, aſſerting, "That it was impoſſible for them to be ſaved, unleſs they renounced the world, and retired themſelves into the deſarts;" which he, with ſix companions, executed immediately, going into a frightful place, called Charteruſe, (x) amongſt the mountains, in the dioceſe of Grenoble; where he was aſſiſted in all things by the biſhop of that place, named Hugues; who, afterwards, became one of his diſciples: they followed the rule of St. Benedict; adding thereto ſeveral other great auſterities; ſome of which were, a total abſtinence from fleſh, (y) even in caſes of deſperate ſickneſs; the living one day in every week on bread and water; always wearing a hair ſhirt next their ſkins; confinement within the walls of their monaſtery, from which none were ever to go out but the prior or procurator, and that only on the neceſſary buſineſs of the convent; a prohibition of walking about their own grounds above once a week; and, beſides all theſe, and more, they were enjoined an almoſt continual ſilence.

THIS rule was confirmed by Pope Alexander III. about the year 1174, and was brought into England, anno 1180, or 1181. Here were only nine houſes of monks of this order, and no nuns; their habit was all white, except an outward plaited cloak (ſometimes worn,) which was black.

THE Ciſtertians were likewiſe produced from the Benedictines; they were ſo called from Ciſtertium, or Ciſteaux, in the biſhopric of Chalons, in Burgundy, where they had their beginning, anno 1098; being inſtituted by one Robert, who had been abbot of Moleſme, in that province; from which he, with twenty of his religious, had withdrawn, on account of the wicked lives of his

(x) FROM whence their monaſteries were ſometimes called charterhouſes.

(y) THE prohibition of eating fleſh is ſtill continued, with this reſtriction: "That fleſh ought to be preſented to thoſe who are thought to draw near their end: if they accept of it, and recover from ſickneſs, they are deprived for ever of any vote; they can never come to any degree of ſuperiority; and are looked upon as infamous men, who have preferred a morſel of meat to a precious death before God." Stevens, vol. ii. p. 239, ſaith, There were but five hunneries of this auſtere order in the world; and but one hundred and ſixty-ſeven houſes of theſe monks.

monks; but they were brought into repute by Stephen Harding, an Engliſhman, their third abbot, who gave them ſome additional rules to thoſe of St. Benedict: theſe were called, Charitatis Chartæ, and confirmed in the year 1107 by Pope Urban II.

STEPHEN is therefore, by ſome, reckoned their principal founder. They were alſo called Bernardines, from St. Bernard, abbot of Clerival, or Clarivaux, in the dioceſe of Langres, about the year 1116; and who, himſelf, founded one hnndred and ſixty monaſteries of this order. Sometimes they were ſtiled white monks, from the colour of their habit; which was a white caſſock, with a narrow ſcapulary, and over that, a black gown, when they went abroad; but a white one, when they went to church. (z) Their monaſteries, which became very numerous, were generally built in ſolitary and uncultivated places, and all dedicated to the Holy Virgin. This order came into England, anno 1128; and had their firſt houſe at Waverley, in Surrey; and, before the diſſolution, had eighty-five houſes here. (a)

THE foundation of the order of Savigni, or Fratres Griſei, is, by ſome, placed before the Conqueſt: but it was not really in being, till about forty years after that event.

ITS author, Vitalis, was born about the middle of the eleventh century, at Tierceville, near Bayeux; and is frequently ſtiled, Vitalis de Mortain, from having been a prebend of the Collegiate Church of Mortain: he was a companion of Robert de Arbriſſel, founder of the order of Fontevrauld; and began, anno 1105, to gather diſciples in the foreſt of Savigni; where, by the aſſiſtance of a nobleman named Roaul de Fugeres, he founded an abbey, about the year 1112: he preſcribed to his diſciples the rule of St. Benedict, with ſome peculiar additional conſtitutions: they wore a grey habit; from whence they were denominated Fratres Griſei.

(z) THEY pretended that the Virgin Mary appeared to St. Bernard, and commanded him to wear, for her own ſake, ſuch white clothes. *Emillianne.*

(a) STEVENS, vol. ii. p. 37, a, and p. 50, a, from A. Wood. All orders, both of monks and friars, were againſt having any houſe of another order near them: but the Ciſtertians would not allow another houſe, even of their own order, to be built within ſuch a diſtance of them.

Vitalis came into England, A. D. 1120; and preaching here, and converting many, probably introduced his order; which was ſhortly after, namely, in the year 1148, united to the Ciſtertians.

The order of Tiron was ſet on foot by St. Bernard, (b) who was born in the territory of Abbeville, in the province of Ponthieu, A. D. 1046, and became a follower of the before-mentioned Robert de Arbriſſel; but inſtituted a different ſort of monks, who took their name Tironenſes, from their firſt monaſtery, which was founded at Tiron, A. D. 1109: they were reformed Benedictines; they wore, at firſt, a grey habit, which was afterwards changed for black.

It does not appear they had any houſe in England; or more than one abbey in Wales, viz. St. Dogmael's (where they were placed about the year 1126,) with its dependant priory at Pille, and cell at Caldey. The Monaſticon mentions the monks of Savigni and Tiron as of the ſame order.

The orders of monks here mentioned, were all we had in England and Wales, (c) except the Culdees, or Cultores Dei, who were Scotch monks, and of the ſame rule with the Iriſh ones; the Scotch writers make them as ancient as the converſion of their country to Chriſtianity, in the times of Decius and Aurelian. But they are neither mentioned by Nennius, who wrote in the ſeventh century, nor Bede, who wrote in the eighth. The firſt account of them is at St. Andrew's about the middle of the ninth century: in England they occur no where, but at St. Peter's, in York.

The next of the religious orders were canons: theſe were either ſeculars or regulars. The ſecular canons were ſo called, becauſe they were converſant in the world, and adminiſtered to the laity on all occaſions, and took upon themſelves the cure of ſouls, which the regulars might not do without a diſpenſation. They

(b) This was a different perſon from St. Bernard of Clairvaux. *Stevens*, vol. ii. p. 256.

(c) Unless there were any Celeſtine monks brought in by King Henry V. as Reymer mentions, tr. i. p. 166, from Walſingham, ſub A. D. 1413; and Weaver p. 138: but I know not on what grounds. *Tanner*.

differed

differed very little from the ordinary prieſts, unleſs that they were under the government of local ſtatutes; for though, in ſome places, they were obliged to live together, yet in general this was not the caſe; moſt of them living apart, and ſubſiſting upon diſtinct portions, called prebends; nearly in the ſame manner as the preſent canons of our cathedrals.

THE regular canons were ſuch as lived in a conventual manner under one roof, had a common refectory and dormitory, and were bound by vows to obſerve the rules and ſtatutes of their order: in fine, they were a kind of religious, whoſe diſcipline was leſs rigid than that of the monks.

THE chief rule of theſe canons was that of St. Auguſtine, who was conſtituted biſhop of Hippo, A. D. 395: but they were not brought into England till after the Conqueſt; and ſeem not to have obtained the appellation of Auguſtine canons, till ſome years after. (d) Their habit was a long black caſſock, with a white rochet

(d) INDEED Bale and Sir Robert Atkins ſay, that theſe canons were brought into England by St. Birinus, in the beginning of the ſeventh century; but thoſe were certainly ſecular canons, whom he then placed at Dorcheſter; and all other hiſtorians agree, that we had no regular canons here till the eleventh, and probably not till the twelfth century.

FOR though they differ about the place of their firſt ſettlement, yet the general opinion is, that they came in after King Henry I. began his reign. Joſeph Pamphilius indeed ſaith, that they were ſeated in London, A. D. 1059; but he ſeems to have been an obſcure writer. Mr. Somner ſaith, that St. Gregory's, in Canterbury, which was built by Archbiſhop Lanfranc, A. D. 1084, was their firſt houſe: but Leland's ſaying, that Archbiſhop Lanfranc placed ſecular canons at St. Gregory's, and that Archbiſhop Corboil changed them into regulars, makes the authority of that judicious antiquary, in this caſe, doubtful.

REYMER ſaith, that they were brought into England by Athelwulphus, or Adulphus, confeſſor to King Henry I. and had their houſe at Noſtell in Yorkſhire: but they ſeem not to have been ſettled there till Thurſtan was archbiſhop of York; and that was not till A. D. 1114.

STOWE ſays, that Norman was the firſt regular canon in England; and that theſe religious were firſt ſeated at the Holy Trinity, or Chriſt Church, within Aldgate, London, A. D. 1108: but that houſe was not built till R. Beaumier was biſhop of London: whereas the houſe of theſe canons at Colcheſter was founded before the death of Biſhop Maurice his predeceſſor, which happened September 26, 1107: and therefore I cannot but think that John Roſſe and Pope Paſchalis II. are right, in placing them firſt at Colcheſter; though it could not be in Roſſe's year 1109, but was rather A. D. 1105.

STEVENS tells us, though there were regular canons who embraced the rule of St. Auſtin, taken from his one hundred and ninth epiſtle, in the eleventh century, (as particularly at the abbey of St. Denis at Rheims, about A. D. 1067) yet the regular canons did not make ſolemn vows till the twelfth century; and did not in general take the name of "Regular Canons of St. Auſtin," till Pope Innocent

chet over it; and over that, a black cloak and hood. The monks were always ſhaved; but theſe canons wore beards, and caps on their heads. There were of theſe canons, and women of the ſame order, called canoneſſes, about one hundred and ſeventy-five houſes.

BESIDES theſe, there were the following ſorts: firſt, ſuch as obſerved the rule of St. Auguſtine, according to the regulations of St. Nicholas of Arroſia; ſecondly, Auguſtines of the order of St. Victor; thirdly, Auguſtines of the inſtitution of St. Mary of Maretune; fourthly, Præmonſtratenſians, or canons who followed a rule laid down, anno 1120, by St. Norbet, afterwards archbiſhop of Magdeburgh, which was a mixture of the monaſtical and canonical diſcipline.

THIS order obtained its appellation of Præmonſtratenſians, from a ſtory told by theſe religious: wherein they aſſerted, that their founder received his rule, curiouſly bound in gold, from the hand of St. Aguſtine himſelf, who appeared to him one night, and ſaid to him, "There is the rule which I have written: if thy brethren obſerve it, they, like my other children, need fear nothing at the day of judgement:" after which, an angel ſhewed him the meadow wherein he was to build his firſt monaſtery, which from thence was called Præmonſtratus. Theſe canons, from their habit, were called white canons: it was a white caſſock, with a rochet over it; a long white cloak, and a white cap. They came into England about the year 1140; and firſt ſettled at Newhouſe in Lincolnſhire.

A CONSERVATOR of their privileges reſided in England; but they neverthelefs were viſited by their ſuperiors of Præmonſtre; who, like thoſe of the Cluniacs and Ciſtertians, raiſed great con-

Innocent II. ordained, in the Lateran Council, A. D. 1139, that all regular canons ſhould ſubmit to that rule of St. Auſtin, in his one hundred and ninth epiſtle; ſo that theſe regular canons certainly fall ſhort of the time of their pretended founder; and therefore when black or regular canons are mentioned before A. D. 1105, the reader muſt thereby underſtand ſecular canons. For it was uſual, in thoſe days, to call ſecular canons of cathedral and collegiate churches, "Canonici Regulares," to diſtinguiſh them from the common parochial clergy; though probably many of thoſe ſocieties might become Auſtin canons afterwards. *Tanner.*

tributions

tributions on them, till reftrained by the parliament held at Carlifle, anno 1307.

THIS ftatute did not reftrain the foreign fuperiors from vifiting their orders; but only from taking money out of the kingdom; fo that the religious of this order continued fubordinate to the general chapter and abbot of Præmonftre, till the year 1512; when they were exempted from it by the bull of Pope Julius II. confirmed by King Henry VIII. and the fuperiority of the houfes of this order in England, which were thirty-five in number, was given to the abbot of Welbeck in Nottinghamfhire. Fifthly, the Gilbertine canons; fo called from St. Gilbert an Englifhman, their firft inftitutor; they were likewife fometimes called Sempringham canons, from the place of their firft monaftery, which was founded at Sempringham in Lincolnfhire, A. D. 1148; and confirmed by Pope Eugenius III.

THIS order confifted of men and women, who lived under the fame roof, but their apartments had no comunication: neverthelefs they could not efcape fcandal, as appears from the verfes in the note. (e) This rule was compofed from thofe of St. Auguftine and St. Benedict: the women following the latter, according to the Ciftertian regulation; and the men that of St. Auguftine, with fome fpecial ftatutes inferted by St. Gilbert. The habit of thefe canons, as defcribed in the Monafticon, was a black caffock, with a cloak over it; and an hood, lined with lamb-fkins: but others fay, it was the fame with the Ciftertians.

THEY were under the directions of a mafter, or prior-general; who frequently vifited them, and had fo much power, that particular priors and convents could do little without him. This order increafed fo faft, that St. Gilbert himfelf founded thirteen monafteries; four of men, and nine for men and women together;

(e) HARUM funt quædam fteriles, quædam parientes
Virginefque tamen nomine cuncta tegunt;
Quæ paftoralis baculi dotatur honore
Illa quidem melius fertiliufque parit.
Vix etiam quævis fterilis reperitur in illis,
Donec ejus ætas talia poffe negat.

thefe,

theſe, together, contained ſeven hundred bretheren, and fifteen hundred ſiſters. At the diſſolution, there were about twenty-five houſes of this order in England and Wales.

THE canons regular of the Holy Sepulchre were inſtituted here, the beginning of the twelfth century, in imitation of thoſe eſtabliſhed anno 1099, after the conqueſt of Jeruſalem, by Godfrey of Boullogne; who committed to their care the keeping of the Holy Sepulchre.

THEY were ſometimes called canons of the Holy Croſs, on account of a double red croſs they wore upon the breaſt of their cloak, or upper garment; in which alone their dreſs differed from that of other Auguſtine canons.

THE firſt houſe of this order was at Warwick, which was begun for them by Henry de Newburgh, earl of Warwick; who dying anno 1123, before it was finiſhed, Roger his ſon completed it before the year 1135. After the loſs of Jeruſalem, A. D. 1188, this order falling to decay, their revenues and privileges were moſtly given to the Maturine friars; and but two houſes of this order continued to the diſſolution.

BESIDES the Benedictine and Gilbertine nuns already mentioned, there were alſo Cluniac, Ciſtertian, Carthuſian, Auguſtine, and Præmonſtratenſian nuns; who followed the ſame rules as the monks of their reſpective orders, omitting only what was not proper for their ſex; and wore habits of the ſame colour, having their heads covered with a veil: and alſo nuns of Fontevraud, St. Clare, and Brigithries.

THE nuns of Fontevraud were inſtituted about the year 1100, by Robert D'Arbriſſel, at Fontevraud, near Poictiers. This order, which was a reformation of the Benedictines, was chiefly for women; yet, in France, both men and women of this order reſided in the ſame convent, but in ſeparate apartments; and, what was peculiar, under the government of an abbeſs, the founder grounding his model on the nineteenth chapter of St. John; where it is written, that Chriſt being on the croſs, recommended St. John to the Virgin Mary, and commanded him to acknowledge

ledge her as his mother: in imitation whereof the male religious were to acknowledge the maternal authority of the abbeſs, or prioreſs.

THIS order was approved of by Pope Paſcal. The abbeſs of Fontevraud was made the general ſuperioreſs of the order. Theſe nuns were brought into England by Robert Boſſu, earl of Leiceſter, before the year 1161, and placed at Nun-Eaton, in Warwickſhire. There were only two other houſes of this order in the kingdom. There is no expreſs account that any monk belonged to them; but that there did is probable, as a prior is mentioned at Nun-Eaton (f). Their habit was a kind of tunic, or caſſock, of the natural colour of the wool, and over it a large black garment.

THE nuns of the order of St. Clare were inſtituted about the year 1212, by one Clara, a religious virgin, at Aſſiſi in Italy, the place of her birth; where ſhe lived ſome time with St. Francis, whoſe diſcipline and habit ſhe adopted for her nuns; on which account they were frequently called Minoreſſes; and their houſe, without Aldgate, the Minories. They were alſo ſometimes, on account of their poverty, ſtiled the Poor Clares.

THIS order was confirmed by the Popes Innocent III. and Honorius III. by the latter, A. D. 1223, after which it was divided into a ſtricter and leſs rigid ſort.

THEY were brought into England by Blanch, queen of Navarre, wife to Edmund, earl of Lancaſter, Leiceſter and Derby, about the year 1293, and placed without Aldgate, London; beſides which, this order had only three houſes in England; viz. Waterbeacle and Denny, in Cambridgeſhire, and Bruſyard, in Suffolk.

THE Bridgettine nuns were ſo called from their inſtitutrix, Bridget, princeſs, or ducheſs of Nerica, in Sweden; who, in the

(f) IN France the nuns wear a black habit, with a white veil and beirs; at church, a long black gown, with large ſleeves. The monks are all in black, as ſecular prieſts; but upon the caſſocks they have a camail, as the French biſhops; at the bottom of which hang two little ſquare pieces of the ſame ſtuff, one before and the other behind. *Emillianne.*

year 1360, went to Rome, and obtained the approbation of Pope Urban V. for an order of nuns which ſhe had inſtituted, as ſhe pretended, by the expreſs command of Chriſt himſelf, by whom the rules were dictated: whence theſe religious were alſo called nuns of Our Holy Saviour: their rule was nearly that of St. Auguſtine.

THIS order, though chiefly for women, had likewiſe men in every convent. Their monaſteries were built double: in one half, which was ſeparated from the other by a high wall, dwelt the women, under the direction of an abbeſs; and the other half was inhabited by the men.

THE church was ſo contrived, that it ſerved for both; the men having the lower, and the nuns the upper part of it. The men were to attend to the ſpiritual matters, the women to the temporal; and, in caſe of a too ſcanty endowment, were to work for the maintenance of themſelves and the brethren: but both men and women were to obey the abbeſs. The men were not permitted to approach the nuns, except in caſes of abſolute neceſſity.

THIS order differed from all others, in requiring a particular number of men and women in every houſe; viz. ſixty nuns, thirteen prieſts, four deacons, and eight lay brothers, in all eighty-five; to repreſent Chriſt's thirteen apoſtles, including St. Paul, and ſeventy-two diſciples. Their habit was a tunic of coarſe grey woollen, with a cloak of the ſame.

THE nuns had on their veils five ſmall pieces of red cloth, repreſenting Chriſt's five wounds: the prieſts, a red croſs on their breaſts, with a circular piece of white cloth in the middle, to repreſent the hoſt; the deacons, a white circle, within which were four ſmall pieces of red cloth, to repreſent tongues; and the laymen wore a white croſs, with five red pieces, repreſenting the five wounds. Of this order there was only one houſe in England; namely, that of Sion in Middleſex, founded by King Henry V. about the year 1414.

THESE conclude the catalogue of the different ſorts of monks, canons, and nuns, formerly reſident in England and Wales. We come next to the friars.

THE

The first were the Dominicans; whose founder was St. Dominic, a Spaniard, born at Calagueraga, a small town in Old Castile, about the year 1070. These were likewise called preaching friars, and black friars: the former, from their office, whereby they were directed to preach, and convert heretics; the latter, from the colour of their garments.

In France, they are also named Jacobins; from the situation of their first house, which stood in St. James's-street, at Paris. Their rule, which was chiefly that of St. Augustine, was verbally approved of by Pope Innocent III. in the Lateran Council, A. D. 1215; and by the bull of Pope Honorius III. A. D. 1216. At first they wore the habit of the Augustine canons; but, about the year 1219, exchanged it for a white cassock, with a white hood over it; and when they went abroad, a black cloak and hood over their white vestments. They came into England, A. D. 1221; and that year had their first house at Oxford. At the dissolution, there were of this order about forty-three houses. There were likewise Dominican nuns, but none of them ever reached England.

The Franciscan, Grey, or Minor Friars, was an order thus variously called: the first, from St. Francis D'Assisi, their founder; the second, from the colour of their habit; and the third, from an affected humility. Their rule was framed by St. Francis, A. D. 1209; approved of by Pope Innocent III. A. D. 1210; and by the General Lateran Council, A. D. 1215.

Their habit was a loose garment of coarse grey cloth, reaching to their heels, a cowl of the same, and, when they went abroad, a cloak. They girded themselves with a cord, and went bare-foot.

Authors differ as to the exact time when they were introduced into England; but the general, and most probable opinion is, that it was about the year 1224. They had their first house at Canterbury, and their second at London.

By degrees, this order relaxing from the strictness of their original discipline, a reformation was set on foot, about the year 1400, by St. Bernard, or Bernardin of Sienna; and was confirmed by by the council of Conſtance, A. D. 1414; and afterwards received the approbation of Eugenius IV. and other popes. Thoſe who profeſſed this reformed rule were called Obſervants, or Recollects. (g)

THEY are commonly ſaid to have been brought into England by King Edward IV. but Tanner ſays, "I find no certain account of their being here, till King Henry VII. built two or three houſes for them."

AT the diſſolution, the Conventual Franciſcans had about fifty-five houſes, under ſeven diſtinct cuſtodies or warderſhips, viz. thoſe of London, York, Cambridge, Briſtol, Oxford, Newcaſtle, and Worceſter.

THE Trinitarians, Maturines, or Friars of the order of the Holy Trinity for the redemption of captives, were inſtituted by John de Martha and Felix de Valois, in France, about the year 1197. They followed the rule of St. Auguſtine; to which were added ſome particular conſtitutions; the chief of theſe were, that all the money or goods that ſhould fall into their hands, were to be divided into three parts; one of which was to be employed in works of charity, one for their maintenance, and the third to be expended in the redemption of captives taken by the Infidels. Their churches were to be all dedicated to the Holy Trinity; which procured them the name of Trinitarians.

THE appellation of Maturines they owed to their firſt houſe being ſituated near St. Mathurine's chapel in Paris: by their rule they were alſo forbidden to travel on horſeback, but might ride on aſſes.

THEIR habit was white, having on the breaſt a croſs, half red and half blue, given them by Pope Innocent III. who confirmed their order, and to whom whilſt ſaying maſs, a hideous phantom had appeared; it was habited in a like dreſs, and holding in its hands two ſlaves, bound in chains; which viſion made him re-

(g) As to the Capuchins, and other diſtinctions of the Franciſcans beyond the ſeas, they chiefly aroſe ſince the Engliſh reformation, and never had any place here.

solve to establish an order, whose business it should be to redeem captive Christians.

These friars were brought into England, A. D. 1224; and on the decay of the order of the canons of the holy sepulchre, their revenues were given to them.

Their first house was at Mottendan in Kent; or, according to some, at Ingham in Norfolk, as long as that house was of this order; from whence they were called of the order of Ingham.(h) These friars had about ten or twelve houses in England and Wales.

The Carmelites pretend that the prophet Elias was the institutor of their order, and was the first Carmelite; and that he never left them any written rule. But the true time of their foundation was the year 1122, by Albert, patriarch of Jerusalem, who with a few hermits, resided on Mount Carmel in Palestine; from whence they were driven, about the year 1238, by the Saracens: they were also called White friars, and friars of the Virgin Mary; the first on account of the colour of their habits; the latter by the direction of Pope Honorius III. who, anno 1224, confirmed their rule, which is chiefly that of St. Basil.

They were brought into England A. D. 1240, by the lords John Vesey and Richard Grey: their first houses were at Alnwick in Northumberland, and Ailesford in Kent; at the latter of these places they held their first European chapter, A. D. 1245. Their habits, it is said, were at first white; but being obliged by the Infidels to make them party-coloured, they continued to wear them so fifty years after their arrival in England; but about the year 1290, changed them again for white. Of this order there were, in England and Wales, about forty houses.

The crossed or crouched friars were instituted, or at least reformed, by one Gerard, prior of St. Mary of Morello, at Bo-

(h) Friars Robertines, instituted by Robert Flower, the devout hermit of Knaresburgh, who lived in King John's reign, are spoken of by Leland as a branch of the Trinitarians; but I have hitherto met with so little concerning these Robertines, that I can say nothing certain of them; and doubt whether there really was any such order. *Tanner.*

logna; and in the year 1169, confirmed by Pope Alexander III. who brought them under the rule of St. Auguſtine; to which he added ſome conſtitutions for their better government. This order came into England, A. D. 1244; their firſt houſe was at Colcheſter. At firſt, they carried in their hands a croſs fixed to a ſtaff; but afterwards wore a croſs of red cloth on their backs and breaſts. Their habit was blue, by the particular direction of Pope Pius II. There were not here, of theſe friars, more than ſix or ſeven houſes.

THE origin of the Auguſtine friars, or friars Eremites, of the order of St. Auguſtine, is extremely uncertain. Their firſt appearance in England was about the year 1250: their habit was, when in the houſe, a white robe, with a ſcapulary; which, when they went abroad, they covered with a ſort of cowl, and a large hood, both black, which were girded with a black leather thong. At the ſuppreſſion they had, in England and Wales, about thirty-two houſes.

OF the original of the friars of the Sack, and the Bethlemite friars, there is no account. They appeared in England both in the ſame year, viz. A. D. 1257; the true ſtile of the former was, friars of the Penance of Jeſus Chriſt; but they were commonly called friars of the Sack; either from the faſhion of their habit, or its materials, which perhaps were of ſackcloth. This order was of ſhort continuance here, being aboliſhed by the Council at Lyons, A. D. 1307; their firſt houſe ſeems to have been near Alderſgate, in London.

THE rule and habit of the Bethlemite friars much reſembled that of the Dominicans; except that the former had a red ſtar, of five rays, with a blue circle in the middle, which they wore on their breaſts, in memory of the ſtar which conducted the wiſe men to Bethlehem. They appear to have had only that houſe in which they were placed at their coming into England. It was in Trumpington Street, at Cambridge.

THE order of St. Anthony of Vienna was inſtituted, A. D. 1095, by one Gaſton Frank. Their principal care was to ſerve thoſe afflicted

afflicted with the diſorder called St. Anthony's Fire, from the relicks of that ſaint being particularly efficacious in its cure. (i) The friars of this order followed the rule of St. Auguſtine, and wore a black habit, with the letter T of a blue colour, on their breaſts. They came hither early in the reign of King Henry III. and had one houſe at London, and another at Hereford.

"Of the Friars de Pica (ſays Tanner) who had an houſe at Norwich, I have met with nothing but what the author there ſays of them; unleſs they were the Freres Pies, a ſort of religious that wore black and white garments, mentioned by Walſingham, page 124."

The laſt order of friars which viſited this kingdom, was that of Bonhommes, or Good Men. They were brought hither, A. D. 1283, by Edmund, earl of Cornwall, and placed at Aſherug in Bucks: beſides which, there occurs but one other houſe of this order in England; viz. at Edingdon in Wiltſhire. Theſe friars followed the rule of St. Auguſtine, and wore a blue habit. The ſuperiors of their convents were called rectors; and one of them was ſtyled preſident of the order.

Of the military orders, there were only two in England; the knights hoſpitalars, and the knights templars.

The order of the knights hoſpitalars, or knights of St. John of Jeruſalem, took its name from an hoſpital built at Jeruſalem, for the uſe of pilgrims viſiting the Holy Sepulchre; ſome mer-

(i) St. Anthony is ſometimes repreſented with a fire by his ſide, ſignifying that he relieves perſons from the inflammation called after his name: but always accompanied by a hog, on account of his having been a ſwine-herd, and curing all diſorders in that animal. Both painters and poets have made very free with this ſaint and his followers: the former, by the many ludicrous pictures of his temptation; and the latter, by divers epigrams on his diſciples, or friars: one of which is the following, printed in Stephens's World of Wonders.

Once fedd'ſt thou, Anthony, an herd of ſwine,
And now an herd of monks thou feedeſt ſtill.
For wit and gut alike both charges bin;
Both loven filth alike: both like to fill
Their greedy paunch alike: nor was that kind
More beaſtly, ſottiſh, ſwiniſh, than this laſt;
All elſe agrees: one fault I only find,
Thou feedeſt not thy monks with oaken maſt.

chants

chants of the city of Melphi, in the kingdom of Naples, who traded into the eaſt, having obtained the permiſſion of the califf of Egypt for its erection. It was dedicated to St. John.

The community afterwards encreaſing, by the foundation of two new churches, they took upon themſelves the protection of pilgrims.

The order was inſtituted about the year 1092; and was particularly favoured by Godfrey of Boullogne, on account of their aſſiſtance in taking the Holy City; and alſo by his ſucceſſor Baldwin.

Their rule was nearly that of St. Auguſtine: beſides which, they obliged themſelves, by their vows, to receive, treat and defend pilgrims; and to maintain by force of arms the Chriſtian religion in their country. This order was compoſed of eight nations; but, ſince the ſeparation of the Engliſh from the church of Rome, has only ſeven.

On the ruin of the Chriſtian affairs in the eaſt, they were obliged to leave Jeruſalem, and ſettled at Rhodes; and, after the loſs of that Iſland, anno 1522, the emperor Charles V. gave them the Iſland of Malta: from theſe changes they have ſucceſſively been called knights hoſpitalars, of Rhodes, and of Malta.

They came into England ſoon after their inſtitution, and had a houſe built for them in London, A. D. 1100. Their habit was a black caſſock, with a white croſs. From a poor and mean beginning, (k) they obtained ſuch riches, honours, and exemptions, that their ſuperior here in England was the firſt lay-baron, and had a ſeat amongſt the lords in parliament; and ſome of their privileges were extended even to their tenants.

There were alſo ſiſters of this order; but we had only one houſe of them in England, viz. Buckland, in Somerſetſhire.

(k) They are ſaid, at firſt, to have had but one horſe between two of them; but, about an hundred and fifty years after their inſtitution, they had nineteen thouſand manors in Chriſtendom. Their wealth and privileges probably made them them ſometimes inſolent; for, by Pat. 45 Ed. III. p. 1, m. 3, vel. 4, "Rex conſtituit Ricardum de Everton viſitatorem hoſpitalis St. Johannis Jeruſalem in Anglia, ad reprimendam religioſorum inſolentiam, et ad obſervandam religionis honeſtatem." Thoſe of this order were all laymen, except two or three to perform divine offices.

The

THE knights templars, ſo called from having their firſt reſidence in ſome rooms adjoining to the Temple of Solomon, aroſe in the year 1118, at Jeruſalem; Hugo of Paganis, Geoffry of St. Omer's, and ſeven others whoſe names have not reached the preſent times, conſecrating themſelves to the ſervice of God, after the manner of the regular canons of St. Auguſtine, and binding themſelves to guard the roads for the ſecurity of pilgrims; at firſt ſubſiſting by alms. Their habit was white, with a red croſs on the left ſhoulder.

THEIR coming into England was in the beginning of the reign of King Stephen; their firſt reſidence in Holborn. They encreaſed very faſt; and, in a ſhort time, obtained great poſſeſſions. (1) Their flouriſhing condition, here and abroad, excited both the avarice and envy of the pope, ſeveral princes, and the whole body of religious.

POPE CLEMENT, in particular, dexterouſly made uſe of the covetous humour of Philip le Bel, king of France, to perſuade him to extirpate them out of his dominions; which he agreed to do, on condition of being inveſted with their eſtates.

THE ſame argument was probably uſed with other princes, who conſidered them as a formidable body. They therefore, to keep up an appearance of juſtice, accuſed the whole order of horrid crimes: whereupon the knights were every where impriſoned, their eſtates ſeized, and their order ſuppreſſed by Pope Clement V. anno 1309; and totally aboliſhed by the Council of Vienna, A. D. 1312. The ſuperior of this order was ſtyled maſter of the temple, and was often ſummoned to parliament.

THE order of St. Lazarus of Jeruſalem (of which we had a few houſes) ſeems to have been founded for the relief and ſupport of lepers and impotent perſons of the military orders.

(1) MATTHEW PARIS ſays, p. 544, That they had nine thouſand manors in Chriſtendom: and at their ſuppreſſion, they had (according to Heylin's Coſmogr. lib. 3.) ſixteen thouſand lordſhips beſides other lands.

See Rapin's Folio Edit. vol. 1. p. 403.

Having thus slightly touched upon the different religious orders (m) which once over-ran this country, it will be necessary to say something of their houses, and the officers thereto belonging.

Under the general title of religious houses, are comprehended cathedral and collegiate churches, abbies, priories, colleges, hospitals, preceptories, and friaries.

Of the cathedral churches as they still remain, little need be said. It may however be necessary to observe, that, in the conventual cathedrals, the bishop was in the place of the abbot, and had the principal stall on the right hand of the entrance into the choir, as he still hath at Ely, and till lately had at Durham and Carlisle.

Collegiate churches and colleges consisted of a number of secular canons, living together, under the government of a dean, warden, provost or master; and had belonging to them, for the more solemn performance of divine service, chaplains, singing men, and choristers.

An abbey was a religious society of men or women, living together under the government of an abbot or abbess. Of these some were so considerable, that the abbots were called to parliament, (n) and sat and voted in the House of Lords, had episcopal

(m) The names of the orders delineated in the annexed plate, follow in the same succession in which the figures stand; beginning with the nun on the left, and reckoning towards the right: the same order is observed with respect to the sitting figures.——A Benedictine nun; a monk of the same order; a Cluniac; a Cistertian and a Carthusian; a nun of St. Gilbert; a regular canon of the same; a Trinitarian; a knight templar; a knight hospitallar; a secular canon; a canon regular of the Premonstratensians. The sitting figures are, a regular canon of St. Augustine; a regular canon of the Holy Sepulche; a canon of the Hospital of St John at Coventry; chaplain of the order of St. John of Jerusalem.

(n) The oracle of the law saith, 2. Instit. p. 585, "Twenty-six abbots and two priors had baronies, and thereby were lords of parliament." In 1 Instit. 97, he saith, "There were an hundred and eighteen monasteries, founded by kings of England; whereof such as held *per baroniam*, and were called to parliament by writ, were lords of parliament, and had places and voices there; but not if they were not called by writ; for Feversham was founded by King Stephen to hold by barony; but the abbot not being called to parliament, did not sit there." This is also in Weaver, p. 183.

Cowel *sub voce* Mitred saith, These abbots were not called to parliament because they were mitred, but because they received their temporals from the king.

Collier,

RELIGIOUS ORDERS

copal power within the limits of their houses, (o) gave solemn benediction, confirmed the lesser orders, wore mitres, (p) sandals, &c. and carried crosses or pastorals in their hands, and some of their houses were exempted from the jurisdiction even of the archbishop, (q) and subject to the pope alone. Fuller says, that

COLLIER, Ecc. Hist. vol. ii. p. 164, saith, they held of the king *in capite per baroniam*; their endowment being at least an entire barony, which consisted of thirteen knights fees, and thereby they were advanced to the state and dignity of spiritual lords: but of the parliamentary abbies, some were founded by subjects, some by kings of Mercia, &c. and about eight only by kings of England.

THE abbot of Thorney pleaded, A. D. 1338, that he did not hold by barony, but by frankalmoigne; Collect. Wren, vol. ii. p. 18, ex reg. Sim. Epist. Elienf. and yet was then called to parliament, as Fuller, book vi. p. 292, and Stevens's Append. p. 15: the prior of Coventry likewise pleaded, 14 Rich. II. that he did not hold *per baroniam*, as Mon. Angl. vol. i. p. 305.

THE abbey of Bardney was valued at no more than 429l. 7s. *per annum* in the whole, and 366l. 6s. 1d. clear: and there were several abbies and priories which had much greater temporals, and consequently were entire baronies, which were not parliamentary: 'tis possible these last might not receive their temporals from the crown, nor hold them *in capite*, and Bardney might; but I rather think this privilege was chiefly owing to the favour of the king; who might, in other cases, as well as that of Tavistock, call an house of the foundation of his ancestors, which was not really so: Fuller's Church Hist. book vi. p. 293.

ALL the parliamentary abbots and priors had houses in Westminster, London, or Southwark, to live in whilst the parliament sat. *Tanner.*

(o) SEE the grant of a mitre to the abbot of Malmsbury, in Wilkins's Councils, vol. iii. p. 142, 143: "Abbas Samson fecit novum sigillum, quod cum mitra esset pingendum, licet predecessores sui tale non haberent; et primus inter abbates Angliæ impetravit, quod daret episcopalem benedictionem solemniter ubicunque fuerit." Joc. Brakeland, in Chron. St. Edm. Bur. M. S. He was abbot from A. D. 1182, to 1211, or 1212.

"THOMAS de MARLEBERG, abbas Evesham primo sculpsit super duas tumbas predecessorum suorum ad honorem et ostensionem dignitatis ecclesiæ imagines episcopales, et sibi ipsi cum eisdem fecit mausoleum, et incidit in lapide marmoreo superposito imaginem episcopalem ad honorem ecclesiæ: obiit A. D. 1236." We may hereby see when these practices began. *Tanner.*

(p) BUT their mitres differed a little from those of the bishops, they also carried their crosiers in their left hands, and the abbots carried them in their right hands: as Austind, in Append. to Dr. Fiddes's Life of Cardinal Wolsey, p. 113.

IN the procession roll, the third of Henry VIII. the parliamentary abbots are drawn with barons caps, not mitres; as M. S. Ashmol. Oxon. n. 13: but in the parliament-house, the fifteenth of Henry VIII. they are drawn with mitres on their heads; as Fiddes's Life of Wolsey, p. 303.

(q) COWEL, *voce* Abbat, saith, such as were mitred were exempted from the jurisdiction of the diocesan, having themselves episcopal authority within their limits; and Godolphin, in Repert. Eccl. hath almost the same words; but Reyner, tr. ii. p. 55, saith, that St. Alban's Westminster, St. Augustine's Canterbury, St. Edmund's Bury, and Eversham, only were exempt, except perhaps Glastonbury.

IT is more likely that several others of them obtained that privilege, as Burnet Reformat. vol. 1. p. 187: however, their exemption from their diocesans, being honoured with the mitre, and called to parliament, certainly depended on different grants; for the abbot of Malmsbury was one of the twenty-five fixed upon for parliamentary abbots, by king Edward III. as Fuller, book vi. p. 292. But he had that in the 49th of Henry III. ſixty-four abbots, and thirty-ſix priors were ſummoned to parliament; but this being thought too many, King Edward III. reduced them to twenty-five abbots, and two priors; to whom were afterwards added the abbots of Taviſtock and Tewkſbury; making in all twenty-nine: theſe, and no more, conſtantly enjoyed this privilege. A liſt of them ſee in the note (r).

A PRIORY was a ſociety of religious, where the chief perſon was termed a prior or prioreſs; and of theſe there were two ſorts.

had not a grant of the epiſcopal ornaments and authority till the third of Richard II; though he was before that exempt from his dioceſan, as appears from the grant in Wilkins's Councils, vol. iii. p. 142.

PETERBOROUGH alſo was allowed to be a parliamentary abbey, by king Edward III; as Fuller, book vi. p. 292; but William Genge was, about the twenty-firſt of Richard II. the firſt mitred abbot: and both abbot and convent were viſited by the biſhop of Lincoln about eighty-years afterwards; viz. in A. D. 1483; as Gunton's Peterborough, with Patrick's Supplement, p. 49, 323, and 328.

THE abbot of Taviſtock obtained the mitre the 36th of Henry VI. but was not called to parliament till the 5th of Henry VIII. and was not exempted from the biſhop of the dioceſe till three years after; as Auſtin. in Append. to Fiddes's Life of Wolſey, p. 112.

THE prior of Durham had the uſe of the mitre and paſtoral ſtaff, from about A. D. 1374; as Ang. Sacr. vol. i. p. 769, and Willis's Abbeys, vol. i. p. 262, though never called to parliament: and in the regiſter of Oliv. King, biſhop of Bath and Wells, there is a grant from Pope Alexander VI. for the priors of Taunton (who were not parliamentary) having epiſcopal authority, and all the ornaments but the mitre, which I never met another inſtance of, and therefore inſert an abſtract of the grant.

"Alexander epiſcopus ſervus ſervorum Dei, dilecto filio Joanni priori et conv. de Tanton, ſalutem: ut tu et ſucceſſores tui annulo paſtorali, baculo almucciis et aliis pontificalibus inſigniis (citra tamen mitram) uti; nec non indicto monaſterio et prioratibus, et eccleſiis illi ſubjectis benedictionem ſolennem poſt miſſarum, veſperarum completorum, et divinorum officiorum ſolennia (dummodo in benedictione hujuſmodi aliquis antiſtes aut apoſtolicæ ſedis legatus præſens non ſit) populo elargiri; canonicos quoque et chorales dicti monaſterii ad minores ordines promovere; licite valeatis, dat. 4 Non. Maii, A. D. 1499."

(r) THE abbots of Tewkſbury, the prior of Coventry, the abbots of Waltham, Cirenceſter, St. John's at Colcheſter, Croiland, Shrewſbury, Selby, Bardney, St. Bennet's of Hulme, Thorney, Hide, Winchelcomb, Battel, Reading, St. Mary's in York, Ramſey, Peterborough, St. Peter's in Glouceſter, Glaſtonbury, St. Edmondſbury, St. Auguſtine Canterbury, St. Alban's, Weſtminſter, Abingdon, Everſham, Malmſbury and Taviſtock, and the prior of St. John's of Jeruſalem, who was ſtyled "Primus Angliæ baro;" but it was with reſpect to the lay barons only, for he was the laſt ſpiritual one.

I HAVE here ſet down the firſt twenty-four of them, in the order they went to parliament the 3d of Henry VIII. Hearne thinks, that they took place in the Houſe of Lords according to the ſeniority of their creation. But Anſtis, Garter king of arms. is of opinion, "that ſome of the abbots, like the biſhops, had by virtue of their abbies, a certain fixed precedency; and that others of them took place according to the priority of their creation." Many have aſſigned the firſt place to the abbot of St. Alban's, becauſe St. Alban was the firſt martyr in this kingdom.

THE abbot of Leiceſter, and the prior of St. James's, near Northampton, was ſometimes called to parliament, after King Edward III. had reduced the number. *Tanner.*

FIRST,

First, when the prior had the ſupreme government, as fully as an abbot in his abbey, and was elected by the convent; ſuch were the cathethral priors, and moſt of the Auguſtine order.

Secondly, where the priory was a cell, ſubordinate to ſome abbey, and the prior was nominated and diſplaced at the diſcretion of the abbot: and in theſe cells there was a conſiderable difference; ſome being ſo entirely ſubjected to their reſpective abbies, that they might ſend them what officers they thought proper, and encreaſe or decreaſe their number of monks at pleaſure; whilſt others conſiſted of a certain ſtated number of monks, who had a prior ſent them from the abbey, to whom they paid an annual ſtipend, as an acknowledgment of their ſubordination, but acted in other matters as an independent body, and had the reſt of their revenues for their own uſe.

These priories or cells were always of the ſame order as the abbies on which they depended, though ſometimes of a different ſex; it being cuſtomary after the conqueſt, for the great abbies to build nunneries in ſome of their manors, which were cells, or priories to them, and ſubject to their viſitation. (s)

Some of thoſe houſes which were originally priories were turned into abbies; as Wymondham in Norfolk, and Walden in Eſſex: but this was looked upon as an injury to the patron, and ſometimes forbidden by the founder; as at Cartmele in Lancaſhire. One inſtance likewiſe occurs of an abbey being degraded

(s) To be ſent to a monaſtery was, in many caſes, the puniſhment of an offending ſecular prieſt; as Can. 61 and 77 of A. D. 740, in Johnſon's Collect. of Canons. To be ſent to a cell was, in ſome caſes, the puniſhment of an offending monk. Mat. Paris, p. 1046. Reyner's Append. p. 125, 160. And that ſome of them were there obliged to hard labour, appears from the regiſter of John Romane, archbiſhop of York, anno primo pontif. "Pænitentia injuncta monacho de Novoburgo qui ſub religioſo habitu diutius vagus in ſeculo extitit: moretur apud hoc cellam, ubi agriculturæ vacet, et caudam aratri teneat loco cujuſdem mercenarii ſoliti hujuſmodi officio deputari; quarta ſexta et feria, pane, cerevіſia, et leguminibus tantum modo ſit contentus; tres diſciplinas in hebdomada recipiat a canonico præſidente ibidem." And when a monk was refractory or quarrelſome in his own houſe, he was ſent to another to be puniſhed; as Reyner's Append. p. 125, 160. "Inobediens monachus de Tanton miſſus ad prioratum St. Germani in Cornubia ad incarcerandum expœnitandum. "Reg. Rad. de Salopia Epiſc. Bath et Wullens, ſub A. D. 1351." *Tanner*.

to a priory, becauſe the revenues were not ſufficient to ſupport the ſtate and dignity of an abbot: this was Cumbwell in Kent.

PRIORIES alien were cells to foreign monaſteries; for when manors or tithes were given to foreign houſes, they, in order to have faithful ſtewards on the ſpot to collect their revenues, built convenient houſes for the reception of a ſmall convent, and peopled them with priors, and ſuch a number of Monks as they thought proper: this at the ſame time encreaſed their order.

THERE was the ſame difference in theſe cells, as between the former: ſome of them being conventual, had the liberty of chooſing their own priors, and of receiving their revenues; of which, at firſt, they remitted to the foreign houſe what was more than neceſſary for their immediate ſubſiſtence: this was afterwards changed into a certain regular annuity, called apportus; which being paid, the ſurplus remained to the convent. The others were immediately dependent on the foreign houſe, who received their income, allowing them ſuch portion for their maintenance as they thought proper: priors were appointed over them from abroad, and the monks were exchanged at pleaſure.

As theſe monaſteries conſiſted chiefly of foreigners, who might give intelligence to our enemies, and who beſides greatly impoveriſhed the kingdom by draining it continually of conſiderable ſums, their eſtates were generally ſeized on the breaking out of a war with France, and reſtored on the return of peace; and at length, moſt of them were, by act of parliament, given to the king; which was a kind of prelude to the general diſſolution.

PRECEPTORIES were a kind of cells to the principal houſes of knights templars in London, under the government of an officer, created by the grand maſter one of the "Preceptores Templi." Their buſineſs was to take care of the lands and rents in that place and neighbourhood.

COMMANDERIES were, under another name, the ſame to the knights hoſpitallars as preceptories were to the templars. The chief officer was called a commander.

HOSPITALS

Hospitals were houſes of relief for poor and impotent perſons; (t) and were incorporated by royal patents, and made capable of gifts and grants in ſucceſſion.

Friaries were erected for the habitation of friars, who being mendicants, and by their rules, incapable of holding any property, they were rarely endowed, (u); yet moſt of their houſes had ſome ſhops and gardens belonging to them. Many of theſe friaries were large and ſtately buildings, and had noble churches, in which many great perſons choſe to be buried. (v)

For the inferior religious foundations, ſuch as hermitages, chauntries and free chapels, ſee the note. (w)

It

(t) Besides the poor and impotent, there generally were in theſe hoſpitals two or three religious; one to be maſter, or prior, and one or two to be chaplains and confeſſors: and theſe obſerved the rule of St. Auſtin, and probably ſubjected the poor and impotent to ſome religious reſtraints, as well as to the local ſtatutes.

Hospitals were originally deſigned for the relief and entertainment of travellers upon the road, and particularly of pilgrims, and therefore were generally built upon the road-ſide: but of later years they have been always founded for fixed inhabitants. *Tanner.*

(u) The Dominicans of King's Langley were endowed with 122l. per annum.

(v) These houſes received conſiderable benefits from the burials of great perſonages within their churches. The friars did not fail to promote it on all occaſions: and, if they could not get the whole body, would at leaſt procure a limb, or part.

Thomas of Walſingham, ſpeaking of the burial of queen Eleanor's heart in the church of the Friars Minors in London, thus expreſſes himſelf: "Qui (meaning the friars) ſicuti & cuncti fratres reliquorum ordinum, aliquod de corporibus quorumcunque potentium morientium ſibimet vindicabant, more canum cadaveribus aſſiſtentium, ubi quiſque ſuam particulam avidè conſumendam expectat."

(w) Hermitages were religious cells, erected in private and ſolitary places, for ſingle perſons, or communities; many times endowed, and ſometimes annexed to larger religious houſes. Vide Kennet's Gloſſary in voce Hermitorium. Mon. Ang. vol. ii. p. 339. Thoreſby's Leeds, p. 91.

The hermits of cells not endowed are ſpoken of as common beggars, in pat. 13 Ed. III. p. 1, m. 8, et p. 2. m. 22. Chauntries were endowments of lands or other revenues, for the maintenance of one or more prieſts, to ſay daily maſs for the ſoul of the founder, and his relations and benefactors: ſometimes at a particular altar, and oftentimes in little chapels added to cathedral and parochial churches for that purpoſe. See Godolph. Repert. p. 329. Fuller, book vi. p. 350. Weaver, p. 733.

Free chapels were places of religious worſhip, exempt from all juriſdiction of the ordinary; ſave only that the incumbents were generally conſtituted by the biſhop, and inducted by the archdeacon of the place. Moſt of theſe chapels were built upon the manors and ancient demeſnes of the crown, whilſt in the king's hands, for the uſe of himſelf and retinue, when he came to reſide there: as Kennet's Gloſſary, in voce Demeſne; and in caſe of appropriations, p. 6. And when the crown parted with thoſe eſtates, the chapels went along with them, and retained their firſt freedom; but ſome lords having had free chapels in manors that do not appear to have been ancient demeſnes of the crown, ſuch are thought to have been built and privileged by grants of the crown. See Biſhop Gibſon's Codex, p. 237. Yet Mr. Newcourt ſaith, that, A. D. 1521, Biſhop Fitzjames converted a decayed chauntry at Rainham

in

It is to be observed, that different founders are frequently assigned by the monastic writers to the same house; a first, second, third, and even a sixth founder sometimes occuring: the fact is, they bestowed that appellation not only on the first endower, to whom only it properly belonged, but also gave it to every great benefactor who either restored the ancient foundation, after it had been ruined by fire or any other calamity, or made any considerable addition to it. (x) The successor of the founders, and patrons or chief lords of the fee, (y) are likewise many times styled founders. (z)

In every abbey, the chief officer was the abbot, or abbess; (a) who presided in great pomp, was generally called the lord abbot, or lady abbess, and had a kitchen, and other offices, distinct from the common ones of the society. The next in rank and authority, in every abbey, was the prior; (b) under whom was the sub-prior; and in great abbies, a third, fourth, and even a fifth prior. These, as well as all the other obedientarii, were removable at the will of the abbot. In every priory, the prior was the supreme head; under whom was the sub-prior, who assisted him when present, and ruled the house in his absence. The priors had the same power in their priories, as the abbots and abbesses in their abbies; but lived in a less expensive and pompous manner: though, in some of the greater houses, they were stiled the lord prior, and lady prioress.

in Essex, with the consent of the patron, into a free chapel; to be held with all its rights, and governed by an honest and literate layman; without mentioning any grant from the crown for it. See his Repert. vol. ii. p. 482.

(x) Sir John Biconill was admitted one of the founders of the Franciscan Friars at Dorchester, for having built mills near to, and for the benefit of the convent. *As Stevens, vol. i. p. 93.*

(y) When the founder's family was extinct, the lord of the fee became patron of course. *As Kennet's Glossary, sub tit. Advowson of Religious Houses.*

(z) In Leland's Collect. we often meet with "Fundator originalis et fundator modernus;" but the last was then the patron only.

(a) From Abba Pater, quia pater monachorum. *Godolph. Repert.*——They were generally wrote "A divinâ permissione abbas." *Decem Script. col. 2059 and 2157.*

(b) Every prior was to be in priest's orders, by decree of the council at London, A. D. 1126. *Wilkins's Councils, vol. i. p. 408.*

The

The following were the ſix principal officers in the monaſtery of Croyland, and perhaps in moſt others:

First, Magiſter Operis, or maſter of the fabric; who probably had the care of the buildings of and belonging to the monaſtery, and whoſe buſineſs it was to ſurvey and keep them in repair.

Eleemosynarius, or the almoner; who ſuperintended the alms of the houſe, which were every day diſtributed to the poor at the gate of the monaſtery; divided the alms upon the founder's day, and at other obits and anniverſaries; and, in ſome places, had the care of the maintenance and education of the choriſters.

Pietantiarius, who had the diſtribution of the pietancies; which were allowances, upon particular occaſions, over and above the common proviſions.

Sacrista, or ſexton, to whoſe care were committed the veſſels, books, and veſtments, belonging to the church; and who looked after, and accounted for the oblations at the great altar, and other altars or images in the church; and ſuch legacies as were given either to the fabric or for utenſils: he likewiſe provided bread and wine for the ſacrament, and took care of burying the dead.

Camerarius, or the chamberlain, had the management of the dormitory, provided the bedding for the monks, with razors and towels for ſhaving them; likewiſe part, if not all their clothing.

Cellerarius, or the cellarer, whoſe office it was to provide all ſorts of proviſions and liquors conſumed in the convent; as alſo firing and kitchen utenſils.

Besides theſe there were theſaurarius, or the burſar; who received all the common rents and revenues of the monaſtery, and paid all the common expences.

Præcentor, or chaunter, who had the chief direction of the choir ſervice; and not only preſided over the ſinging-men and choriſters, but provided them with books, paid their ſalaries, and repaired the organs: he had alſo the cuſtody of the ſeal, kept the Liber Diurnalis, or Chapter Book, and provided parchment and ink for the writers, and colours for the limners employed in writing and illuminating books for the library.

Hostilarius, or Hoſpitilarius, whoſe buſineſs it was to manage the entertainment of ſtrangers, and to provide them with neceſſaries.

Infirmarius, who had the care of the infirmary, and of the ſick monks carried there, for whom he was to provide phyſic, and other neceſſaries; and to waſh and prepare for burial the bodies of the dead: he was likewiſe to ſhave all the monks in the convent.

Refectionarius, who looked after the refectory, and provided table cloths, napkins, glaſſes, diſhes, plates, ſpoons, and other requiſites, and even ſervants to wait at table: he had the cuſtody of the cups, ſalts, ewers, and all the ſilver utenſils whatſoever belonging to the houſe, except the church plate. (c)

There was likewiſe coquinarius, or the cook; gardinarius, or the gardener; and portorius, or the porter; et in cœnobiis quæ jus archidiaconale in prædiis et eccleſiis ſuis obtinuerant, erat monachus qui archidiaconi titulo et munere inſignitus eſt. (d)

Every great abbey had a room called the ſcriptorium; where ſeveral ſcribes were employed in tranſcribing books for the library. They ſometimes, indeed, wrote the ledger-books of the houſe, the miſſals, and other books uſed in divine ſervice; but were chiefly employed on other works, ſuch as the fathers, claſſics, or hiſtory: the monks in general, were ſo zealous for this work, that they often procured gifts of lands and churches, to be ſolely appointed to the carrying of it on. Beſides this, they had alſo particular perſons appointed to take notice of and record the principal events which happened in the kingdom; which at the end of the year, were digeſted and formed into annals.

The foregoing accounts of the riſe and progreſs of monaſtic foundations, with the particular deſcription of the ſeveral orders,

(c) In nunneries there was a correſpondence of all theſe offices and officers, abbeſs, prioreſs, ſubprioreſs, ſacriſtan or ſexton, treſorier, chamberesſ, capellan, &c. *Willis's Abbies, vol. ii. Append. p.* 1, 8, 20.

(d) The Worceſter hiſtorian, in Ang. Sacr. p. 547. *See alſo Mon. Ang. vol. ii. p.* 378.

having rather ſtretched beyond the intended limits, I ſhall but briefly treat of the circumſtances attending the general diſſolution; and that the rather, as they are minutely mentioned in the general hiſtories of England, and the memoirs of thoſe times.

ANNO 1534, King Henry having thrown off the papal yoke, and procured himſelf to be acknowledged by parliament the ſupreme head of the Engliſh church, the next year ſet on foot a general viſitation of the religious houſes; undoubtedly, in order to find a pretence for their ſuppreſſion. It was begun in October, 1535, by one Doctor Layton, and others: many of their letters are extant; two of them, never before printed, are in the notes. (e) Burnet ſays, "the viſitors went over England, and found, in many places, monſtrous diſorders; the ſin of Sodom

(e) PLEASITH it your worſhip to underſtand that yeſternight we came from Glaſtonbury to Briſtow. I here ſend you for relicks two flowers, wrapped up in black ſarcenet; that on Chriſtmas even (hora ipſa qua natus Chriſtus fuerat) will ſpring and burgen, and bear flowers. Ye ſhall alſo receive a bag of relicks, wherein ye ſhall ſee ſtrange things; as God's coat, our Lady's ſmock, part of God's ſupper in cœna Domini; pars petræ ſuper quam natus erat Jeſus in Bethlehem; belike Bethlehem affords plenty of ſtone. Theſe are all of Maiden Bradley; whereof is a holy father priour, who hath but ſix children, and but one daughter married yet of the goods of the monaſtery, but truſting ſhortlie to marrie the reſt: his ſons be tall men, waiting upon him.

HE thanks God he never meddled with married women; but all with maidens, faireſt that could be gotten, and always married them right well. The pope, conſidering his fragilitie, gave him his licence to keep a whore; and he has good writing, ſub plumbo, to diſcharge his conſcience, and to chuſe Mr. Underhill to be his ghoſtly father, and he to give him plenam remiſſionem. I ſend you alſo our Lady's girdle of Bruton, red ſilke, a ſolemn relick, ſent to women in travail; Mary Magdalen's girdle, which Matilda the empreſs, founder of Fairley, gave with them, as ſayeth the holy father of Fairley.—I have croſſes of ſilver and gold, Sir, which I ſend you not now; becauſe I have more to be delivered this night, by the priour of Maiden Bradley. There is nothing notable; the bretheren be kept ſo ſtreight, that they cannot offend; but fain they would if they might, as they confeſs, and ſuch fault is not in them.

R. LAYTON.

From St. Auſtin's without Briſtol.

MY ſingular good lord, &c. As touching the abbot of Bury, nothing ſuſpect as touching his living; but it was detected he lay much forth at Grainges, and ſpent much money in playing at cards and dice.—It is confeſſed and proved, that there was here ſuch frequence of women, comyn and reſortyng, as to no place more.—Among the relicks are found the coles St. Laurence was roſted withal; the paring of St. Edmund's nails; St. Thomas of Canterbury's penknife and books; and divers ſculls for the head-ach; pieces of the Holy Croſs, able to make a whole croſs: other relicks, for rain, and for avoiding the weeds growing in corn, &c. From Bury St. Edmund's, Your ſervant bounden,

JOSEPH AP RICE.

THESE were copied from the original letters, written by R. Layton, and others, viſitors of the religious houſes, to Lord Cromwell, about the year 1537, preſerved among Dodſworth's MS. collections, in the Bodleian library.

was

was found in many houſes; great factions and barbarous cruelties were in others; and in ſome were found tools for coining; the report contained many abominable things, that are not fit to be mentioned; ſome of them were printed, but the greateſt part is loſt: only a report of one hundred and forty-four houſes is yet extant." Five houſes made a voluntary ſurrender this year.

In 1536, an act was paſſed, ſuppreſſing all thoſe monaſteries whoſe revenues were under 200l. per annum. This act ſets forth the great diſorders of thoſe houſes, and the many unſucceſful attempts that had been made for their reformation. The religious who belonged to them, were directed to be put into the greater houſes, where better diſcipline was obſerved, and their eſtates and goods were given to the king; and, by another act, a new court was erected, entitled the court of the augmentations of the king's revenue; which was to take care that the king was not defrauded of them.

It is to be noted, that the revenues of moſt of theſe houſes, though valued at only 200l. per annum, greatly exceeded that ſum, many of them being worth ſeveral thouſands: this was owing to the monks never having raiſed their ancient rents; chuſing rather to make their tenants pay a conſiderable fine, at the renewal of their leaſes; and according to theſe ancient rents they were eſtimated.

Visitors were now appointed to ſurvey the leſſer monaſteries: "they were," ſays Burnet, "required to carry along with them the concurrence of the gentry near them, and to examine the eſtate of the revenues and goods, and take inventories of them; and to take their ſeals into their keeping: they were to try how many of the religious would take capacities, and return to a ſecular courſe of life; and theſe were to be ſent to the archbiſhop of Canterbury, or the Lord Chancellor for them; and an allowance was to be given them for their journey: but thoſe who intended to continue in that ſtate, were to be ſent to ſome of the great monaſteries that lay next.

A pension

A PENSION was alſo to be aſſigned to the abbot or prior during life; and of all this they were to make their report by Michaelmas: and they were particularly to examine what leaſes had been made all laſt year. The abbots hearing of what was coming on them, had been raiſing all the money they could; and ſo it was intended to recover what was made away by ill bargains.

THERE were great complaints made of the proceedings of the viſitors, of their violences and briberies; and perhaps not without reaſon. Ten thouſand of the religious were ſet to ſeek for their livings, with forty ſhillings and a gown a man. Their goods and plate were eſtimated at 100,000l. and the valued rents of their houſes was 32,000l. but was really above ten times ſo much. The churches and cloiſters were in moſt places pulled down, and the materials ſold." This gave a general diſcontent, and cauſed ſeveral unſucceſsful inſurrections.

HENRY having taſted the ſweets ariſing from the ſuppreſſion of the leſſer monaſteries, now reſolved to poſſeſs himſelf of the revenues of the great ones; and accordingly, the next year, a freſh viſitation was appointed; when the viſitors were directed to enquire into the lives of the monks, how they ſtood affected towards the pope, and whether they acknowledged and promoted the king's ſupremacy.

THEY were likewiſe directed to enquire whether they made uſe of any impoſtures, or pretended miraculous images, to work upon the ſuperſtition of the credulous people; and, above all, underhand to endeavour, both by promiſes and threats, to influence them to ſurrender their houſes to the king: which many of them, either conſcious of their evil lives, having been engaged in the late inſurrections, or attracted by the offer of a conſiderable penſion, accordingly did; when they and their monks had penſions aſſigned them, proportionable to the value of the houſe.

SOME abbots, relying on their innocence and irreproachable conduct, were more reſolute, and abſolutely refuſed: againſt theſe charges of high treaſon were inſtituted, on various pretences, and ſeveral of them were unjuſtly executed. Burnet is very particular in theſe tranſactions; ſee his account in the notes. (f) In 1539, the ſurrender of all mo aſteries was confirmed by act of parliament; and in that year the total diſſolution was completed.

THIS

(f) A NEW viſitation was appointed, to enquire into the converſation of the monks, to examine how they ſtood affected to the pope, and how they promoted the king's ſupremacy: they were likewiſe ordered to examine what impoſtures might be among them, either in images or relics; by which the ſuperſtition of the credulous people was wrought on.

SOME few houſes, of greater value, were prevailed with, the former year, to ſurrender to the king. Many houſes that had not been diſſolved, though they were within the former act, were now ſuppreſſed; and many of the greater abbots were wrought on to ſurrender by ſeveral motives. Some had been faulty during the rebellion, and ſo, to prevent a ſtorm, offered a reſignation: others liked the reformation, and did it on that account: ſome were found guilty of great diſorders in their lives, and to prevent a ſhameful diſcovery, offered their houſes to the king: and others had made ſuch waſtes and dilapidations, that, having taken care of themſelves, they were leſs concerned for others. At St. Alban's, the rents were let ſo low, that the abbot could not maintain the charge of the abbey.

AT Battel, the whole furniture of the houſe and chapel was not above 100l. in value, and their plate was not 300l. In ſome houſes, there was ſcarce any plate or furniture left. Many abbots and monks were glad to accept of a penſion for life; and that was proportioned to the value of their houſe, and to their innocence.

THE abbots of St. Alban's and Tewkſbury had 400 marks a-year. The abbot of St. Edmund's Bury was more innocent and more reſolute: the viſitors wrote that they found no ſcandals in that houſe: but at laſt he was prevailed with, by a penſion of 500 marks, to reſign.

THE inferior governors had ſome 30, 20, or 10l. penſions; and the monks had generally ſix pounds, or eight marks a-piece.

IF any abbot died, the new abbot (they being choſen as the biſhops were, upon a congé d'elire, and a miſſive letter) was named for that purpoſe, only to reſign the houſe; and all were made to hope for advancement, that they ſhould give good example to others, by a quick and chearful ſurrender: by theſe means, one hundred and twenty one of thoſe houſes were this year reſigned to the king.

IN moſt houſes, the viſitors made the monks ſign a confeſſion of their former vices and diſorders, of which there is only one original extant, that eſcaped the general raſure of all ſuch papers in Queen Mary's time; in which they acknowledged, in a long narrative, "their former idleneſs, gluttony and ſenſuality; for which the pit of hell was ready to ſwallow them up: others acknowledged, that the manner of their former pretended religion conſiſted in ſome dumb ceremonies, by which they were blindly led, having no true knowledge of God's laws; but that they had procured exemption from their dioceſans, and had ſubjected themſelves wholly to a foreign power, that took no care to reform their abuſes; and therefore, ſince the moſt perfect way of life was revealed by Chriſt and his apoſtles, and that it was fit they ſhould be governed by the king their ſupreme head, they reſigned to him."

OF this ſort, I have ſeen ſix. Some reſigned in hopes that the king would found them of new; theſe favoured the reformation, and intended to convert their houſes to better uſes; for preaching, ſtudy, and prayer: and Latimer preſſed Cromwell earneſtly, that two or three houſes might be reſerved for ſuch purpoſes in every county. But it was reſolved to ſurpreſs all; and therefore, neither could the interceſſions of the gentry of Oxfordſhire, nor the viſitors, preſerve the nunnery of Godſtow; though they found great ſtrictneſs of life in it, and it was the common place of the education of young women

of

THIS measure, though only fully accomplished by Henry VIII. had, fron time to time, been attempted, and even partially put in execution, by many of our bishops, kings, and even some of the popes. From the days of Edgar to that prince, several of the instances have already been mentioned in this work; but to bring them under one point of view, see the note. (g)

THE chief reasons urged in its defence were, that the monks, notwithstanding their subscriptions, still retained their attachment to the pope; and would, on all occasions, have excited troubles in the kingdom against an excommunicated king. Their luxurious and debauched manner of living, (h) their pretended miracles

of quality in that county. The common preamble to most surrenders was, "That upon full deliberation, and of their own proper motion, for just and reasonable causes moving their consciences, they did freely give up their houses to the king." Some surrendered, without any preamble, to the visitors, as feoffees, in trust for the king. In short, they went on at such a rate, that one hundred and fifty-nine resignations were obtained before the parliament met; and of these, the originals of one hundred and fifty-four are yet extant. Some thought that these resignations could not be valid, since the incumbents had not the property, but only the trust for life of those houses; but the parliament did afterwards declare them good in law. It was also said, that they, being of the nature of corporations, all deeds under their seals were valid; and that at least by their resignation and quitting their houses, they forfeited them to the king: but this was thought to subsist rather on a nicety in law, than natural equity.

(g) As to the dissolution of religious foundations, we may observe, that King Edgar, Archbishop Dunstan, and the bishops Ethelwold and Oswald, in the tenth century, ejected seculars, and put in regulars, as hath been before mentioned. Richard de Belmeis, by the authority of Pope Eugenius III. and King Stephen, turned a secular college into an abbey of Augustine canons, at Lilleshull: and Pope Alexander III. and King Henry II. turned the secular canons out of Waltham, and placed regulars there in their stead: and the order of templars was suppressed by Pope Clement V. A dissolution of the alien priories was brought about in the reign of Henry V. with the concurrence of several bishops, who purchased and procured their revenues, for the endowment of divers colleges by them founded: amongst these were William of Wickham, bishop of Winchester, and Archbishop Chicheley.——King Henry VI. founded the college of Eaton, and King's College, Cambridge, about the year 1441, and endowed them chiefly with alien priories: and William Wainfleet, bishop of Winchester, procured revenues of the priory of Sile, or Atsile, in Sussex, and the priory of Shelburn, in Hampshire, (though the founder of the latter had carefully forbiden such alteration) for the endowment of his foundation of Magdalene College, Oxford.——Cardinal Wolsey also obtained the bull of Pope Clement VII. for the suppression of several religious houses, for the founding his colleges at Oxford and Ipswich.—Besides these, there are many more instances, too numerous to insert.

(h) THE luxurious manner of living of the monks, so early as the reign of Henry II. may be gathered from the following stories, related of those of Canterbury and Winchester, by Giraldus Cambrensis. "Their table," says he, speaking of the first, "consisted regularly of sixteen covers, or more, of the most costly dainties, dressed with the most exquisite cookery to provoke the appetite, and please the taste: they had an excessive abundance of wine, particularly claret; of mulberry wine, of mead, and of other strong liquors; the variety of which was so great in these repasts, that no place could

miracles and impostures, (i) shocking accounts of which were undoubtedly transmitted by the visitors; though one may venture to believe, they were not softened in their relation: but above all, the damage sustained by the nation, in the loss of so many hands, who might have made useful manufacturers and husbandmen, as well as the great check to population, by the number of men and women bound by their vows to celibacy. Cogent as these reasons were, probably they would not have brought about this great event, but for that delicious incentive, their goods and manors, which the king's necessities, as well as his avarice, made him so extremely desirous to seize.

ALTHOUGH the general suppression of religious houses, even considered in a political light only, was of a vast national benefit, yet it must be allowed, that at the time they flourished, they were not entirely useless. Monasteries were then the repositories, as well as seminaries of learning; many valuable books, and national records, as well as private evidences, have been preserved in their libraries; the only places wherein they could have been safely lodged, in those turbulent times: many of them, which had

could be found for ale, though the best was made in England, and particularly in Kent." And of the prior and monks of St. Swithin at Winchester, he says, "They threw themselves prostrate at the feet of King Henry II. and with many tears complained to him, that the bishop of that diocese, to whom they were subject as their abbot, had withdrawn from them three of the usual number of their dishes. Henry enquired of them how many there still remained; and being informed they had ten, he said that he himself was contented with three, and imprecated a curse on the bishop, if he did not reduce them to that number."

(i) THEY (the visitors) discovered many impostures about relicks and wonderful images, to which pilgrimages had been wont to be made. At Reading they had an angel's wing, which brought over the spear's point that pierced our Saviour's side; and as many pieces of the cross were found, as joined together would have made a big cross. The rood of grace, at Boxley in Kent, had been much esteemed, and drawn many pilgrims to it: it was observed to bow and roll its eyes, and look at times well pleased, or angry; which the credulous multitude imputed to a divine power: but all this was discovered to be a cheat, and it was brought up to St. Paul's cross, and all the springs were openly shewed that governed its several motions. At Hales in Gloucestershire, the blood of Christ was shewed in a phial; and it was believed that none could see it who were in mortal sin: and so, after good presents were made, the deluded pilgrims went away well satisfied, if they had seen it. This was the blood of a duck, renewed every week, put in a phial, very thick of one side, as thin on the other; and either side turned towards the pilgrim, as the priests were satisfied with their oblations. Several other such like impostures were discovered, which contributed much to the undeceiving of the people. *Burnet's Abridg. Hist. Refor.*

escaped

escaped the ravages of the Danes, were destroyed, with more than Gothic barbarity, at their dissolution. (k)

Every abbey had at least one person, whose office it was to instruct youth; and to the monks, the historians of this country are chiefly beholden for the knowledge they have of former national events. The arts of painting, architecture, and printing, were also successfully cultivated within their walls.

Religious houses were likewise the hospitals for the sick and poor, many of both being daily relieved by them: they also afforded lodging and entertainment for travellers, at a time when there were no inns.

The nobility and gentry, who were heirs to their founders, in them could provide for a certain number of ancient and faithful servants by procuring them corodies, or stated allowances of meat, drink and clothes. It was also an asylum or retreat for aged indigent persons of good family.

The places near the site of these abbies were considerably benefited, both by the concourse of people resorting to them, by fairs procured for them, and by their exemption from the forest laws; add to which, the monastic estates were generally let at very easy rents, the fines given at renewals included.

(k) The barbarous ravages committed on the libraries of the monks, are thus set forth and lamented by John Bale, in his declaration upon Leland's Journal, anno 1549. "Covetousness," saith he "was at that time so busy about private commodity, that public wealth in that most necessary, and of respect, was not any where regarded. A number of them, which purchased those superstitious mansions, reserved of those library books, some to serve their jakes, some to scour the candlesticks, and some to rub their boots; some they sold to the grocer and soap-seller; and some they sent over sea, to the book-binders, not in small numbers; but, at times, whole ships full; yea, the universities of this realm are not at all clear in this detestable fact. But cursed is that belly, which seeketh to be fed with so ungodly gains, and so deeply shameth his natural country. I know (says he) a merchantman (which shall at this time be nameless) that bought the contents of two noble libraries for forty shillings price: a shame it is to be spoken! This stuff hath he occupied instead of grey paper, by the space of more than these ten years, and yet he hath store enough for as many years to come: a prodigious example is this, and to be abhorred by all men, which loved their nation as they should do. Yea, what may bring our realm to more shame and rebuke, than to have it noised abroad, that we are despisers of learning. I shall judge this to be true, and utter it with heaviness, that neither the Britons under the Romans and Saxons, nor yet the English people, under the Danes and Normans, had ever such damage of their learned monuments, as we have seen in our time. Our posterity may well curse this wicked fact of our age; this unreasonable spoil of England's most noble antiquities."

To

To conclude, their ſtately buildings and magnificent churches were ſtriking ornaments to the country; the furious zeal with which theſe were demoliſhed, their fine carvings deſtroyed, and their beautiful painted windows broken, would almoſt tempt one to imagine, that the perſons who directed theſe depredations, were actuated with an enmity to the fine arts, inſtead of a hatred to the popiſh ſuperſtition.

☞ An alphabetical liſt of all the religious houſes in England and Wales, to whom dedicated, when founded, with their valuation at the time of the diſſolution, will be added in the Index, at the concluſion of the work.

ARCHITECTURE.

MOST of the writers who mention our ancient buildings, particularly the religious ones, notwithſtanding the ſtriking difference in the ſtyles of their conſtruction, claſs them all under the common denomination of Gothic: a general appellation by them applied to all buildings not exactly conformable to ſome one of the five orders of architecture. Our modern antiquaries, more accurately, divide them into Saxon, Norman and Saracenic; or that ſpecies vulgarly, though improperly, called Gothic.

AN opinion has long prevailed, chiefly countenanced by Mr. Somner, (a) that the Saxon churches were moſtly built with timber; and that the few they had of ſtone, conſiſted only of upright walls, without pillars or arches; the conſtruction of which, it is pretended, they were entirely ignorant of. Mr. Somner ſeems to have founded his opinion on the authority of Stowe, and a diſputable

(a) INDEED, it is to be obſerved, that before the Roman Advent, moſt of our monaſteries and church buildings were all of wood: "All the monaſteries of my realm," ſaith King Edgar, in his charter to the abbey of Malmſbury, dated in the year of Chriſt 974, "to the ſight are nothing but worm-eaten and rotten timber and boards:" and that upon the Norman Conqueſt, ſuch timber fabricks grew out of uſe, and gave place to ſtone buildings, raiſed upon arches; a form of ſtructure introduced by that nation, furniſhed with ſtone from Caen in Normandy.

"IN the year 1087," (Stowe's words of the cathedral of London) "this church of St. Paul was burnt with fire, and therewith moſt part of the city. Mauricius, then biſhop, began therefore the new foundation of a new church of St. Paul; a work that men of that time judged would never have been finiſhed, it was then ſo wonderful for length and breadth: as alſo the ſame was builded upon arches, or vaults of ſtone, for defence of fire, which was a manner of work before that time unknown to the people of this nation, and then brought from the French, and the ſtone was fetched from Caen in Normandy."——"St. Mary Bow Church in London, being built much about the ſame time and manner, that is on arches of ſtone, was therefore called," ſaith the ſame author, "New Mary Church, or St. Mary le Bow; as Stratford Bridge, being the firſt builded with arches of ſtone was therefore called Stratford le Bow." This doubtleſs is that new kind of architecture, the continuer of Bede (whoſe words Malmſbury hath taken up) intends, when ſpeaking of the Normans income, he ſaith, "You may obſerve every where, in villages churches, and in cities and villages monaſteries, erected with a new kind of architecture."——And again, ſpeaking doubtfully of the age of the eaſtern part of the choir of Canterbury, he adds, "I dare conſtantly and confidently deny it to be elder than the Norman Conqueſt; becauſe of the building it upon arches; a form of architecture, though in uſe with and among the Romans long before, yet, after their departure, not uſed here in England, till the Normans brought it over with them from France. *Somner's Antiq. Canterbury.*

inter-

interpretation of ſome words in King Edgar's charter; (b) " Meaning no more, as I apprehend," ſays Mr. Bentham, in his Curious Remarks on Saxon Churches, " than that the churches and monaſteries were in general ſo much decayed, that the roofs were uncovered or bare to the timber; and the beams rotted by neglect, and overgrown with moſs." It is true, that Bede and others ſpeak of churches built with timber; but theſe appear to have been only temporary erections, haſtily run up for the preſent exigency: (c) and for the other poſition, that the Saxons had neither arches nor pillars in their buildings, it is not only contradicted by the teſtimony of ſeveral cotemporary or very ancient writers, who expreſsly mention them both, but alſo by the remains of ſome edifices univerſally allowed to be of Saxon workmanſhip; one of them the ancient conventual church at Ely.

The writers here alluded to, are Alcuin, an eccleſiaſtic, who lived in the eighth century; and in a poem, entitled, De Pontificibus et Eccleſiæ Ebor. publiſhed by Doctor Gale, A. D. 1691, deſcribes the church of St. Peter at York; which he himſelf, in conjunction with Eanbald, had aſſiſted Archbiſhop Albert to rebuild. In this poem he particularizes, by name, both columns and arches, as may be ſeen in note. (d)

(b) " Quæ velut muſcivis ſcindulis carioſiſque tabulis, tigno tenus viſibiliter diruta."

(c) " Baptizatus eſt (Sc. Rex Edwinus, A. D. 627) autem Eboraci in die Sancto Paſchæ.—— In eccleſia St. Petri apoſtoli quam ipſe de ligno citato opere erexit." *Bedæ Hiſt. Eccl. lib. ii. c. 14.*—— " Curavit majorem ipſo in loco et auguſtiorem de lapide fabricare baſilicam, in cujus medio ipſum quod prius fecerat oratorium includeretur." *Ibid.*

(d) " Ast nova baſilicæ miræ ſtructura diebus
Præſulis hujus erat jam cæpta, peracta, ſacrata.
Hæc nimis alta domus ſolidis, ſuffulta columnis,
Suppoſita quæ ſtant curvatis arcubus, intus
Emicat egregiis laquearibus atque feneſtris,
Pulchraque porticibus fulget circumdata multis,
Plurima diverſis retinens ſolaria tectis,
Quæ triginta tenet variis ornatibus aras.
Hoc duo diſcipuli templum, Doctore jubente,
Ædificarunt Eanbaldus et Alcuinus, ambo
Concordes operi devota mente ſtudentes.
Hoc tamen ipſe pater ſocio cum Præſule templum,
Ante die decima quam clauderet, ultima vitæ
Lumina præſentis, Sophiæ ſacraverat almæ."

The

The author of the deſcription of the abbey of Ramſay in Huntingdonſhire, which was founded A. D. 974, by Ailwood, ſtyled Alderman of all England, aſſiſted therein by Oſwald, biſhop of Worceſter, in that account names both arches and columns, as is ſhewn in note. (e)

Richard Prior, of Hexham, who flouriſhed about the year 1180, and left a deſcription of that church, part of which was ſtanding in his time, though built by Wilfred, anno 674; he likewiſe ſpeaks of arches, and columns with their capitals richly ornamented: ſee note. (f)

Many more authorities might be cited, was not the matter ſufficiently clear. Indeed, it is highly improbable, that the Saxons could be ignorant of ſo uſeful a contrivance as the arch: many of them, built by the Romans, they muſt have had before their eyes; ſome of which have reached our days: two particularly are now remaining in Canterbury only; one in the caſtle-yard, the other at Riding-gate. And it is not to be believed, that once knowing them, and their convenience, they would neglect to make uſe of them; or having uſed, would relinquiſh them. Beſides, as it appears, from undoubted authorities, they procured

(e) "Duce quoque turres ipſis tectorum culminibus eminebant, quarum minor verſus occidentem, in fronte Baſilicæ pulchram intrantibus inſulam a longe ſpectaculum præbebat; major vero in quadrifidæ ſtructuræ medio columnas quatuor, porrectis de alia ad aliam arcubus ſibi invicem connexus, ne laxi defluerunt, deprimebat."

Hiſt. Rameſienſis, inter xv. Scriptores, Edit. per Gale.

(f) Profunditatem ipſius eccleſiæ criptis, et oratoriis ſubterraneis, et viarum amfractibus, inferius cum magna induſtria fundavit: parietes autem quadratis, et variis, et bene politis columpnis ſuffultos, et tribus tabulatis diſtinctos immenſæ longitudinis, et altitudinis erexit: ipſos etiam et capitella columpnorum quibus ſuſtentatur, et arcum ſanctuarii hiſtoriis, et imaginibus, et variis celaturarum figuris ex lapide prominentibus, et picturarum, et colorum grata varietate mirabilique decore decoravit: ipſum quoque corpus eccleſiæ appenticiis, et porticibus nudique circumcinxit. Quæ miro atque inexplicabili artificio per parietes, et cocleas inferius, et ſuperius diſtinxit; in ipſis vero cocleis, et ſuper ipſas, aſcenſoria ex lapide, et deambulatoria, et varios viarum amfractus modo, ſurſum modo deorſum artificioſſiſſime item machinari fecit, ut innumera hominum multitudo ibi exiſtere, et ipſum corpus eccleſiæ circumdare poſſit, cum a nemine tamen infra in ea exiſtentium videri queat: oratoria quoque quamplurima ſuperius, et inferius ſecretiſſima, et pulcherrima in ipſis porticibus cum maxima diligentia, et cautela conſtituit, in quibus altaria in honore B. Dei Genetricis ſemperque Virginis Mariæ, et St. Michaelis Archangeli, ſanctique Johannis Bapt. honeſtiſſime preparari fecit. Unde etiam uſque hodie quædam illorum ut turres, et propugnacula ſupereminent. *Richardi Prioris Haguſt. lib. i. cap. 3.*

workmen from the Continent (g) to conſtruct their capital buildings "according to the Roman manner," this alone would be ſufficient to confute that ill-grounded opinion; and at the ſame time proves, that what we commonly call Saxon, is in reality Roman architecture,

THIS was the ſtyle of building practiſed all over Europe; and it continued to be uſed by the Normans, after their arrival here, till the introduction of what is called the Gothic, which was not till about the end of the reign of Henry II. ſo that there ſeems to be little or no grounds for a diſtinction between the Saxon and Norman architecture. Indeed, it is ſaid, the buildings of the latter were of larger dimenſions, both in height and area; and they were conſtructed with a ſtone brought from Caen in Normandy, of which their workmen were peculiarly fond: but this was ſimply an alteration in the ſcale and materials, and not in the manner of the building. The ancient parts of moſt of our cathedrals are of this early Norman work.

(g) CUM centoribus Ædde et Eona, et cementariis omniſque pene artis miniſterio in regionem ſuam revertens, cum regula Benedicti inſtituta eccleſiarum Dei bene melioravit. *Eddii vit. St. Wilfridi, cap.* 14. *Bedæ Hiſt. Ecc. lib. iv. cap.* 2.——De Roma quoque, et Italia, et Francia, et de aliis terris ubicumque invenire poterat, cæmentarios et quoſlibet alios induſtrios artifices ſecum retinuerat, et ad opera ſua facienda ſecum in Angliam adduxerat. *Rich. Prior Haguſt, lib.* 1. *cap.* 5.

ST. PETER's church, in the monaſtery of Weremouth, in the neighbourhood of Gyrwi, was built by the famous Benedict Biſcopius, in the year 675. This abbot went over into France, to engage workmen to build his church after the Roman manner (as it is called by Bede in his hiſtory of Weremouth) and brought them over for that purpoſe: he proſecuted this work with extraordinary zeal and diligence, inſomuch that, within the compaſs of a year after the foundations were laid, he cauſed the roof to be put on, and divine ſervice to be performed in it. Afterwards, when the building was near finiſhed, he ſent over to France for artificers ſkilled in the myſtery of making glaſs (an art till that time unknown to the inhabitants of Britain) to glaze the windows, both of the porticos, and the principal parts of the church; which work they not only executed, but taught the Engliſh nation that moſt uſeful art. *Bentham's Hiſtory of Ely, p.* 21.

WHAT Bede here affirms of the abbot Benedict, that he firſt introduced the art of making glaſs into this kingdom, is by no means inconſiſtent with Eddius's account of Biſhop Wilfrid's glazing the windows of St. Peter's church at York, about the year 669, *i. e.* ſeven or eight years before this time; for glaſs might have been imported from abroad by Wilfred. But Benedict firſt brought over the artiſts who taught the Saxons the art of making glaſs.——That the windows in churches were uſually glazed in that age abroad, as well as in theſe parts, we learn from Bede; who, ſpeaking of the church on Mount Olivet, about a mile from Jeruſalem, ſays, "In the weſt front of it were eight windows, which on ſome occaſions, uſed to be illuminated with lamps; which ſhone ſo bright through the glaſs, that the mount ſeemed in a blaze." *Bedæ lib. de Locis Sanctis, cap.* 6.

THE

The grand[l] Door of Barfreston Church in Kent

ARCHITECTURE.

The characteriſtic marks of this ſtyle are theſe: The walls are very thick, generally without buttreſſes; the arches, both within and without, as well as thoſe over the doors and windows, ſemicircular, and ſuported by very ſolid, or rather clumſy columns, with a kind of regular baſe and capital: in ſhort, plainneſs and ſolidity conſtitute the ſtriking features of this method of building. Neverthleſs, the architects of thoſe days ſometimes deviated from this rule: their capitals were adorned with carvings of foliage, and even animals; and their maſſive columns decorated with ſmall half columns united to them, and their ſurfaces ornamented with ſpirals, ſquares, lozenge network and other figures, either engraved, or in relievo: various inſtances of theſe may be ſeen in the cathedral of Canterbury, particularly the under-croft; the monaſtery at Lindisfarn or Holy Iſland, the cathedral at Durham, and the ruined choir at Orford in Suffolk. (h) Their arches too, though generally plain, ſometimes came in for more than their ſhare of ornaments: particularly thoſe over the chief doors: ſome of theſe were overloadedwith a profuſion of carving.

It would be impoſſible to deſcribe the different ornaments there crowded together; which ſeem to be more the extemporaneous product of a groteſque imagination, than the reſult of any particular deſign. On ſome of theſe arches is commonly over the key-ſtone repreſented God the Father, or our Saviour ſurrounded with angels; and below a melange of foliage, animals, often ludicrous, and ſometimes even indecent ſubjects. Partly of this ſort is the great door at Barfreſton Church in Kent. The friſes round churches were alſo occaſionally ornamented, with groteſque, human heads, monſters, figures playing on different muſical inſtruments, and other whimſical devices, of which the

(h) The columns No. 1, in the plate of architecture, are at the monaſtery of Lindisfarn or Holy Iſland. Thoſe No. 2, belong to the ruined chancel at Orford in Suffolk. No. 4, at Chriſt church, Canterbury. No. 3, an arch in Romſey church, Hampſhire, containing a ſegment greater than a ſemicircle. No. 5, a column with two remarkable projections like claws: in the ſouth aiſle of the ſame building there are ſeveral others ſimilar to it. No. 6, 7, 8, ornaments in the cathedral at Rocheſter.

church

church of Barfreston, above mentioned, and that of Adderbury in Suffolk afford ſtriking ſpecimens.

THE idea of theſe artiſts ſeems to have been, that the greater number of ſmall and diſſimilar ſubjects they could there aſſemble, the more beautiful they rendered their work. It is not however to be denied, that the extreme richneſs of theſe inferior parts ſerved, by their ſtriking contraſt, to ſet off the venerable plainneſs of the reſt of the building; a circumſtance wanting in the Gothic ſtructures: which, being equally ornamented all over, fatigue and diſtract, rather than gratify the eye.

I WOULD not here be underſtood to aſſert, that all the Saxon ornamented arches were devoid of beauty and taſte; on the contrary, there are ſeveral wherein both are diſplayed, particularly in ſome belonging to the church of Ely. Beſides the ornaments here mentioned, which ſeem always to have been left to the fancy of the ſculptor, they had others, which were in common uſe, and are more regular. Moſt of them, as mentioned by Mr. Bentham, in his ingenious preface to the Hiſtory of Ely, the reader will find in the note; (i) and ſpecimens of them are given in the miſcellaneous

(i) As to their arches, though they were for the moſt part plain and ſimple, yet ſome of their principal ones, as thoſe over the chief entrance at the weſt end, and others moſt expoſed to view, were abundantly charged with ſculpture of a particular kind; as the chevron work, or zig zag moulding, the moſt common of any; and various other kinds, riſing and falling, jetting out and receding inward alternately, in a waving or undulating manner: the embattled frette, a kind of ornament formed by a ſingle round moulding, traverſing the face of the arch, making its returns and croſſings always at right angles, ſo forming the intermediate ſpaces into ſquares alternately open above and below. Specimens of this kind of ornament appear on the great arches in the middle of the weſt front at Lincoln; and within the ruinous part of the building adjoining to the great weſtern tower at Ely: the triangular frette, where the ſame kind of moulding, at every return, forms the ſide of an equilateral triangle, and conſequently incloſes the intermediate ſpace in that figure: the nail-heads, reſembling the heads of great nails, driven in at regular diſtances; as in the nave of old St. Paul's, and the great tower at Hereford (all of them found alſo in more ancient Saxon buildings):—the billeted moulding, as if a cylinder ſhould be cut into ſmall pieces of equal length, and theſe ſtuck on alternately round the face of the arches; as in the choir of Peterborough, at St. Croſs, and round the windows of the upper tire on the outſide of the nave at Ely:—this latter ornament was often uſed (as were alſo ſome of the others) as a faſcia, band, or fillet, round the outſide of their buildings.—Then to adorn the inſide walls below, they had rows of little pillars and arches; and applied them alſo to decorate large vacant ſpaces in the walls without (capitals of theſe were frequently ornamented with groteſque work):—and the corbel-table, conſiſting of a ſeries of ſmall arches without pillars, but with the heads of men or animals, ſerving inſtead of corbels or brackets to ſupport them, which they

PREFACE

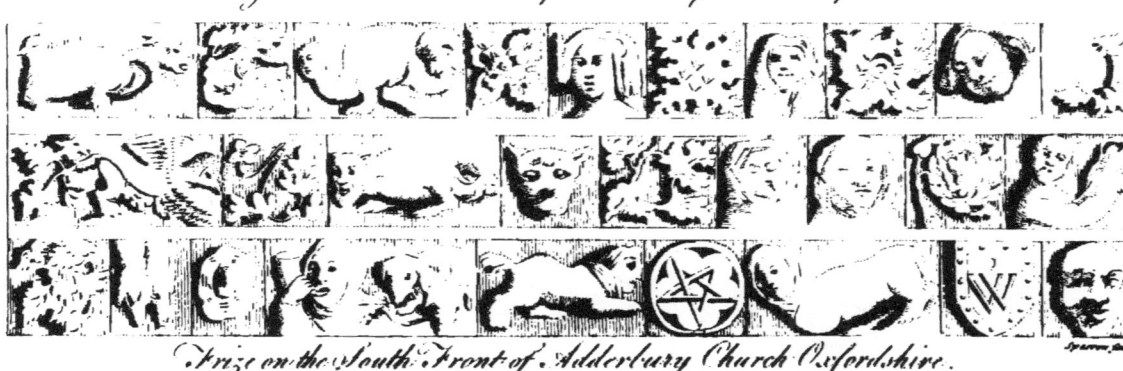

Frize on the North Front of Adderbury Church Oxfordshire.

Frize on the South Front of Adderbury Church Oxfordshire.

BARFRESTON CHURCH, *KENT*.

Stranger's Hall, Christ Church Canterbury.

laneous plate, in the view of the eaſt end of Barfreſton church; and in the entrance into what was the ſtrangers hall, in the monaſtery of Chriſt's Church, Canterbury, built by Archbiſhop Lanfranc; the ſmall pillars, or columns whereof, were formerly richly ornamented; but by order of one of the deans, were chipped plain. The eſcutcheons over theſe are remarkable; they not being cuſtomary at the time of its erection.

About the time of Alfred probably, but certainly in the reign of Edgar, (k) high towers and croſs aiſles were firſt introduced: the Saxon churches till then being only ſquare, or oblong buildings, generally turned ſemicircularly at the eaſt end. Towers at firſt ſcarcely roſe higher than the roof; being intended chiefly as a kind of lanthorn, for the admittance of light. An addition to their height was in all likelihood ſuggeſted on the more common uſe of bells; which, though mentioned in ſome of our monaſteries in the ſeventh century, were not in uſe in churches till near the middle of the tenth.

To what country, or people, the ſtyle of architecture called Gothic owes its origin, is by no means ſatisfactorily determined. (l) It

they placed below the parapet, projecting over the upper and ſometimes the middle tire of windows:—the hatched moulding, uſed both on the faces of the arches, or as a faſcia on the outſide; as if cut with the point of an axe, at regular diſtances, and ſo left rough:—and the nebule, a projection terminated by an undulating line, as under the upper range of windows at Peterborough. To theſe marks that diſtinguiſh the Saxon or Norman ſtyle, we may add, that they had no tabernacles, (or niches with canopies) or pinnacles or ſpires, or, indeed, any ſtatues to adorn their buildings on the outſide, which are the principal grace of what is now called the Gothic; unleſs thoſe ſmall figures we ſometimes meet with over their door-ways; ſuch as is that little figure of Biſhop Herbert Loſing, over the north tranſept door at Norwich, ſeemingly of that time; or another ſmall figure of our Saviour, over one of the ſouth doors of Ely, &c. may be called ſo. But theſe are rather mezzo relievos than ſtatues; and it is known, that they uſed reliefs ſometimes with profuſion; as in the Saxon or Norman gateway at Bury, and the two ſouth doors at Ely. Eſcutcheons of arms are hardly (if ever) ſeen in theſe fabrics, though freqent enough in after times; neither was there any tracery in their vaultings. Theſe few particularities in the Saxon and Norman ſtyle of building, however minute they may be in appearance, yet will be found to have their uſe, as they contribute to aſcertain the age of an edifice, at firſt ſight.

(k) Vide note (c), Page 108.

(l) The ſtyle of building with pointed arches is modern, and ſeems not to have been known in the world, till the Goths ceaſed to make a figure in it. Sir Chriſtopher Wren thought this ſhould rather be called the Saracenic way of building. The firſt appearance of it here, was indeed in the time of the Cruſades; and that might induce him to think the archetype was brought hither by ſome who had been engaged in thoſe expeditions, when they returned from the Holy Land. But the obſervations of ſeveral learned

It is indeed generally conjectured to be of Arabian extraction, and to have been introduced into Europe by some persons returning from the Crusades in the Holy Land. Sir Christopher Wren (m) was

learned travellers, who have accurately surveyed the ancient mode of building in those parts of the world, do by no means favour that opinion, or discover the least traces of it. Indeed, I have not yet met with any satisfactory account of the origin of pointed arches, when invented, or where first taken notice of. Some have imagined they might possibly have taken their rise from those arcades we see in the early Norman or Saxon buildings on walls, were the wide semicircular arches cross and intersect each other, and form at their intersection a narrow and sharp-pointed arch.

In the wall, south of the choir, at St. Cross, is a facing of such wide round interlaced arches, by way of ornament to a flat vacant space; only so much of it as lies between the legs of the two neighbouring arches, where they cross each other, is pierced through the fabric, and forms a little range of sharp-pointed windows; it is of King Stephen's time: whether they were originally pierced, I cannot learn. *Bentham.*

(m) These surveys, and other occasional inspections of the most noted cathedral churches and chapels in England, and foreign parts; a discernment of no contemptible art, ingenuity, and geometrical skill in the design and execution of some few, and an affectation of height and grandeur, though without regularity and good proportion in most of them, induced the surveyor to make some enquiry into the rise and progress of this Gothic mode, and to consider how the old Greek and Roman style of building, with the several regular proportions of columns, entablatures, &c. came, within a few centuries, to be so much altered, and almost universally disused.

He was of opinion (as has been mentioned in another place) that what we now vulgarly call the Gothic, ought properly and truly to be named the Saracenic architecture, refined by the Christians; which first of all began in the East, after the fall of the Greek empire, by the prodigious success of those people that adhered to Mahomet's doctrine; who, out of zeal to their religion, built mosques, caravanseras, and sepulchres wherever they came.

These they contrived of a round form, because they would not imitate the Christian figure of a cross; nor the old Greek manner, which they thought to be idolatrous; and for that reason all sculpture became offensive to them.

They then fell into a new mode of their own invention, though it might have been expected with better sense, considering the Arabians wanted not geometricians in that age; nor the Moors, who translated many of the most useful old Greek books. As they propagated their religion with great diligence, so they built mosques in all their conquered cities in haste.

The quarries of great marble, by which the vanquished nations of Syria, Egypt, and all the East had been supplied for columns, architraves, and great stones, were now deserted; the Saracens therefore were necessitated to accommodate their architecture to such materials, whether marble or free-stone, as every country readily afforded. They thought columns and heavy cornices impertinent, and might be omitted; and affecting the round form for mosques, they elevated cupolas in some instances with grace enough.

The Holy War gave the Christians, who had been there, an idea of the Saracen works; which were afterwards by them imitated in the West: and they refined upon it every day, as they proceeded in building churches. The Italians (among which were yet some Greek refugees) and with them French, Germans, and Flemings, joined into a fraternity of architects: procuring papal bulls for their encouragement, and particular privileges: they stiled themselves Free-masons, and ranged from one nation to another, as they found churches to be built (for very many in those ages were every where in building, through piety or emulation).

Their government was regular, and where they fixed near the building in hand, they made a camp of huts. A surveyor governed in chief; every tenth man was called a warden, and overlooked each nine: the

the gentleman of the neighbourhood, either out of charity, or commutation of penance; gave the materials and carriages. Those who have seen the exact accounts in records of the charge of the fabrics of some of our cathedrals, near four hundred years old, cannot but have a great esteem for their œconomy, and admire how soon they erected such lofty structures. Indeed, great height they thought the greatest magnificence: few stones were used, but what a man might carry up a ladder on his back from scaffold to scaffold; though they had pullies, and spoked wheels, upon occasion; but having rejected cornices, they had no need of great engines: stone upon stone was easily piled up to great heights; therefore, the pride of their works was in pinnacles and steeples.

In this they essentially differed from the Roman way, who laid all their mouldings horizontally, which made the best perspective: the Gothic way, on the contrary, carried all their mouldings perpendicular; so that the ground-work being settled, they had nothing else to do but to spire all up as they could. Thus they made their pillars of a bundle of little Torus's, which they divided into more, when they came to the roof; and these Torus's, split into many small ones, and traversing one another, gave occasion to the tracery work, as they call it, of which this society were the inventors. They used the sharp-headed arch, which would rise with little centering, required lighter key-stones, and less buttment, and yet would bear another row of doubled arches, rising from the key-stone: by the diversifiying of which, they erected eminent structures; such as the steeples of Vienna, Strasburg, and many others. They affected steeples, though the Saracens themselves most used cupolas. The church of St. Mark at Venice is built after the Saracen manner. Glass began to be used in windows; and a great part of the outside ornaments of churches consisted in the tracery works of disposing the mullions of the windows for the better fixing in of the glass. Thus the work required fewer materials, and the workmanship was for the most part performed by flat moulds, in which the wardens could easily instruct hundreds of artificers. It must be confessed, this was an ingenious compendium of work, suited to these northern climates; and I must also own, that works of the same height and magnificence in the Roman way, would be very much more expensive, than in the other Gothic manner, managed with judgment. But as all modes, when once the old rational ways are despised, turn at last into unbounded fancies, this tracery induced too much mincing of the stone into open battlements, and spindling pinnacles, and little carvings without proportion of distance; so the essential rules of good perspective and duration were forgot. But about two hundred years ago, when ingenious men began to reform the Roman language to the purity which they assigned and fixed to the time of Augustus, and that century; the architects also, ashamed of the modern barbarity of building, began to examine carefully the ruins of old Rome and Italy, to search into the orders and proportions, and to establish them by inviolable rules; so, to their labours and industry, we owe, in a great degree, the restoration of architecture.

The ingenious Mr. Evelyn makes a general and judicious comparison, in his Account of Architecture, of the ancient and modern styles; with reference to some of the particular works of Inigo Jones, and the Surveyor; which, in a few words, give a right idea of the majestic symmetry of the one, and the absurd system of the other.—"The ancient Greek and Roman architecture answer all the perfections required in a faultless and accomplished building; such as for so many ages were so renowned and reputed by the universal suffrages of the civilized world; and would doubtless have still subsisted, and made good their claim, and what is recorded of them, had not the Goths, Vandals, and other barbarous nations, subverted and demolished them; together with that glorious empire where those stately and pompous monuments stood: introducing in their stead, a certain fantastical and licentious manner of building, which we have since called Modern, or Gothic. Congestions of heavy, dark, melancholy, and monkish piles, without any just proportion, use, or beauty, compared with the truly ancient; so as when we meet with the greatest industry, and expensive carving, full of fret and lamentable imagery, sparing neither of pains nor cost, a judicious spectator is rather distracted, or quite confounded, than touched with that admiration which results from the true and just symmetry, regular proportion, union, and disposition; and from the great and noble manner in which the august and glorious fabrics of the ancients are executed." *Accounts of Architecture*, p. 9.

It was after the irruption of swarms of those truculent people from the north, the Moors and Arabs from the south and east, over-running the civilized world, that wherever they fixed themselves, they began to debauch this noble and useful art; when, instead of those beautiful orders, so majestical and proper

was of that opinion; (n) and it has been ſubſcribed to by moſt writers who have treated on this ſubject. (o) If the ſuppoſition is

proper for their ſtations, becoming variety, and other ornamental acceſſories, they ſet up thoſe ſlender and miſhapen pillars, or rather bundles of ſtaves, and other incongruous props, to ſupport incumbent weights, and ponderous arched roofs, without entablature; and though not without great induſtry, (as Mr. D'Aviler well obſerves) not altogether naked of gaudy ſculpture, trite and buſy carvings, it is ſuch as gluts the eye, rather than gratifies and pleaſes it with any reaſonable ſatisfaction. For proof of this, without travelling far abroad, I dare report myſelf to any man of judgment, and that has the leaſt taſte of order and magnificence, if, after he has looked a while upon King Henry the Seventh's Chapel at Weſtminſter, gazed on its ſharp angles, jetties, narrow lights, lame ſtatues, lace, and other cut work, and crinkle crankle, and ſhall then turn his eyes on the Banquetting-houſe, built at Whitehall, by Inigo Jones, after the ancient manner; or on what his Majeſty's ſurveyor, Sir Chriſtopher Wren, has advanced at St. Paul's; and conſider what a glorious object the cupola, porticos, colonades, and other parts preſent to the beholder: or compare the ſchools and library at Oxford with the theatre there; or what he has built at Trinity College, in Cambridge: and ſince all theſe, at Greenwich and other places, by which time our home traveller will begin to have a juſt idea of the ancient and modern architecture; I ſay, let him well conſider, and compare them judicially, without partiality and prejudice, and then pronounce which of the two manners ſtrikes the underſtanding as well as the eye, with the more majeſtic and ſolemn greatneſs; though in ſo much a plainer and ſimple dreſs, conform to the reſpective orders and entablature; and accordingly determine to whom the preference is due: not as we ſaid, that there is not ſomething of ſolid, and oddly artificial too, after a ſort. But the univerſal and unreaſonable thickneſs of the walls, clumſy buttreſſes, towers, ſharp-pointed arches, doors, and other apertures without proportion: nonſenſical inſertions of various marbles impertinently placed; turrets and pinnacles, thick ſet with monkies and chimeras, and abundance of buſy work, and other incongruities, diſſipate and break the angles of the ſight, and ſo confound it, that one cannot conſider it with any ſteadineſs, where to begin or end; taking off from that noble air and grandeur, bold and graceful manner, which the ancients had ſo well and judiciouſly eſtabliſhed. But in this ſort have they and their followers, ever ſince, filled not Europe alone, but Aſia and Africa beſides, with mountains of ſtone; vaſt and gigantic buildings indeed! but not worthy the name of architecture, &c. *Wren's Parentalia.*

(n) THIS we now call the Gothic manner of architecture, (ſo the Italians called what was not after the Roman ſtyle) though the Goths were rather deſtroyers than builders; I think it ſhould with more reaſon be called the Saracen ſtyle; for thoſe people wanted neither arts nor learning; and after we in the weſt had loſt both, we borrowed again from them, out of their Arabic books, what they with great diligence had tranſlated from the Greeks.—They were zealots in their religion; and wherever they conquered, (which was with amazing rapidity) erected moſques and caravanſeras in haſte, which obliged them to fall into another way of building; for they built their moſques round, diſliking the Chriſtian form of a croſs. The old quarries, whence the ancients took their large blocks of marble for whole columns and architraves, were neglected; and they thought both impertinent. Their carriage was by camels; therefore, their buildings were fitted for ſmall ſtones, and columns of their own fancy, conſiſting of many pieces; and their arches pointed without key-ſtones, which they thought too heavy.——The reaſons were the ſame in our northern climates, abounding in free-ſtone, but wanting marble.

(o) MODERN Gothic, as it is called, is deduced from a different quarter: it is diſtinguiſhed by the lightneſs of its work, by the exceſſive boldneſs of its elevations, and of its ſections; by the delicacy, profuſion, and extravagant fancy of its ornaments. The pillars of this kind are as ſlender as thoſe of the ancient Gothic are maſſive; ſuch productions, ſo airy, cannot admit the heavy Goths for their author; how can be attributed to them, a ſtyle of architecture, which was only introduced in the tenth century of our æra? Several years after the deſtruction of all thoſe kingdoms, which the Goths had

is well grounded, it ſeems likely that many ancient buildings of this kind, or at leaſt their remains, would be found in thoſe countries from whence it is ſaid to have been brought; parts of which have at different times been viſited by ſeveral curious travellers, many of whom have made deſigns of what they thought moſt remarkable. Whether they over-looked or neglected theſe buildings, as being in ſearch of thoſe of more remote antiquity, or whether none exiſted, ſeems doubtful. Cornelius le Brun, an indefatigable and inquiſitive traveller, has publiſhed many views of eaſtern buildings, particularly about the Holy Land: in all theſe, only one Gothic ruin, the church near Acre, and a few pointed arches, occur; and thoſe built by the Chriſtians, when in poſſeſſion of the country. Near Iſpahan, in Perſia, he gives ſeveral buildings with pointed arches; but theſe are bridges and caravanſeras, whoſe age cannot be aſcertained; conſequently, are as likely to have been built after as before the introduction of this ſtyle into Europe.

had raiſed upon the ruins of the Roman empire, and at a time when the very name of Goth was entirely forgotten: from all the marks of the new architecture, it can only be attributed to the Moors; or, what is the ſame thing, to the Arabians or Saracens; who have expreſſed, in their architecture, the ſame taſte as in their poetry; both the one and the other falſely delicate, crowded with ſuperfluous ornaments, and often very unnatural; the imagination is highly worked up in both; but it is an extravagant imagination; and this has rendered the edifices of the Arabians (we may include the other orientals) as extraordinary as their thoughts. If any one doubts of this aſſertion, let us appeal to any one who has ſeen the moſques and palaces of Fez; or ſome of the cathedrals in Spain, built by the Moors; one model of this ſort, is the church at Burgos; and even in this iſland there are not wanting ſeveral examples of the ſame; ſuch buildings have been vulgarly called Modern Gothic, but their true appellation is Arabic, Saracenic, or Moreſque.—This manner was introduced into Europe through Spain: learning flouriſhed among the Arabians, all the time that their dominion was in full power; they ſtudied philoſophy, mathematics, phyſic and poetry. The love of learning was at once excited; in all places, that were not at too great a diſtance from Spain, theſe authors were read; and ſuch of the Greek authors as they had tranſlated into Arabic, were from thence turned into Latin. The phyſic and philoſophy of the Arabians ſpread themſelves in Europe, and with theſe their architecture: many churches were built after the Saracenic mode; and others with a mixture of heavy and light proportions, the alteration that the difference of the climate might require, was little, if at all conſidered. In moſt ſouthern parts of Europe, and in Africa, the windows, (before the uſe of glaſs) made with narrow apertures, and placed very high in the walls of the building, occaſioned a ſhade and darkneſs within ſide, and were all contrived to guard againſt the fierce rays of the ſun; yet were ill ſuited to thoſe latitudes, where that glorious luminary ſhades its feebler influences, and is rarely ſeen but through a watery cloud. *Rious's Architecture.*

At Iſpahen itſelf, the mey doen, or grand market-place, is ſurrounded by divers magnificent Gothic buildings; particularly the royal moſque, and the Talael Ali-kapie, or theatre. The magnificent bridge of Alla-werdie-chan, over the river Zenderoet, five hundred and forty paces long, and ſeventeen broad, having thirty-three pointed arches, is alſo a Gothic ſtructure: but no mention is made when or by whom theſe are built. The Chiaer Baeg, a royal garden, is decorated with Gothic buildings; but theſe were, it is ſaid, built only in the reign of Scha Abbas, who died anno 1629.

One building indeed, at firſt ſeems as if it would corroborate this aſſertion, and that the time when it was erected might be in ſome degree fixed; it is the tomb of Abdalla, (p) one of the apoſtles of Mahomet, probably him ſurnamed Abu Becr. If this tomb is ſuppoſed to have been built ſoon after his death, eſtimating that even to have happened according to the common courſe of nature, it will place its erection about the middle of the ſeventh century: but this is by far too conjectural to be much depended on. It alſo ſeems as if this was not the common ſtyle of building at that time, from the temple of Mecca; where, if any credit

(p) Le vingt-troſieme de ce mois nous allames encore en ceremonie au village de Kaladoen, à une bonne lieuë de la ville, pour y voir le tombeau d'Abdulla. On dit que ce ſaint avoit autrefois l'inſpection des eux d'Emoen Oſſeyn, & qu'il étoit un des 12 deſciples, ou à ce qu'ils pretendent; un des apôtres de leur prophete, ce tombeau qui eſt placé entre quatre murailles, revetues de petites pierres, eſt de marbre gris, ornè de caracteres Arabes, & entouré de lampes, de cuivre étamées; on y monte par 15 Marches d'un pied de haut, & l'on y en trouve 15 autres un peu plus élevées qui conduiſent, à une platte forme quarée, qui a 32 pieds de large de chaque côte, a ſur le devant, de la quelle il y a deux colomnes de petites pierres, entre les quelles il s'en trouve de blues. La baſe en a 5 pieds de large, & une petite porte, avec un eſcalier à noyau qui a auſſi 15 Marches. Elles ſont fort endommagées par les injures du temps, & ill paroit qu'elles ont eté une fois plus élevées quelles ne ſont a preſent. L'eſcalier en eſt ſi étroit qu'il faut qu'un homme de taille ordinaire ſe deſhabille pour y monter, comme je fis, & paſſai la moitié du corps au deſſus de la colomne. Mais ce qu'il y a de plus extraordinaire, eſt que lors qu'on ébranle une des colomnes en faiſant un mouvement du corps; l'autre en reſſent les ſecouſſes, & eſt agitèe du même; une choſe dont j'ai fait l'epreuve, ſans en pouvoir comprendre, ni apprendre la raiſon. Pendant que j'etois occupé à deſſiner ce batiment, qu'on trouve au Num. 71, un jeun garçon de 12 a 13 ans, boſſu par devant, grimpa en dehors, le long de la muraille, juſqu'au haut de la colomne dont il fit le tour, & redeſcendit de même ſans ſe tenir à quoi que ce ſoit, qu'aux petites pierres, de ce bâtiment, aux endroits où la chaux en étoit détachée; & il ne le fit que pour nous devertir.

is to be given to the print of it, in Sale's Koran, the arches are ſemicircular. The tomb here mentioned, has one evidence to prove its antiquity; that of being damaged by the injuries of time and weather. Its general appearance much reſembles the eaſt end of the chapel belonging to Ely Houſe, London; except that, which is filled up there by the great window: in the tomb is an open pointed arch; where alſo, the columns, or pinnacles, on each ſide, are higher in proportion.

SOME have ſuppoſed that this kind of architecture was brought into Spain by the Moors (who poſſeſſed themſelves of a great part of that country the beginning of the eighth century, which they held till the latter end of the fifteenth); and that from thence, by way of France, (q) it was introduced into England. This at firſt ſeems plauſible; though, the only inſtance which ſeems to corroborate this hypotheſis, or at leaſt the only one proved by authentic drawings, is the moſque at Cordua in Spain; where, according to the views publiſhed by Mr. Swinburn, although moſt of the

(q) THE Saracen mode of building ſeen in the eaſt, ſoon ſpread over Europe, and particularly in France, the faſhions of which nation we affected to imitate in all ages, even when we were at enmity with it. Nothing was thought magnificent that was not high beyond meaſure, with the flutter of arch buttreſſes, ſo we call the ſloping arches that poiſe the higher vaultings of the nave. The Romans always concealed their butments, whereas the Normans thought them ornamental. Theſe I have obſerved are the firſt things that occaſion the ruin of cathedrals, being ſo much expoſed to the air and weather; the coping, which cannot defend them, firſt failing, and if they give way the vault muſt ſpread. Pinnacles are of no uſe, and as little ornament. The pride of a very high roof, raiſed above reaſonable pitch, is not for duration, for the lead is apt to ſlip; but we are tied to this indiſcreet form, and muſt be contented with original faults in the firſt deſign. But that which is moſt to be lamented, is the unhappy choice of the materials, the ſtone is decayed four inches deep, and falls off perpetually in great ſcales. I find after the conqueſt all our artiſts were fetched from Normandy; they loved to work in their own Caen ſtone, which is more beautiful than durable. This was found expenſive to bring hither; ſo they thought Ryegate ſtone in Surry the neareſt like their own, being a ſtone that would ſaw and work like wood, but not durable, as is manifeſt: and they uſed this for the aſhlar of the whole fabrick, which is now disfigured in the higheſt degree. This ſtone takes in water, which being frozen, ſcales off; whereas good ſtone gathers a cruſt and defends itſelf, as many of our Engliſh free-ſtones do. And though we have alſo the beſt oak timber in the world, yet theſe ſenſeleſs artificers, in Weſtminſter hall and other places, would work their cheſnuts from Normandy: that timber is not natural to England, it works finely, but ſooner decays than oak. The roof in the abbey is oak, but mixed with cheſnut, and wrought after a bad Norman manner, that does not ſecure it from ſtretching and damaging the walls; and the water of the gutters is ill carried off. All this is ſaid, the better, in the next place, to repreſent to your lordſhip what has been done, and is wanting ſtill to be carried on; as time and money is allowed to make a ſubſtantial and durable repair. *Wren's Parentalia, p.* 298.

arches

arches are circular, or horſe-ſhoe faſhion, there are ſome pointed arches, formed by the interſection of two ſegments of a circle. This moſque, was as it is there ſaid, begun by Abdoulrahman, the firſt, who laid the foundation, two years before his death, and was finiſhed by his ſon Hiſſem or Iſcan about the year 800. If theſe arches were part of the original ſtructure it would be much in favour of the ſuppoſition; but, as it is alſo ſaid, that edifice has been more than once altered and enlarged by the Mahometans, before any well grounded concluſion can be drawn, it is neceſſary to aſcertain the date of the preſent building.

There are alſo ſeveral pointed arches in the Mooriſh Palace, at Grenada, called the Alhambra, but as that was not built till the year 1273, long after the introduction of pointed arches into Europe, they are as likely to be borrowed by the Moors from the Chriſtians, as by the Chriſtians from the Moors. The greateſt peculiarity in the Mooriſh architecture is the horſe-ſhoe arch, (r) which containing more than a ſemicircle, contracts towards its baſe, by which it is rendered unfit to bear any conſiderable weight, being ſolely calculated for ornament. In Romeſy Church Hampſhire, there are ſeveral arches ſomewhat of that form, one of them is repreſented in the plate of architecture, No. 3.

The drawings of the Mooriſh buildings given in Les Delices de L'Eſpagne, ſaid to be faithful repreſentations, there are no traces of the ſtyle called Gothic architecture, there as well as in the Mooriſh Caſtle at Gibraltar, the arches are all repreſented circular. Perhaps a more general knowledge of theſe buildings would throw ſome lights on the ſubject, at preſent almoſt entirely enveloped in obſcurity: poſſibly the Moors may, like us, at different periods, have uſed different manners of building. Having thus in vain attempted to diſcover from whence we had this ſtyle, let us turn to what is more certainly known, the time of its introduction into this kingdom, and the ſucceſſive improvements and changes it has undergone.

(r) As delineation gives a much clearer idea of forms and figures, than the moſt laboured deſcription, the reader is referred to the plates in Swinburns Travels, where there are many horſe ſhoe arches, both round and pointed.

Its

Its firſt appearance here was towards the latter end of the reign of King Henry II. but was not at once thoroughly adopted; ſome ſhort ſolid columns, and ſemicircular arches, being retained, and mixed with the pointed ones. An example of this is ſeen in the weſt end of the Old Temple Church; and at York, where, under the choir, there remains much of the ancient work; the arches of which are but juſt pointed, and riſe on ſhort round pillars: both theſe were built in that reign. More inſtances might be brought, was not the thing probable in itſelf; new inventions, even when uſeful, not being readily received. The great weſt tower of Ely Cathedral was built by Biſhop Rydel, about this time: thoſe arches were all pointed.

In the reign of Henry III. this manner of building ſeems to have gained a complete footing; the circular giving place to the pointed arch, and the maſſive column yielding to the ſlender pillar. Indeed, like all novelties, when once admitted, the rage of faſhion made it become ſo prevalent, that many of the ancient and ſolid buildings, erected in former ages, were taken down, in order to be re-edified in the new taſte; or had additions patched to them, of this mode of architecture. The preſent cathedral church of Saliſbury was begun early in this reign, and finiſhed in the year 1258. It is entirely in the Gothic ſtyle; and, according to Sir Chriſtopher Wren, may be juſtly accounted one of the beſt patterns of architecture of the age in which it was built. Its excellency is undoubtedly in a great meaſure owing to its being conſtructed on one plan; whence ariſes that ſymmetry and agreement of parts, not to be met with in many of our other cathedral churches; which have moſtly been built at different times, and in a variety of ſtyles. The faſhionable manner of building at this period, and till the reign of Henry VIII. as is deſcribed by Mr. Bentham, ſee in note. (s)

In

(s) During the whole reign of Henry III. the faſhionable pillars to our churches were of Purbec marble, very ſlender and round, encompaſſed with marble ſhafts a little detached, ſo as to make them appear of a proportionable thickneſs; theſe ſhafts had each of them a capital richly adorned with foliage,

In the beginning of the reign of Henry VIII. or rather towards the latter end of that of Henry VII. when brick building became common, a new kind of low pointed arch grew much in uſe: it was deſcribed from four centers, was very round at the haunches, and

foliage, which together in a cluſter formed one elegant capital for the whole pillar. This form, though graceful to the eye, was attended with an inconvenience, perhaps not apprehended at firſt; for the ſhafts, deſigned chiefly for ornament, conſiſting of long pieces cut horizontally from the quarry, when placed in a perpendicular ſituation, were apt to ſplit and break; which probably occaſioned this manner to be laid aſide in the next century. There was alſo ſome variety in the form of the vaultings in the ſame reign: theſe they generally choſe to make of chalk, for its lightneſs; but the arches and principal ribs were of free-ſtone. The vaulting of Saliſbury cathedral, one of the earlieſt, is high pitched, between arches and croſs ſpringers only, without any further decorations: but ſome that were built ſoon after are more ornamental, riſing from their impoſt with more ſpringers, and ſpreading themſelves to the middle of the vaulting, are enriched at their interſecting with carved orbs, foliage, and other devices: as in Biſhop Norwood's work in the Preſbytery, at the eaſt end of the cathedral of Ely. As to the windows of that age, we find them very long, narrow, ſharp pointed, and uſually decorated on the inſide and outſide with ſmall marble ſhafts: the order and diſpoſition of the windows varied in ſome meaſure according to the ſtories of which the building conſiſted: in one of three ſtories the uppermoſt had commonly three windows within the compaſs of every arch, the center one being higher than thoſe on each ſide; the middle tire or ſtory had two within the ſame ſpace; and the loweſt only one window, uſually divided by a pillar or mullion, and after ornamented on the top with a trefoil, ſingle roſe, or ſome ſuch ſimple decoration; which probably gave the hint for branching out the whole head into a variety of tracery and foliage, when the windows came afterwards to be enlarged. The uſe of painting and ſtained glaſs, in our churches, is thought to have begun about this time: this kind of ornament, as it diminiſhed the light, induced the neceſſity of making an alteration in the windows: either by encreaſing the number or enlarging their proportions; for ſuch a gloomineſs rather than overmuch light, ſeems more proper for ſuch ſacred edifices, and better calculated for recollecting the thoughts, and fixing pious affections: yet without that alteration, our churches had been too dark and gloomy; as ſome of them now, being diveſted of that ornament, for the ſame reaſon appear over light. As for ſpires and pinnacles, with which our oldeſt churches are ſometimes, and more modern ones are frequently decorated, I think they are not very ancient; the towers and turrets of churches built by the Normans, in the firſt century after their coming, were covered as platforms, with battlements or plain parapet walls; ſome of them indeed built within that period we now ſee finiſhed with pinnacles or ſpires; which were additions ſince the modern ſtyle of pointed arches prevailed, for before we meet with none. One of the earlieſt ſpires we have any account of is that of old St. Paul's, finiſhed in the year 1222: it was, I think, of timber, covered with lead; but not long after, they began to build them with ſtone, and to finiſh all their buttreſſes in the ſame manner. Architecture under Edward I. was ſo nearly the ſame as in his father Henry the Third's time, that it is no eaſy matter to diſtinguiſh it. Improvements no doubt were then made, but it is difficult to define them accurately. The tranſition from one ſtyle to another, is uſually affected by degrees, and therefore not very remarkable at firſt, but it becomes ſo at ſome diſtance of time: towards the latter part indeed of his reign, and in that of Edward II. we begin to diſcover a manifeſt change of the mode, as well in the vaulting and make of the columns, as the formation of the windows. The vaulting was, I think, more decorated than before; for now the principal ribs ariſing from their impoſt, being ſpread over the inner face of the arch, ran into a kind of tracery; or rather, with tranſoms divided the roof into various angular compartments, and were uſually ornamented in the angles, with gilded orbs, carved heads or figures, and other emboſſed work. The columns retained ſomething of their general form already

and the angle at the top was very obtufe. This fort of arch is to be found in every one of Cardinal Wolfey's buildings; alfo at Weft Sheen; an ancient brick gate at Mile End, called King John's Gate; and in the great gate of the palace of Lambeth. From this time Gothic architecture began to decline, and was

already defcribed; that is as an affemblage of fmall pillars or fhafts: but thefe decorations were now not detached or feparate from the body of the columns, but made part of it, and being clofely united and wrought up together, formed one entire, firm, flender, and elegant column. The windows were now greatly enlarged, and divided into feveral lights by ftone mullions, running into various ramifications above, and dividing the head into numerous compartments of different forms, as leaves, open flowers, and other fanciful fhapes: and more particularly the eaftern and weftern windows (which became fafhionable about this time) took up nearly the whole breadth of the nave, and were carried up almoft as high as the vaulting; and being fet off with painted and ftained glafs of moft lively colours, with portraits of kings, faints, martyrs and confeffors, and other hiftorical reprefentations, made a moft fplendid and glorious appearance. The three firft arches of the Prefbytery, adjoining to the dome and lantern of the cathedral church of Ely, began the latter part of Edward the Second's reign, A. D. 1322, to exhibit elegant fpecimens of thefe fafhionable pillars, vaultings and windows. St. Mary's chapel, (now Trinity parifh church) at Ely, built about the fame time, is conftructed on a different plan, but the vaultings and windows are in the fame ftyle. The plan of this chapel, generally accounted one of the moft perfect ftructures of that age, is an oblong fquare; it has no pillars nor fide aifles, but is fupported by ftrong fpiring buttreffes, and was decorated on the outfide with ftatues over the eaft and weft windows; and withinfide alfo with ftatues, and a great variety of other fculpture, well executed. The fafhion of adorning the weft end of our churches with rows of ftatues, in tabernacles or niches, with canopies over them, obtained very foon after the introduction of pointed arches, as may be feen at Peterborough and Salifbury, and in latter times we find them in a more improved tafte, as at Litchfield and Wells. The fame ftyle and manner of building prevailed all the reign of Edward III. and with regard to the principal parts and members, continued in ufe to the reign of Henry VII. and the greater part of Henry VIII. only towards the latter part of that period, the windows were lefs pointed and more open, a better tafte for ftatuary began to appear, and indeed a greater care feems to have been beftowed on all the ornamental parts, to give them a lighter and higher finifhing; particularly the ribs of the vaulting, which had been large, and feemingly formed for ftrength and fupport, became at length divided into fuch an abundance of parts, iffuing from their impofts as from a center, and fpreading themfelves over the vaulting, where they were intermixed with fuch delicate fculpture, as gave the whole vault the appearance of embroidery, enriched with clufters of pendent ornaments, refembling the works Nature fometimes forms in caves and grottos hanging down from their roofs. To what height of perfection modern architecture (I mean that with pointed arches, its chief characteriftic) was carried on in this kingdom, appears by one complete fpecimen of it, the chapel founded by King Henry VI. in his college at Cambridge, and finifhed by King Henry VIII. The decorations, harmony, and proportions of the feveral parts of this magnificent fabric, its fine painted windows, and richly ornamented roof, its gloom and perfpective, all concur in affecting the imagination with pleafure and delight, at the fame time that they infpire awe and devotion. It is undoubtedly one of the moft complete, elegant, and magnificent ftructures in the kingdom; and if, befides thefe larger works, we take into our view thofe fpecimens of exquifite workmanfhip we meet with in the fmaller kinds of oratories, chapels, and monumental edifices, produced fo late as the reign of Henry VIII. fome of which are ftill in being, or at leaft fo much of them, as to give an idea of their former grace and beauty, one can hardly help concluding, that architecture arrived at its higheft point of glory in this kingdom, but juft before its final period. *Bentham.*

foon

ſoon after ſupplanted by a mixed ſtyle, if one may venture to call it one; wherein the Grecian and Gothic, however diſcordant and irreconcileable, are jumbled together. Concerning this mode of building, Mr. Warton, in his obſervations on Spencer's Fairy Queen, has the following anecdotes and remarks:

———————————" Did riſe
On ſtately pillars, fram'd after the Doric guiſe.

Although the Roman or Grecian architecture did not begin to prevail in England till the time of Inigo Jones, yet our communication with the Italians, and our imitation of their manners, produced ſome ſpeciments of that ſtile much earlier. Perhaps the earlieſt is Somerſet Houſe in the Strand, built about the year 1549, by the duke of Someſet, uncle to Edward VI. The monument of Biſhop Gardiner, in Wincheſter Cathedral, made in the reign of Mary, about 1555, is decorated with Ionic pillars; Spenſer's verſes, here quoted, bear an alluſion to ſome of theſe faſhionable improvements in building, which, at this time, were growing more and more into eſteem. Thus alſo Biſhop Hall, who wrote about the ſame time; viz. 1598:

There findeſt thou ſome ſtately Doricke frame,
Or neat Ionicke work.——————

But theſe ornaments were often abſurdly introduced into the old Gothic ſtyle: as in the magnificent portico of the ſchools at Oxford, erected about the year 1613; where the builder, in a Gothic edifice, has affectedly diſplayed his univerſal ſkill in the modern architecture, by giving us all the five orders together. However, moſt of the great buildings of Queen Elizabeth's reign, have a ſtyle peculiar to themſelves both in form and finiſhing; where, though much of the old Gothic is retained, and great part of the new taſte is adopted, yet neither predominates; while both, thus diſtinctly blended, compoſe a fantaſtic ſpecies, hardly reducible to any claſs or name. One of its characteriſtics is the affectation of large and lofty windows; where, ſays Bacon, you ſhall have ſometimes

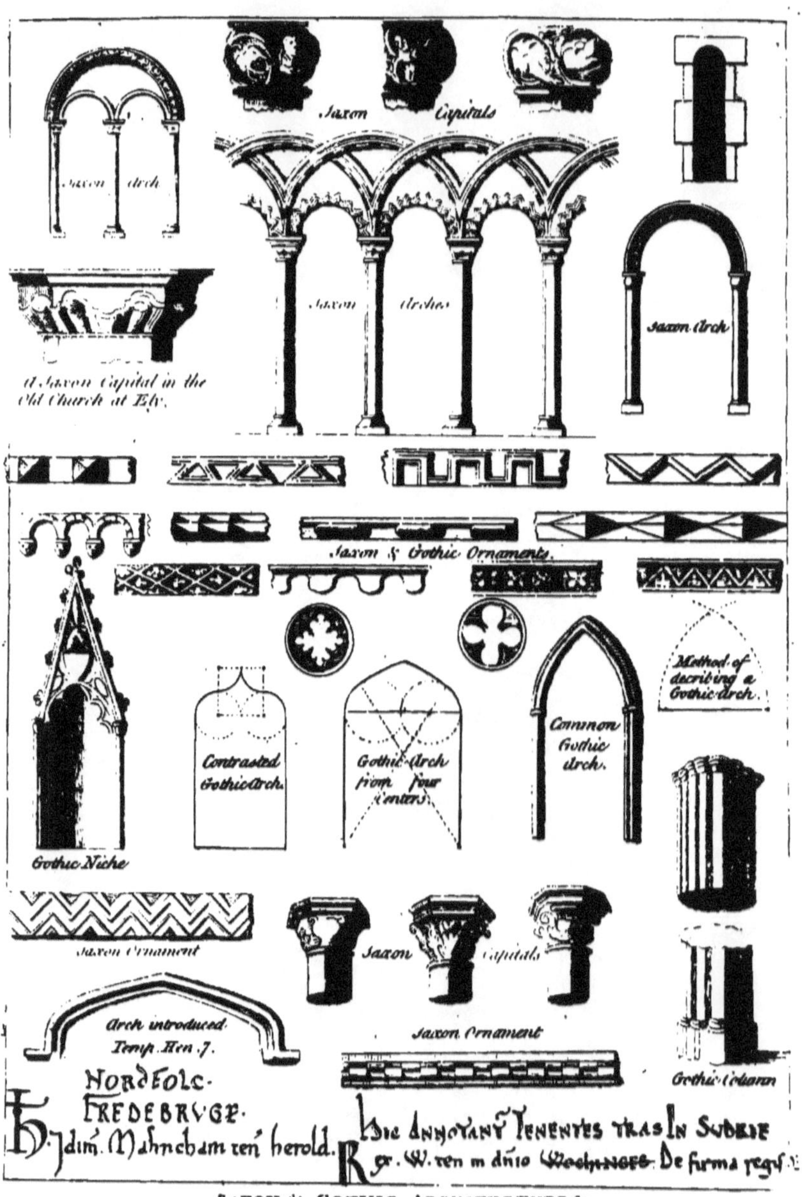

SAXON & GOTHIC ARCHITECTURE &c.

ſometimes fair houſes ſo full of glaſs, that one cannot tell where to become, to be out of the ſun."

The marks which conſtitute the character of Gothic, or Saracenical architecture, are its numerous and prominent buttreſſes, its lofty ſpires and pinnacles, its large and ramified windows, its ornamental niches or canopies, its ſculptured ſaints, the delicate lace-work of its fretted roofs, and the profuſion of ornaments laviſhed indiſcriminately over the whole building: but its peculiar diſtinguiſhing characteriſtics are, the ſmall cluſtered pillars and pointed arches, formed by the ſegments of two interſecting circles; which arches, though laſt brought into uſe, are evidently of more ſimple and obvious conſtruction than the ſemicircular ones; two flat ſtones, with their tops inclined to each other, and touching, form its rudiments, a number of boughs ſtuck into the ground oppoſite each other, and tied together at the top, in order to form a bower, exactly deſcribe it: whereas a ſemicircular arch appears the reſult of deeper contrivance, as conſiſting of more parts; and it ſeems leſs probable, chance, from whence all theſe inventions were firſt derived, ſhould throw ſeveral wedge-like ſtones between two ſet perpendicular, ſo as exactly to fit and fill up the interval.

Bishop Warburton, in his notes on Pope's Epiſtles, in the octavo editition, has ſome ingenius obſervations on this ſubject, which are given in the note: (t) to which it may not be improper to

(t) Our Gothic anceſtors had juſter and manlier notions of magnificence, on Greek and Roman ideas, than theſe mimics of taſte, who profeſs to ſtudy only claſſic elegance: and becauſe the thing does honour to the genius of thoſe barbarians, I ſhall endeavour to explain it. All our ancient churches are called without diſtinction Gothic, but erroneouſly. They are of two ſorts; the one built in the Saxon times, the other in the Norman. Several cathedral and collegiate churches of the firſt ſort are yet remaining, either in whole or in part; of which this was the original: when the Saxon kings became Chriſtians, their piety (which was the piety of the times) conſiſted chiefly in building churches at home, and performing pilgrimages abroad, eſpecially to the Holy Land: and theſe ſpiritual exerciſes aſſiſted and ſupported one another. For the moſt venerable as well as moſt elegant models of religious edifices were then in Paleſtine. From theſe, the Saxon builders took the whole of their ideas, as may be ſeen by comparing the drawings which travellers have given us of the churches yet ſtanding in that country, with the Saxon remains of what we find at home; and particularly in that ſameneſs of ſtyle in the latter religious edifices of the knights templars (profeſſedly built upon the model of the church of the Holy Scripture at Jeruſalem) with the earlier remains of our Saxon edifices. Now the architecture

to add ſome particulars relative to Caen ſtone, with which many of our ancient cathedrals are built, as extracted from ſome curious records, originally given in Doctor Ducarrel's Anglo Norman Antiquities.

I SHALL cloſe this article, with recommending it to ſuch as deſire more knowledge of theſe matters than is communicated in this

architecture of the Holy Land was Grecian, but greatly fallen from its ancient elegance. Our Saxon performance was indeed a bad copy of it; and as much inferior to the works of St. Helene and Juſtinian, as theirs were to the Grecian models they had followed: yet ſtill the footſteps of ancient art appeared in the circular arches, the entire columns, the diviſion of the entablature into a ſort of architrave, frize, and corniche, and a ſolidity equally diffuſed over the whole maſs. This, by way of diſtinction, I would call the Saxon architecture. But our Norman works had a very different original. When the Goths had conquered Spain, and the genial warmth of the climate, and the religion of the old inhabitants had ripened their wits, and inflamed their miſtaken piety, both kept in exerciſe by the neighbourhood of the Saracens, through emulation of their ſervice, and averſion to their ſuperſtition) they ſtruck out a new ſpecies of architecture, unknown to Greece and Rome; upon original principles, and ideas much nobler than what had given birth even to claſſical magnificence. For this northern people having been accuſtomed, during the gloom of paganiſm, to worſhip the deity in groves (a practice common to all nations) when their new religion required covered edifices, they ingeniouſly projected to make them reſemble groves, as nearly as the diſtance of architecture would permit; at once indulging their old prejudices, and providing for their preſent conveniences, by a cool receptacle in a ſultry climate; and with what ſkill and ſucceſs they executed the project, by the aſſiſtance of Saracen architects, whoſe exotic ſtyle of building very luckily ſuited their purpoſe, appears from hence, that no attentive obſerver ever viewed a regular avenue of well grown trees, intermixing their branches over head, but it preſently put him in mind of the long viſto through the Gothic cathedral; or even entered one of the larger and more elegant edifices of this kind, but it preſented to his imagination an avenue of trees; and this alone is what can be truly called the Gothic ſtyle of building. Under this idea of ſo extraordinary a ſpecies of architecture, all the irregular tranſgreſſions againſt art, all the monſtrous offences againſt nature diſappear; every thing has its reaſon, every thing is in order, and an harmonious whole ariſes from the ſtudious application of means proper and proportioned to the end. For could the arches be otherwiſe than pointed, when the workmen were to imitate that curve, which branches of two oppoſite trees make by their inſertion with one another; or could the columns be otherways than ſplit into diſtinct ſhafts, when they were to repreſent the ſtems of a clump of trees, growing cloſe together? On the ſame principles they formed the ſpreading ramification of the ſtone work in the windows, and the ſtained glaſs in the interſtices; the one to repreſent the branches, and the other the leaves of an opening grove, and both concurred to preſerve that gloomy light which inſpires religious reverence and dread. Laſtly, we ſee the reaſon of their ſtudied averſion to apparent ſolidity in theſe ſtupendous maſſes, deemed ſo abſurd by men accuſtomed to the apparent as well as real ſtrength of Grecian architecture. Had it been only a wanton exerciſe of the artiſt's ſkill, to ſhew he could give real ſtrength without the appearance of any, we might indeed admire his ſuperior ſcience, but we muſt needs condemn his ill judgment. But when one conſiders, that this ſurpriſing lightneſs was neceſſary, to complete the execution of his idea of a ſylvan place of worſhip, one cannot ſufficiently admire the ingenuity of the contrivance. This too will account for the contrary qualities in what I call the Saxon architecture. Theſe artiſts copied, as has been ſaid, from the churches in the Holy Land, which were built on the models of the Grecian architecture, but corrupted by prevailing barbariſm; and ſtill further depraved by a religious idea. The firſt places of Chriſtian worſhip were ſepulchres and ſubterraneous caverns, low

this ſlight compilation, to peruſe Wren's Parentalia, Wharton's Thoughts on Spenſer's Fairy Queen, and the Ornaments of Churches conſidered; but, above all, Mr. Bentham's Diſſertation on Saxon and Norman Architecture, prefixed to his Hiſtory of Ely, to which the author of this account eſteems himſelf much beholden.

low and heavy from neceſſity. When Chriſtianity became the religion of the ſtate, and ſumptuous temples began to be erected, they yet in regard to the firſt pious ages, preſerved the maſſive ſtyle, made ſtill more venerable by the church of the Holy Sepulchre; where this ſtyle was, on a double account, followed and aggravated.

IN page 7 of this preface, it is ſaid, that the keeps of the ancient caſtles were coined, and their arches faced with ſtone, brought from Caen in Normandy: a curious gentleman has favoured me with the following particular, reſpecting this ſtone. Formerly vaſt quantities of this ſtone were brought to England; London Bridge, Weſtminſter Abbey, and many other edifices, being built therewith. *See Stowe's Survey of London, edit.* 1633, *p.* 31, 32, *&c. See alſo Rot. Liter. patent. Norman. de anno* 6 *Hen. V. P.* 1 *m.* 22.—"De quarreris albæ petræ in ſuburbio villæ de Caen annexandis dominio regis pro reparatione eccleſiarum, caſtrorum, et fortalitiorum, tam in Anglia quam in Normannia." *See alſo Rot. Normanniæ, de anno* 9 *Hen. V. m.* 31, *dors.*—Arreſtando naves pro tranſportatione lapidum et petrarum, pro conſtructione abbatiæ Sancti Petri de Weſtminſter a partibus Cadomi." *Ibid. m.* 30. —"Pro domo Jeſu de Bethleem de Shene, de lapidibus in quarreris circa villam de Cadomo capiendis pro conſtructione eccleſiæ, clauſtri, et cellarum domus prædictæ." *See alſo Rot. Franciæ, de anno* 35 *Hen. VI. m.* 2.—"Pro ſalvo conductu ad ſupplicationem abbatis et conventus Beati Petri Weſtmonaſterii, pro mercatoribus de Caen in Normannia, veniendis in Angliam cum lapidibus de Caen pro reparatione monaſterii prædicti. Teſte rege, apud Weſtm. 15 die Auguſti." *See alſo Rot. Franciæ, de anno* 38 *Hen. VI. m.* 23.—"De ſalvo conductu pro nave de Caen in regnum Angliæ revenienda, cum lapidibus de Caen pro reparatione monaſterii de Weſtminſter. Teſte rege apud Weſt. 9 die Maii. Now, however, the exportation of this ſtone out of France, is ſo ſtrictly prohibited, that, when it is to be ſent by ſea, the owner of the ſtone, as well as the maſter of the veſſel on board which it is ſhipped, is obliged to give ſecurity that it ſhall not be ſold to foreigners."

DOMES-

DOMESDAY BOOK.

DOMESDAY Book, according to Sir Henry Spelman, if not the moſt ancient, yet, without controverſy, (a) the moſt venerable monument of Great Britain, contains an account of all the lands of England; except the four northern counties, Northumberland, Cumberland, Weſtmoreland, Durham, and part of Lancaſhire; and deſcribes the quantity and particular nature of them, whether meadow, paſture, arable, wood, or waſte land: it mentions their rents and taxations; and records the ſeveral poſſeſſors of lands, their number, and diſtinct degrees. King Alfred, about the year 900, compoſed a book of like nature; of which this was in ſome meaſure a copy.

THIS work, according to the Red Book in the Exchequer, was begun, by order of William the Conqueror, with the advice of his parliament, in the year of our Lord 1080, and completed in the year 1086. (b) The reaſon given for doing it, as aſſigned by ſeveral ancient records and hiſtories, was, that every man ſhould be ſatisfied with his own right; and not uſurp with impunity, what belonged to another. (c) Beſides theſe other motives ſeem to

(a) Mr. Selden, in his preface to Eadmerus, p. 4, ſpeaking of Domeſday, ſays, "Neque puto alibi in orbe Chriſtiano actorum publicorum autographa, quorum ſaltem ratio aliqua habenda eſt, extare quæ non ſæculis aliquot his cedunt."

(b) This alſo appears, from the concurrent teſtimony of divers ancient writers; and from an entry written at the end of the ſecond volume of the work itſelf; where, in a large coeval hand, in capitals, are the words following: "Anno milleſimo octogeſſimo ſexto ab incarnatione Domini, vigeſimo vero regni Willi, facta eſt iſta deſcriptio, non ſolum per hos tres comitatus, ſed etiam per alios."——My Lord Littleton, in his Hiſtory of Henry II. vol. ii. page 289, ſays, "It was made by order of William I. with the advice of his parliament, the year 1086; but it ſeems not to have been finiſhed till the following year." His Lordſhip does not cite any authority, to prove this ſuppoſition.

(c) THE author of the Dialogues de Scaccario, who wrote in the time of Henry II. book i. cap. xvi. gives this account of it, ſpeaking of William the Conqueror: "Demum ne quid deeſſe videretur ad omnem totius providentiæ ſummam, communicato conſilio, diſcretiſſimos a latere ſuo deſtinavit viros per regnum in circuitu, ab his itaque totius terræ deſcriptio diligens facta eſt, tam in nemoribus quam paſcuis, et pratis, nec non et agriculturis, et verbis communibus annotata, in librum redacta eſt; ut videlicet quilibet jure ſuo contentus alienum non uſurpet impune. Fit autem deſcriptio per comitatus, per

to have occasioned this survey. Sir Martin Wright, in his Introduction to the Law of Tenures, appears to be of this opinion; which he expresses in the following words: "It is very remarkable, that William I. about the twentieth year of his reign, just

per centuriatas et hydas, prænotato in ipso capite regis nomine et deinde seriatim aliorum procerum nominibus appositis secundum statum sui dignitatem, qui videlicet de rege tenent in capite. Apponuntur autem singulis numeri secundum ordinem sic dispositis, per quos inferius in ipsa libri serie, quæ ad eos pertinent facilius occurrant. Hic liber ab indigenis Domus Dei nuncupatur, id est, dies judicii, per metaphoram. Sicut enim districti et terribilis examinis illius novissimi sententia, nulla tergiversationis arte valet eludi: sic cum orta fuit in regno contentio de his rebus quæ illic annotantur; cum ventum fuerit ad librum, sententiæ ejus infatuari non potest, vel impune declinari. Ob hoc nos eundem librum judiciorum nominavimus; non quod in eo de præpositis aliquibus dubiis feratur sententia; sed quod ab eo, sicut a prædicto judicio non licet ulla ratione discedere. *Dialog. de Scacc. page* 30, 31, *published by Mr. Madox.*

The Saxon Chronicle, published by Bishop Gibson, thus mentions it; "Post hæc tenuit rex magnum concilium, et graves sermones habuit cum suis proceribus de hac terra, quo modo incoleretur, et a quibus hominibus. Mittebat idcirco per totam Anglorum terram in singulos comitatus suos servos, quibus permisit scrutari quot hydarum centenæ essent in comitatu, et quantum census annui deberet percipere, ex eo comitatu. Permisit etiam describi, quantum terrarum ejus archiepiscopi haberent, et diœcesani episcopi, ac ejus abbates, ejus comites; et ne longior in hoc sim, quid aut quantum unusquisque haberet, qui terras possideret in Anglorum gente, sive terrarum, sive pecoris quantum illud pecunia valeret. Tam diligenter lustrari terram permisit ut ne unica esset hyda, aut virgata terræ, nequidem (quod dictu turpe, verum in factu turpe, non existimarit) bos, aut vacca, aut porcus prætermittebatur, quod non is retulerat in censum: omniaque postea scripta ad eum efferebantur. *Page* 186, *anno* 1085.

In the Escheat Rolls of Edward III. the occasion and manner of making this survey, and its authority, are declared nearly in the same words of the Author of the Dialogues de Scaccario. It is thus spoken of in the Annals of Waverly: "Misit rex Willielmus justitiarios suos per unamquamque Scyram, id est provinciam Angliæ, et inquirere fecit per jus jurandum quot hidæ, id est jugera uni aratro sufficientia per annum, essent in unaquaque villa, et quot animalia; hinc autem fecit inquiri quid unaquaque urbs, castellum, vicus, villa, flumen, palus silva reddit per annum; hæc autum omnia in chartis scripta delata sunt ad regem, et in thesauros reposita usque hodie servantur. Rex tenuit curiam suam in natali apud Glocestre, ad pascha apud Wintoniam, ad pentecostem apud Londoniam: deinde accipiens hominum omnium terrariorum Angliæ cujuscunque feodi essent, juramentum fidelitatis, recipere non distulit." *Page* 133.

Mr. Agard, in his Preface to the Obsolete words in Domesday Book, assigns an additional reason for the Conqueror's making this survey; "Conquestor sub ipso suo ingressu regnum, hoc annuo tributo (Danegelt vocatum) taxatum invenit; pro quo colligendo, Rex Ethelredus totum regnum in hidas divisit, quarum singula sex solidos persolvere tenetur. Cum vero Rex Willielmus illud aliquando majoris, aliquando minoris emolumenti esse in comperto habuisset, optimum esse duxit, ut inquisitio per totum regnum haberetur, qua dignosceret, quantum singula oppida, villæ, et hamletta numerare tenerentur; et ut libro Domesday scriberetur in verbis, pro vi solidis. Hidæ, vel carucatis se defendit, quod æque valet ac si diceret, pro tot solidis. Hidæ, vel carcucatis Danegelt persolvit." The author of the notes to the Register of Original Writs, p. 14, erroneously asserts that this book was made in the time of Edward the Confessor. His words are: "Fait assavoir que le livre de Domesday fuit fait en temps de St. Edw. le roy, et touts les terres que furent en le mein de dit Seint E. all. temps que le livre fuist fait sount ancien demene, et les terres que furent adonques en auter main sount Frankfee." This mistake hath been adopted by Fitzherbert.

 when

when the general survey of England, called Domesday Book, is supposed to be finished, and not till then, summoned all the great men and landholders in the kingdom to London and Salisbury, to do their homage, and swear their fealty to him; by doing whereof, the Saxon Chronicler supposes, that, at that time, the proceres, et omnes prædia tenentes, se illi subdidere, ejusque facti sunt Vasalli; so that we may reasonably suppose, First, That this general homage and fealty was done at this time, (nineteen or twenty years after the accession of William I.) in consequence of something new; or else that engagements so important to the maintenance and security of a new establishment, had been required long before; and if so, it is probable that tenures were then new; inasmuch as homage and fealty were, and still are, mere feudal engagements, binding the homager to all the duties and observances of a feudal tenant. Secondly, That as this general homage and fealty was done about the time that Domesday Book was finished, and not before, we may suppose that that survey was taken upon or soon after our ancestors consent to tenures, in order to discover the quantity of every man's fee, and to fix his homage. This supposition is the more probable, because it is not likely that a work of this nature was undertaken without some immediate reason; and no better reason can be assigned why it was undertaken at this time, or indeed why this survey should be taken at all: there being at that time extant a general survey of the whole kingdom, made by Alfred."

For the execution of this survey, commissioners were sent into every county and shire; and juries summoned in each hundred, out of all orders of freemen, from barons down to the lowest farmers; who were, upon oath, to inform the commissioners the name of each manor, and that of its owner; also by whom it was held in the time of Edward the Confessor; the number of hides, the quantity of wood, of pasture, and meadow land; how many ploughs were in the demesne, and how many in the tenanted part of it; how many mills, how many fish-ponds, or fisheries belonged to it; with the value of the whole together in the

the time of King Edward, as well as when granted by King William, and at the time of this ſurvey; alſo whether it was capable of improvement, or of being advanced in its value: they were likewiſe directed to return the tenants of every degree, the quantity of lands now and formerly held by each of them; and what was the number of the villains or ſlaves; and alſo the number and kinds of their cattle and live ſtock. Theſe inquiſitions being firſt methodized in the county, were afterwards ſent up to the king's Exchequer; ſome of the particulars, concerning which the jury were directed to enquire, were thought unneceſſary to be inſerted. This ſurvey, at the time in which it was made, gave great offence to the people; and occaſioned a jealouſy that it was intended for the foundation of ſome new impoſition.

NOTWITHSTANDING the precaution taken by the Conqueror to have this ſurvey faithfully and impartially executed, it appears, from indiſputable authority (d) that a falſe return was given in by ſome of the commiſſioners; and that, as it is ſaid, out of a pious motive. This was in the caſe of the abbey of Croyland in Lincolnſhire; the poſſeſſions of which were greatly under-rated, both with regard to quantity and value. Perhaps ſimilar, or more intereſted inducements, may have operated in other inſtances. A deviation from truth, ſo clearly proved, fully juſtifies a ſuſpicion of the veracity of any record or teſtimony. Perhaps more of theſe pious returns were diſcovered; as it is ſaid, Ralph Flambard, miniſter to William Rufus, propoſed the making a freſh and more rigorous inquiſition; but it was never executed.

(d) INGULPHUS, abbot of Croyland, himſelf confeſſes it in his account of this ſurvey. His own words are: "Totam teram deſcripſit, nec erat hida in tota Anglia, quin valorem ejus et poſſeſſorem ſuum ſcivit: nec lacus, nec locus aliquis, quin in regis rotulo extitit deſcriptus, ac ejus reditus et proventus, ipſa poſſeſſio et ejus poſſeſſor regiæ notitiæ manifeſtatus, juxta taxatorum fidem qui electi de qualibet patria territorium proprium deſcribebant. Iſti penes noſtrum monaſterium benevole et amantes non *ad verum pretium* nec *ad verum ſpatium* noſtrum monaſterium librabant, miſericorditer præcaventes in futurum regiis exactionibus et aliis oneribus *piiſſima* nobis benevolentia providentes. In illo vero deſcripti ſunt, non tantum totius terræ comitatus, centuriæ et decuriæ, ſylvæ, ſaltus, et villæ univerſæ; ſed in omni territorio quot carucatæ terræ, quot jugera, et quot acræ, quæ paſcua et paludes, quæ tenementa, et qui tenentes continebantur."

Ingulphus, printed among the Scriptores Ang. vol. i. p. 80. 81.

NEVER

Nevertheless, in despight of this impeachment of its credibility, "the authority of Domesday Book (e) in point of tenure, hath never been permitted to be called in question; for instance, when it hath been necessary to distinguish whether lands were held in ancient demesne, or in what other manner, recourse hath always been had to Domesday Book, and to that only, to determine the doubt. If lands were set down in that book, under the title of Terra Regis, or if it was said there, Rex Habet such land, or such a town, it was determined to be the king's ancient demesne. If the land or town was therein set down under the name of a private lord or subject, then it was determined to have been at the time of the survey the land of such private person, and not ancient demesne." Indeed, its name is said to have been derived from its definitive authority, from which, as from the sentence

(e) The tallages formerly affessed upon the king's tenants in ancient demesne, were usually greater than the tallages upon persons in the counties at large; and therefore, when persons were wrongfully tallaged with those in ancient demesne, it was usual for them to petition the crown to be tallaged with the community of the county at large: upon this the king's writ issued to the barons of the Exchequer, to acquit the party aggrieved of such tallage, in case, upon search of Domesday Book, the barons found the lands were not in ancient demesne.

Madox Firma Burgi, p. 5 and 6. - Hist. of the Exchequer, p. 499, 500.

The pound so often mentioned in Domesday Book (says Sir Robert Atkins, in his History of Gloucestershire) for reserved rent, was the weight of a pound in silver, consisting of twelve ounces, which is equal in weight to three pounds and two shillings of our present money: the same weight in gold is now worth forty-eight pounds.

The shilling mentioned in the same book, consisted of twelve pence, and is equal in weight to three shillings of our money. The denomination of a shilling was of different value in different nations; and often of a different value in the same nation, as the government thought fit to alter it. There was no such piece of money ever coined in this kingdom, untill the year 1504, in the latter end of the reign of King Henry VII. In the Saxon times, there went forty-eight shillings to the pound; then the shilling was accounted at five pence; and every one of those pence being of the weight of our three pence, a shilling then must make fifteen pence; and forty-eight times fifteen pence, a pound weight. In the Norman time, and ever since, a shilling was accounted twelvepence; and every penny as aforesaid, weighing threepence, there must be the weight of three of our shillings in one shilling of the Norman computation; and consequently twenty Norman shillings do likewise make a pound weight. Silver pence were anciently the only current coin of England; and afterwards about the reign of King John, silver halfpence and silver farthings were introduced. The penny was the greatest piece of silver coin until the year 1353, when King Edward III. began to coin groats; and they had their name from their large size, for Gross did signify Great. Crowns and half crowns were first coined in the reign of King Edward VI. in the year 1551, about one hundred and sixty years since. *Page 5.* It may not be improper to add, that a carucate, hide or plow-land, was a certain quantity of land, about one hundred and twenty acres.

pronounced

pronounced at Doomsday, or the Day of Judgment, there could be no appeal. But Stowe assigns another reason for this appellation; Domesday Book being, according to him, a coruption of Domus Dei Book; a title given it, because heretofore deposited in the king's treasury, in a place of the church of Westminster, or Winchester, called Domus Dei; but this last explanation has but few advocates. This record is comprised in two volumes; one a large folio, the other a quarto. The first is written on three hundred and eighty-two double papers of vellum, in a small, but plain character; each page having a double column. Some of the capital letters and principal passages are touched with red ink, and some have strokes of red ink run cross them, as if scratched out. This volume contains the description of thirty-one counties, arranged and written as follows:

	Chent —	fol. 1		Wiricestrescire	fol. 172
	Sudsex —	16		Herefordscire —	179
	Sudrie —	30		Grantbr'scire —	189
	Hantscire —	38		Huntedunscire —	203
5	Berrochescire —	56	20	Bedefordscire —	209
	Wiltscire —	64		Northantscire —	219
	Dorsette —	75		Ledecestrescire —	230
	Sumersite —	86		Warwicscire —	238
	Devenescire —	100		Staffordscire —	245
10	Cornualgie —	120	25	Sciropescire —	252
	Midelsex —	126		Cestrescire —	262
	Hertfordscire —	132		Derbyscire —	272
	Bockinghamscire —	143		Snotingh'scire —	280
	Oxenfordscire —	154		Roteland —	f. 293, 367
15	Glowcest'scire —	162		Eurvicscire —	298, 379

Lindesig, or Lincolnshire, fol. 336, divided into the West Riding, North Riding, and East Riding.

Towards the beginning of each county, there is a catalogue of the capital lords or great land-holders, who possessed any thing in in it; beginning with the king, and then naming the great lords, according to their rank and dignity.

THE other volume is in quarto; it is written on four hundred and fifty double pages of vellum, but in a ſingle column, and in a large but very fair character. It contains the counties of Eſſex, fol. 1, Norfolk, fol. 109, Suffolk, fol. 281, to the end. Part of the county of Rutland is included in that of Northampton; and part of Lancaſhire in the counties of York and Cheſter.

FROM the great care formerly taken for the preſervation of this ſurvey, may be gathered the eſtimation of its importance; the Dialogue de Scaccario ſays, "Liber ille (Domeſday) ſigilli regis comes eſt individuus in theſauro."

UNTIL of late years, it has been kept under three different locks and keys, one in the cuſtody of the treaſurer, and the others of the two chamberlains of the Exchequer. It is now depoſited in the Chapter Houſe at Weſtminſter, where it may be conſulted on paying to the proper officers a fee of 6s. 8d. for a ſearch, and four-pence per line for a tranſcript.

MANY parts of this ancient record have been printed in different county hiſtories, and many more are to be found in public and private libraries. A catalogue of them are given in an account of Domeſday-Book, written by Philip Carteret Webb, Eſq; and publiſhed in 1756, by the Antiquarian Society: another has been ſince publiſhed by Richard Gough, Eſq; in his uſeful book, entitled, Anecdotes of Britiſh Topography, ranged under the different counties. The whole has been lately printed at the public expence, with types caſt for that purpoſe, for the uſe of the members of parliament.

DRUIDICAL

DRUIDICAL ANTIQUITIES.

Pub.d by S. Hooper April 16: 1784.

DRUIDICAL MONUMENTS.

DRUIDICAL Monuments confift of Obelifques, being large ftones or pillars fet up perpendicularly, Carnes or Carnedes, Cromlehs or Cromleiches, Kift vaens, Rocking ftones, Tolmen or ftones of paffage, Rock bafons, and circles or ovals.

OF SINGLE STONES.

THESE monuments are the moft fimple and undoubtedly of more ancient date than druidifm itfelf, they were placed as memorials recording different events, fuch as remarkable inftances of God's mercies, contracts, fingular victories, boundaries, and fometimes fepulchres; various inftances of thefe monuments erected by the patriarchs, occur in the Old Teftament. Such was that raifed by Jacob at Lug, afterwards by him named Bethel, fuch alfo was the pillar placed by him over the grave of Rachael. They were likewife marks of execrations and magical talifmans.

THESE ftones from having long been confidered as objects of veneration, at length were by the ignorant and fuperftitious idolatroufly worfhiped; wherefore, after the introduction of chriftianity fome had croffes cut on them, which was confidered as fnatching them from the fervice of the devil.

VULGAR fuperftition of a later date has led the common people to confider them as perfons transformed into ftone for the punifhment of fome crime, generally that of fabbath breaking, but this tale is not confined to fingle ftones, but is told alfo of whole circles: witnefs the monuments called the Hurlers in Cornwall and Rollorick ftones in Warwickfhire.

THE firft are by the vulgar fuppofed to have been once men, and thus transformed as a punifhment for playing on the Lord's day at a game called hurling, the latter a pagan king and his army.

CARNES

CARNES.

Carnes or carneds were commonly ſituated on eminences ſo that they might be viſible one from the other, they are formed of ſtones of all dimenſions, thrown together in a conical form, a flat ſtone crowning the apex, the ramp or aſcent is generally pretty eaſy, though Toland ſuppoſes the Druids aſcended them by means of ladders. Carnes are of different ſizes, ſome of them containing at leaſt an hundred cart loads of ſtones. According to the writer above cited, fires were kindled on the tops or flat ſtones, at certain times of the year, particularly on the eves of the firſt of May and the firſt of November, for the purpoſe of ſacrificing, at which time all the people having extinguiſhed their domeſtic hearths, rekindled them from the ſacred fires of the carnes.

Mr. Rowland in his Mona Antiqua, ſuppoſes the ſmaller Carnedes to be ſepulchral monuments, formed with ſtones thrown on the grave by the friends of the deceaſed, not only with an intent to mark the place of their interment, but alſo to protect their corps from wild beaſts and other injuries, but allows the larger monuments of this kind, particularly where accompanied by ſtanding pillars of ſtone, to have been erected as marks of ſacrifices or ſome religious ceremony, ſuch as the ſolmn convention, recorded by Moſes to have been made between Jacob and Laban.

KIST VAENS.

Kist vaens, that is, ſtone cheſts, commonly conſiſt of four flaggs or thin ſtones, two of which are ſet up edgeways, nearly parallel, a third ſhorter than the other two, is placed at right angles, to them thus forming the ſides, and cloſing the end of the cheſt, the fourth laid flat on the top, makes the lid or cover, which on account of the inequality of its ſupporters, inclines to the horizon at the cloſed end. Mr. Toland ſuppoſes Kiſt Vaens to have been altars for ſacrifice, moſt of them having originally belonged

belonged to a circle or temple, the inclination of the covering he imagines to have been intended to facilitate the draining of the blood from the victim into the holy veſſel placed to receive it; he denies their having been places of burial, ſaying the bones frequently found near them were remains of the victims. Theſe monuments are in the iſlands of Guernſey and Jerſey ſtill called autels, or altars and poquelays, i. e. a heap of ſtones. Mr. Borlace, in his Hiſtory of Cornwall, combats the notion of their being altars for ſacrifice, and on the contrary judges them to be ſepulchral monuments, and in ſupport of his opinion urges the following reaſons. Firſt, that they were not altars, becauſe on account of their general height, the prieſt could not officiate ſtanding on the ground, that to aſcend them would have been dangerous and difficult, and when mounted, his footing from the irregularity of moſt of theſe ſtones, would have been extremely unſtable, added to which he could not have been ſufficiently diſtant to avoid being ſcorched by the fire, which beſides ſeveral of the coits or covers being Moore ſtone would not reſiſt, but be likely to ſplit aſunder; to prove their being ſepulchral monuments, he mentions a ſimilar inſtance in altar tombs, which probably obtained their denomination from their reſemblance to an altar, not from ſacrifices being performed on them, and adds, that the area commonly encloſed within a Keſt vaen is nearly equal to that occupied by a human body. Mr. Rowland takes the middle between both, ſaying, " their being ſepulchral monuments I deny not, but there may be ſome appearance of truth, yet conſiſtent enough of what I have ſaid of them, for they may be both ſepulchers and altars in a different ſenſe, I mean thoſe of latter erection, becauſe when the great ones of the firſt ages fell, who were eminent among the people for ſome extraordinary qualities and virtues, their enamoured poſterity continued their veneration of them to their very graves, over which they probably erected ſome of theſe altars or cromleche, on which when the true religion became depraved and corrupted, they might make oblations and other ſacrifices to their departed ghoſts.

ROCK BASONS.

Rock Basons are cavities or artificial basons of different sizes, from six feet to a few inches diameter, cut in the surface of the rocks, for the purpose, as is supposed, of collecting the dew and rain, pure as it descended from the heavens, for the use of ablutions and purifications, prescribed in the druidical religion, these, especially the dew, being deemed the purest of all fluids. There are two sorts of these basons, one with lips or communications between the different basons, the other simple cavities. The lips as low as the bottom of the basons, which are horizontal and communicate with one somewhat lower, so contrived that the contents fell by a gradual descent through a succession of basons either to the ground, or into a vessel set to receive it, this will be better explained by the plate.

The basons without lips might be intended for reservoirs to preserve the rain or dew in its original purity, without touching any other vessel, and was perhaps used for the druid to drink, or wash his hands, previous to officiating at any high ceremony, or else to mix with their missletoe.

Some of these basons are so formed as to receive the head and part of the human body; one of this kind is found on a rock called King Arthur's bed, in the parish of North Hall in Cornwall, where are also others, called by the country people Arthur's troughs, in which they say he used to feed his dogs.

LOGGON OR ROCKING STONES.

These are huge stones so exactly poised on a point, as to be easily caused to rock or vibrate, if touched at a certain place, some of these are artificial, and others natural rocks cleared of the circumjacent earth. These were probably used by the druids as instruments of pious fraud, like the statue of St. Rumbold by the monks of a monastery in Kent; which statue, though only the size and figure of an infant, could not, it was pretended, be lifted by any one labouring under an unexpiated offence, that is, one who

who had not by alms and offerings purchaſed their abſolution. The figure ſtood on a kind of pedeſtal againſt the wall, to which it was ſecured by a ſecret peg, which might be put in or withdrawn on the other ſide. If the penitent was nigardly in his offering to the ſaint, the peg was applied, and the figure became immoveable even by the ſtrongeſt man, and on the contrary a liberal benefaction made it eaſy to be lifted by the moſt delicate girl. In like manner theſe ſtones might be ſo managed as to vibrate, or not, according to the will of the druids, who might impede its motion by wedges, or direct the application to be made at the wrong point. Some of theſe ſtones had rock baſons on them, as perhaps a ſacred ablution made a part of the ceremonial.

THE CROMLEH.

THE cromlech or cromleh chiefly differs from the Kiſt vaen, in not being cloſed up at the end and ſides, that is, in not ſo much partaking of the cheſt like figure, it is alſo generally of larger dimenſions, and ſometimes conſiſts of a greater number of ſtones; the terms cromleh and kiſt vaen are however indiſcriminately uſed for the ſame monument. The term cromlech is derived from the armoric word crum, crooked or bowing, and leh ſtone, alluding to the reverence which perſons paid to them by bowing. Rowland derives it from the Hebrew words, ſignifying a devoted or conſecrated ſtone, they are thus deſcribed by him.

THESE altars of ſtone, where ſtone ſerved to raiſe them up, were huge broad flattiſh ſtones mounted up and laid upon erect ones, and leaning with a liitle declivity in ſome places, on thoſe pitched ſupporters, which poſture for ſome unaccountable reaſons they ſeem to have affected.

THEY are called by the vulgar Coetne Arthur, or Arthurs Quoits, it being a cuſtom in Wales as well as Cornwall, to aſcribe all great or wonderful objects to Prince Arthur, the hero of thoſe countries.

CIRCLES,

CIRCLES, OVALS, &c.

THESE, it is now generally agreed were temples, and many writers think alſo places of ſolemn aſſemblies for councils or elections, and ſeats of judgement. Mr. Borlace is of this opinion, "inſtead, therefore, (ſays he) of detaining the reader with a diſpute, whether they were places of worſhip or council, it may with great probability be aſſerted that they were uſed for both purpoſes, and having for the moſt part been firſt dedicated to religion, naturally became afterwards the curiæ and foræ of the ſame community."

THESE temples though generally circular, occaſionally differ as well in figure as magnitude, with relation to the firſt, the moſt ſimple were compoſed of one circle, Stonehenge conſiſted of two circles and two ovals, reſpectively concentric, whilſt that at Bottalch near St. Juſt in Cornwall is formed by four interſecting circles. And the great temple at Abiry in Wiltſhire, it is ſaid, deſcribed the figure of a ſeraph or fiery flying ſerpent, repreſented by circles and right lines. Some beſides circles have avenues of ſtone pillars. Moſt, if not all of them, have pillars or altars within their penetralia or center.

IN the article of magnitude and number of ſtones, there is the greateſt variety. Some circles being only twelve feet diameter and formed only of twelve ſtones, whilſt others, ſuch as Stonehenge and Abury, contained, the firſt one hundred and forty, and the ſecond ſix hundred and fifty two, and occupied many acres of ground.

ALL theſe different numbers and meaſures and arrangements had its pretended reference; either to the aſtronomical diviſions of the year or ſome myſteries of the druidical religion. Mr. Borlace, however, ſuppoſes that thoſe very ſmall circles ſometimes formed of a low bank of earth, ſometimes of ſtones erect, and frequently of looſe ſmall ſtones thrown together in a circular form, encloſing an area of about three yards diameter, without any larger circle round them, were originally places of burial.

THE

THE TOLMEN.

THE word *Tolmen* ſignifies *the hole of ſtone:* this monument is formed by a large orbicular ſtone, ſupported by two ſmaller, betwixt which there is an aperture or paſſage. " What uſe the ancients made of theſe paſſages (ſays Mr. Borlace) we can only gueſs; but we have reaſon to think, that when ſtones were once ritually conſecrated, they attributed great and miraculous virtues to every part of them, and imagined that whatever touched, lay down upon, was ſurrounded by, or paſſed through or under theſe ſtones, acquired thereby a kind of holineſs, and became more acceptable to the Gods. This paſſage might alſo be a ſanctuary for the offender to fly to, and ſhelter himſelf from the purſuer; but I imagine it chiefly to have been intended and uſed for introducing proſelytes or novices, people under vows, or about to ſacrifice, into their more ſublime myſteries; for the ſame reaſon I am apt to think the vaſt architraves or croſs ſtones reſting upon the uprights at Stonehenge, were erected; namely, with an intent to conſecrate and prepare worſhippers, by paſſing through thoſe holy rocks, for the better entering upon the offices which were to be performed in the penetralia, the moſt ſacred part of the temple."

THERE is a rock of the Tolmen kind at Bombay in the Eaſt-Indies, which is held in great veneration by the Gentoos, it is called *The Rock of Purification*; a paſſage through it is conſidered as a purifying the penitent from all ſins; and ſuch is its eſtimation in the neighbouring countries, that tradition ſays, the famous pirate, Conagee Angria, ventured by ſtealth into the iſland, on purpoſe to perform that ceremony; the aperture is deſcribed as ſo ſmall that a man of any corpulence cannot poſſibly ſqueeze through; perhaps it may be uſed as a gage to aſcertain whether the party has ſufficiently reduced himſelf, by faſting and other mortifications.

Having thus enumerated the different kinds of what are uſually ſtyled *Druidical Monuments*, and generally pointed out the uſes for which they are ſuppoſed to have been erected or appropriated, I ſhall conclude this article with remarking, that in all the different parts of this kingdom, where theſe monuments are found, the common people retain a kind of traditionary reverence for them, without being able to aſſign any reaſon for their veneration; and all relate almoſt ſimilar ſtories, ſerving to prove, that great and uncommon misfortunes have attended thoſe perſons who have ventured to break or remove them.

The ſame tale that is told of Stonehenge is alſo related of almoſt every other large Druidical Circle, by its local hiſtorian, namely, that no one has ever been able to count the ſtones of which it is compoſed, ſo as to make the numbers of two ſucceſſive reckonings agree. Although a baker once eſſayed to do it, by placing a loaf on every ſtone, and afterwards counting the loaves, yet on a ſecond trial he always found the former number of loaves either too many or too few.

ADDEN-

ADDENDA

TO THE

PREFACE.

MONUMENTS.

AS ſepulchral monuments and fonts make a conſiderable part of the eccleſiaſtical antiquities of this kingdom, although they do not come immediately under my firſt plan, yet having been prevailed on to make this Preface a kind of introduction to the general ſtudy of Britiſh Antiquities, I ſhall, in order to compleat it, briefly point out the different kinds of both, with the leading principles by which we may be enabled to gueſs with ſome degree of probability at the time of their conſtruction. In this inveſtigation I ſhall not carry my enquiries beyond the period of the Conqueſt, nor bring them farther down than the laſt century; neither ſhall I enter into a detail of the different manners of preparing the corpſe, or the various kinds of coffins for containing it; but confine my obſervations to the forms of the external tomb, or ornaments on incumbent ſtones laid over it, to mark whoſe remains were there depoſited.

THE earlieſt monuments, at leaſt thoſe in churches, were in all likelihood flat coffin-ſhaped ſtones, making part of the pavement; at firſt they were only inſcribed with the name and rank of the perſon there buried; the figure of the croſs was not engraved on them, to avoid the indignity of its being trampled under foot.

Afterwards Kenneth, king of Scotland, is ſaid to have iſſued an order ſor cutting the croſs on all grave-ſtones; but directed that care ſhould be taken not to trample on them. Some regulation of this nature might poſſibly take place in England.

THAT the firſt monuments admitted into churches, and making part of the pavement, were flat, and not raiſed to a ridge, as was afterwards the faſhion, ſeems probable; as the latter would have been very likely to trip up the prieſts walking and ſinging in proceſſion, with their eyes directed to their books. Thus the great Earl of Devon is buried under the ſteps of the high altar at Chriſt-Church, Hampſhire, with only this inſcription:—BALDEWIN FILI. WILLI. COMITIS DEVONIÆ, rudely cut, without any ornament whatſoever.

THE monuments of perſons of diſtinction, about the time of, or ſoon after the Conqueſt, were formed like the ſhrines in which the relicks of ſaints were depoſited; theſe were ſimilar to the ancient coffins, the bottoms being ſhaped like thoſe of the preſent time, that is, broadeſt near the ſhoulders, and tapering towards the feet, but covered with a lid *en dos d'ane, i. e.* riſing to a ridge or angle in the middle, with both ends ſloped off triangularly, the whole reſembling the roof of a houſe; and indeed the intent was the ſame in the conſtruction of both, namely, to prevent the rain or any moiſture lodging on the top: a ſtone of this kind is ſhewn in plate I. figure 2; ſuch is the monument of King William Rufus, in the cathedral of Wincheſter, and ſuch alſo is that of the Lady Juga, in Little Dunmow church, but both are conſiderably elevated above the ground. Lady Juga's monument at preſent ſtands under an arch in the church wall. See repreſentation of both in plate I. Fig. 3. is the tomb of William Rufus. Fig. 1. that of the Lady Juga.

ELEVATED table monuments, adorned with cumbent figures, were uſed very early; but they were chiefly for kings, or very great perſonages, and were placed under magnificent erections like oratories, having ornamented flat canopies called Teſtoons over them.

ANOTHER

Another ſpecies of early monuments were thoſe of biſhops, abbots, or other dignitaries of the church; theſe are generally flat coffin-ſhaped ſtones, level with the floor, and ſerving both as tomb-ſtone and pavement, commonly ornamented with croſſes of different kinds, occaſionally held by a hand coming as it were from under the ſtone. One of this ſort is in the cathedral of Wincheſter, engraved in the antiquarian repertory, and another in Mr. Gough's elegant publication on ſepulchral monuments. Some of theſe have inſcriptions deeply cut in Saxon characters, about their ſides, which it is ſaid were formerly filled up with lead. Theſe inſcriptions are ſometimes Latin, but oftener old French, beginning at the head with *Cy Giſt*, and frequently promiſing a certain number of days' indulgence or pardon for thoſe who will pray for them. Some of theſe have croſſes at the beginning and end of the inſcription; a ſpecimen of this kind of monument is given in plate II. fig. 1, where there are alſo ſeveral other of this kind of grave-ſtones. Monuments of this ſort occur as early as the beginning of the fourteenth century, and are found as late as the beginning of the ſixteenth; but the latter have the common Gothic letter. Dates are rarely found on ancient monuments, though there are inſtances where we meet with them.

Where an abbot, as lord of the manor, had temporal authority, and was entitled to the privilege of the furcâ, &c. he had the ſword joined to the croſier. An inſtance of which appears in the tomb of the abbot of Bala Sala, in the Iſle of Man, repreſented in plate II. fig. 2.

The cruſades gave riſe to a particular ſort of ſepulchral monument, whereon the figure of the perſon contained is always repreſented with his right leg croſſed over his left. This figure is completely armed, generally in the hawberk, or coat, and hood of mail; over it a ſurcoat, girded about the middle with a belt, and ſometimes, but not often, charged with armorial bearings. On the head an open cylindrical helmet, flat at the top; the legs covered with hoſe of mail; and on the heels pryck ſpurs, having only one point, ſuch as are repreſented on the great ſeals of of many of our early kings and barons. On the left arm a triangular ſhield, occaſionally adorned with his arms, but more commonly plain. At the feet, a lion, or ſome other emblematical figure. Effigies of this kind are commonly on altar or table tombs, placed againſt the walls of churches, under elegant Gothic arches, richly adorned with foliage, and terminating, pinnacle faſhion, in a ſingle flower, or leaf.

THE hands of theſe croſs-legged knights are often joined, as in the act of prayer; ſometimes employed in drawing their ſwords. When their ſhields are braced, that is, fixed on their arms, their right hands are laid by their ſides, or over their bodies.

THESE croſs-legged figures have very improperly obtained the title of knights templars; the abſurdity of which muſt be immediately recognized, when it is recollected that the knights templars were a religious order, profeſſing celibacy, and wearing a particular habit; whereas many of the perſons repreſented croſs legged on their tombs are known to have been married men, or perſons who never profeſſed any religious order. One inſtance we have in the monument of Robert, ſurnamed Courthoſe, brother to William Rufus, preſerved in the cathedral of Glouceſter, who is repreſented croſs legged. Nor is the dreſs ſimilar to the habit of the knights templars, a repreſentation of which may be ſeen among the religious orders in this preface.

THE true appellation for theſe figures ſeems to be Cruſaders, or the knights of the cruſade; as not only thoſe who had actually ſerved in the Holy Land were entitled to this monumental diſtinction, but it was alſo aſſumed by, and permitted to perſons who had taken up the croſs, or made the vow, to go thither, but died before the accompliſhment; and frequently by thoſe who in lieu of perſonal attendance had contributed a conſiderable ſum of money towards the expences of that ſervice; even ladies who had accompanied their huſbands on theſe expeditions, were, it is ſaid, diſtinguiſhed by having their arms croſſed over their breaſts; but of this I have never been able to ſee a ſpecimen. Children born in the Holy Land were repreſented on their monuments with

with their legs croſſed. The church of Ayot St. Laurence, in Hertfordſhire, furniſhed an inſtance of this kind in a monument called the Boy Templar, which was, as I have been told by perſons who had ſeen it, the figure of a boy, of about twelve years of age, caſed in knight's armour, and having his legs croſſed. This church was, not many years ago, pulled down, and rebuilt on another ſpot. Some of theſe figures were of oak; that of Robert Courthoſe, before-mentioned, and another in St. Mary Overy's, in Southwark, are of that wood. See the latter, pl. III. fig. 2.

The age of theſe monuments may be pretty nearly gueſſed from the following data:—The cruſades began anno 1096, and ended in 1291, by the Saracens retaking the laſt place in the poſſeſſion of the Chriſtians; but as many who were perſonally preſent at that ſiege might ſurvive it fifty years, or even longer, genuine tombs of the cruſaders might be erected as late as the middle of the fourteenth century. Although dates to theſe monuments are extremely rare, Hutchins in his Hiſtory of Dorſetſhire ſays, that in Horton church in that county, in the Haſtings' aiſle, was an effigy of a perſon croſs legged, with an imperfect inſcription, of which only remained, "Anno Domini - - - - - - - - - - nunc quieſcit anima."

Covered monuments, that is, conſiſting of cumbent figures on altar tombs, under canopies or Teſtoons, were introduced into general uſe in the fourteenth century, and laſted till the fifteenth. Very few inſtances are to be found of theſe monuments in open air. One however we meet with in Newland churchyard, Glouceſterſhire, in the tomb of Jenkyn Worral; part of the irons which ſupported the Teſtoon was remaining in 1775, and is ſhewn in the engraving of this monument in the antiquarian repertory; as are alſo three female figures, of barbarous workmanſhip, lying on the ground near it, traditionally called his wife and daughters.

Another order of monuments were flat ſtones, even with the pavement, inlaid with engraved braſs plates. Some of theſe are as old as the latter end of the thirteenth century. Among the

the oldeſt of this kind is that of Longſpee, biſhop of Saliſbury, who died anno 1297. There are alſo ſome croſs-legged figures engraved on braſs, but they are by no means common. Theſe for the reaſons before given, may be aſcribed to the middle of the fourteenth century, unleſs, as has been ſuggeſted, they were put down in remembrance of, or in the places of ſtatues of the ſame perſons decayed, removed, or otherwiſe deſtroyed, and thus replaced by ſome of their deſcendants, deſirous of perpetuating their family honours at a ſmaller expence than rebuilding or repairing theſe monuments. Not more than four or five of theſe engraved cruſaders are known. A very fine one at Trumpington, in Cambridgeſhire, is engraved in the repertory; and another in Acton church, Suffolk, in Mr. Gough's work.

From about the year 1380, theſe braſs plates grew into common uſe; and till the fifteenth century, had commonly the inſcription round the ſide of the ſtone.

On theſe monuments the deceaſed are repreſented commonly at full length, though there are ſome demi figures; both their hands are uſually joined as in the act of prayer. They are dreſſed in habits that denote their profeſſion; knights and gentlemen are delineated in armour, frequently bareheaded; the oldeſt diſtinguiſhed by their picked toes, and rounded hair radiating from the centre of the head, a peculiarity alſo found on divers ſculptured figures of the 13th century. Their heads are often reſting on a helmet; ſome are repreſented with open head-pieces, without bever or viſor, the chaperon of mail, and offenſively armed with ſword and dagger.

Persons of the law, or in civil departments, are habited in fur gowns; their hair and beards according to the faſhion of the times.

Bishops, abbots, and other dignified eccleſiaſtics, appear in pontificalibus, bearing their croſiers and paſtoral ſtaves in their left hands, their right elevated, and all the fingers, but the firſt two, cloſed as in the act of benediction. The parochial prieſts have ſometimes the chalice, and are dreſſed in their rich altar veſt-

ments;

ments; theſe have often the emblems of the four Evangeliſts at the corners of the ſtone; ſometimes from the mouths of theſe, and other figures, a label is projected, charged with ſome text or pious ſentence.

In monuments of this ſort, where man and wiſe are repreſented, the lady is placed on the left ſide of her huſband, like him, with joined hands, as in a praying poſture, their children frequently ranged in a rank beneath them; the boys under the father, the girls under the mother. Frequently the man has a lion at his feet, to denote generoſity and courage, and the lady a dog, the emblem of fidelity.

After the time of Edward VI. or Queen Mary, the petition of *Orate pro Anima* is omitted; and towards the latter end of the reign of Queen Elizabeth, or the beginning of that of King James I. the Gothic letter is changed for the Roman. On ſome of theſe monuments the coats of arms are enamelled, but theſe are chiefly of the 17th century. In ſeveral places we meet with figures engraved on ſtone, but theſe are in general very modern, chiefly of the 17th century. Several of this ſort are found in Cornwall, particularly in the church of Fowey; and one is engraved on marble in a church in London, I think St. Helen's in Biſhopſgate-ſtreet.

Mural monuments, that is, monuments ſupported by brackets againſt a wall, were not introduced into common uſe till the 16th century. Here the figures are repreſented kneeling and praying at a kind of deſk, the man and wife frequently oppoſite each other, he on the right, ſhe on the left of it; their children ſometimes behind, and ſometimes under their parents; the boys behind or under the father, the girls behind or under the mother. The figures are frequently repreſented in natural colours, and the architecture adorned with gilding.

About the latter end of the reign of King James I. a ſpecies of mixed architecture is to be found on theſe monuments, where we ſee Doric, Ionic, or Corinthian columns, ſupporting Gothic ſuperſtructures. Shortly after, Grecian architecture appears to have been generally adopted in these erections; and in some late performances, amends seems to have been made to the heathen gods for turning them out of the Pantheon, by admitting them into our churches, particularly Westminster-Abbey.

BESIDES these general observations, much assistance may be drawn from the following circumstances:

THOSE monuments ornamented with circular and intersecting arches, are of greater antiquity than those having pointed ones, described by the intersection of two circles; and these are more ancient than those low pointed arches described from four centers; the latter being scarcely older than the reign of King Henry VII.

IN figures of armed knights, those with the mail armour and cylindrical helmets flat at the top, are always older than those with plate armour and a head-piece, having a visor and bever. The radiating hair curling inwards towards the head, is a mark of a monument of the 13th or 14th century.

THE female head-dress of that period was the tiara or mitre-like cap. The Lady Fitzwalter, in Little Dunmow church, and a lady of —— Chidiok, in Christ-Church, Hants, both have this kind of coiseure.

A MONUMENT adorned with armorial bearings cannot be older than the latter end of the eleventh century, as arms were not used in England before that period, Mr. Gale says, not before the year 1147; Mr. Edmonson places the introduction of them before the commencement of the tenth century: the medium as stated above may perhaps be nearer the truth than either.

THE first instance of quartering arms by any subject, was given by John Hastings, earl of Pembroke, following the example of King Edward III. therefore monuments adorned with different quarterings must be posterior to that period.

MONUMENTS with supporters to coats of arms, mark them to have been erected since the time of King Richard II. that prince being the first who used them.

TILL

TILL the time of Henry III. the heads of the peers were not adorned with coronets. John of Eltham, fecond fon of King Edward II. who died A. D. 1334, and is buried in Weftminfter Abbey, has on a coronet with leaves, and is the moft ancient of its kind.

WHERE the arms of France contain only three *fleurs de lis*, or lilies, the monument has been erected fince the reign of King Henry V.; before that time they were femeé with thofe flowers.

THOSE monuments on which the heads of the cumbent figures are fupported by two pillows, are prior to the 16th century; after that period, mats were reprefented as ufed for that purpofe.

IN eftimating the age of monuments, we muft not always judge of their æra from the time in which the perfon lived to whofe honour they are erected, as in many inftances they have been conftructed long after their deceafe. Of this the tomb of King Athelftan in Malmfbury abbey, and that of St. Etheldred king of the Weft Saxons, in Winborne Minfter, Dorfetfhire, are ftriking examples; and if I am not much miftaken, fomething of that kind occurs in the cathedral of St. David, or Landaff, and likewife in the church of Chefter-le-Street, where there is a feries of monuments of the Lumley family, moftly made at the fame time, and that long after their deceafe. To exalted characters a future age has perhaps done that honour which the envy of their contemporaries, or the poverty of their families denied. The cenotaphs of Shakefpeare, Ben Johnfon, and a variety of others, afford plenty of inftances of fuch erections.

IT is alfo probable that many of the ancient monuments in parochial churches are at prefent only cenotaphs; for it is faid, that at the diffolution of the religious houfes, moft of their churches were granted to lay ufes, on which the reprefentatives of many of the great families there buried, removed the monuments of their anceftors to the neareft parifh church, leaving the bodies in their original place of interment.

A PARTICULAR kind of monuments, found in divers churches, require explanation. Thefe are commonly tombs of bifhops or other ecclesiastics, whereon are two figures of the person there deposited, one in full flesh and vigour, dressed in the ceremonial robes of his office, with mitre, crosier, and every other ensign of dignity, and beneath it, as in a coffin, another representing him a corpse, emaciated almost to a skeleton, and wrapped up in his winding-sheet. Instances of this sort of figures occur in the monuments of Archbishop Chicheley at Canterbury, and Bishop Fox at Salisbury. Some, as at Landaff, St. Mary Overy's, and that of Sir William Weston, the last prior of the order of St. John of Jerusalem, in Clerkenwell church, have only the emaciated figure. The common story told by the sexton or verger who shews the church where they are found is, that the person represented endeavoured, in imitation of Christ, to fast forty days, but died in the attempt, having reduced himself from the figure represented above, to the state shewn below; or that by a long sickness he was from a fine lusty man brought down to the skeleton there exhibited. Both these are in fact vulgar errors, calculated to astonish their holiday visitors; for by these sculptures it was only meant to inculcate the vanity and mutability of human felicity and greatness, and to remind the spectators that every man, however rich, powerful, dignified, adorned or handsome, must inevitably, some time or another, put on the disgusting appearance there represented.

Fig. 1.

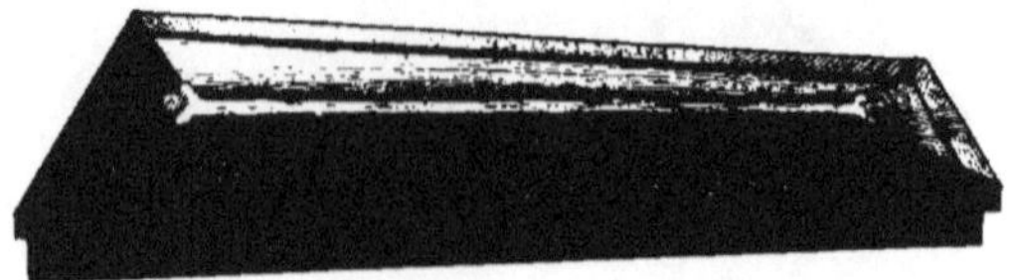

Fig. 2.

Fig. 3.

ANCIENT MONUMENTS. Pl. I.

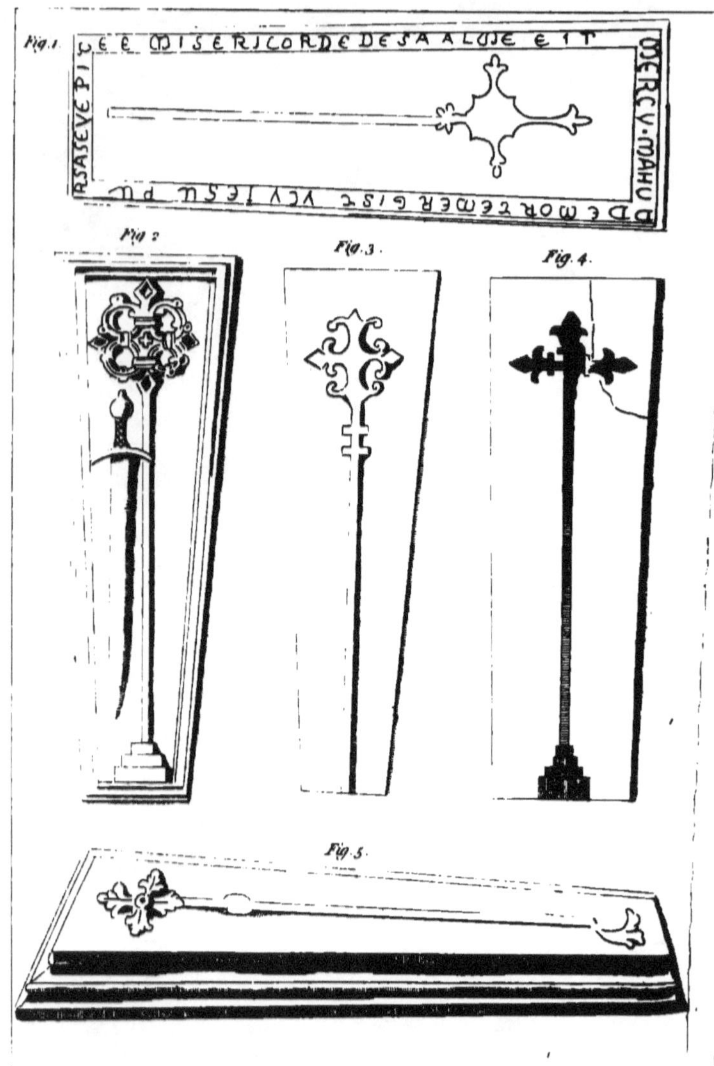

MONUMENTS. *Pl. II.*

Fig. 1

Fig. 2

Pub. 29 Sep. 1787 by S. Hooper

MONUMENTS. Pl. III.

DESCRIPTION OF THE PLATES IN THE ADDENDA TO THE PREFACE.

PLATE I.

FIG. 1. The monument of Lady Juga Baynard, in Little Dunmow, Eſſex; ſhe founded the priory there in 1111.

FIG. 2. A coffin-ſhaped ſtone, here repreſented to illuſtrate the deſcription.

FIG. 3. The monument of King William Rufus, in the cathedral of Wincheſter.

PLATE II.

FIG. 1. Grave-ſtone of Maud de Mortimer, in Tiltey Abbey, Eſſex.

FIG. 2. Grave-ſtone of the abbot of Bala Sala, in the Iſle of Man.

FIG. 3. Another near the church-door in Pevenſey chancel, Suſſex.

FIG. 4. Another, Weſtham church, Suſſex.

FIG. 5. Another in the cathedral at Wincheſter.

PLATE III.

FIG. 1. A ſkeleton-like figure in the church of St. Mary Overy's, in the Borough of Southwark, of which the uſual ſtory is told, *i. e.* that the perſon thereby repreſented, attempted to faſt forty days.

FIG. 2.

Fig. 2. A crusader, carved in oak, in the same church.

PLATE IV.

Figure of an ancient knight clad in the hawberk, and armed with a battle-axe and roundel. It lyes on a table monument in the abbey church of Great Malvern, Worcestershire, and is supposed to represent a Richard Corbet, and to have been erected before the 14th century. It is broken off at the legs.

PLATE V.

Fig. 1. The figure of Joan, wife of Richard, son and heir to Robert Lord Poynings, from a brass plate in St. Helen's church, Bishopsgate Ward; the inscription adds, she died a virgin A. D. 1420.

Fig. 2. The representation of a woman in her winding-sheet, from a brass plate in Bodiam church, Sussex.

PLATE VI.

Edmund Flambert and Elizabeth his wife, from a brass plate in Harrow church; to which, according to Weaver, were the following inscriptions:

> Edmund Flamberd et ELisabeth, gisont icy
> Dieu de salmes eyt mercy. Amen.

> FLambard Edmundus jacet hic tellure sepultus
> Conjux addetur Elisabeth et societur.

PLATE VII.

Fig. 1. A figure of an ancient warrior in singular armour, from an impression of a brass plate, late in the collection of Gustavus Brander, Esq. name unknown. His hair is of the kind mentioned, as radiating from a center; his head rests on what seems to be a saddle.

Fig. 2.

MONUMENT. *Pl:IV.*

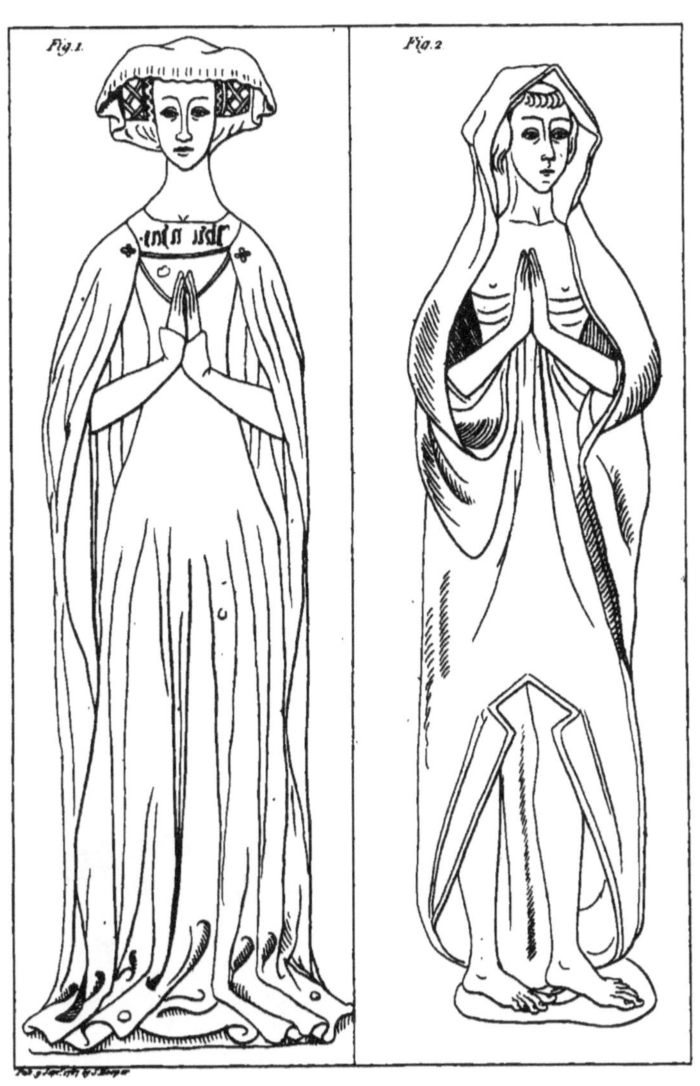

MONUMENTS. Pl. V.

Pub. 5 Sept. 1787 by S. Hooper

MONUMENTS . Pl. IV.

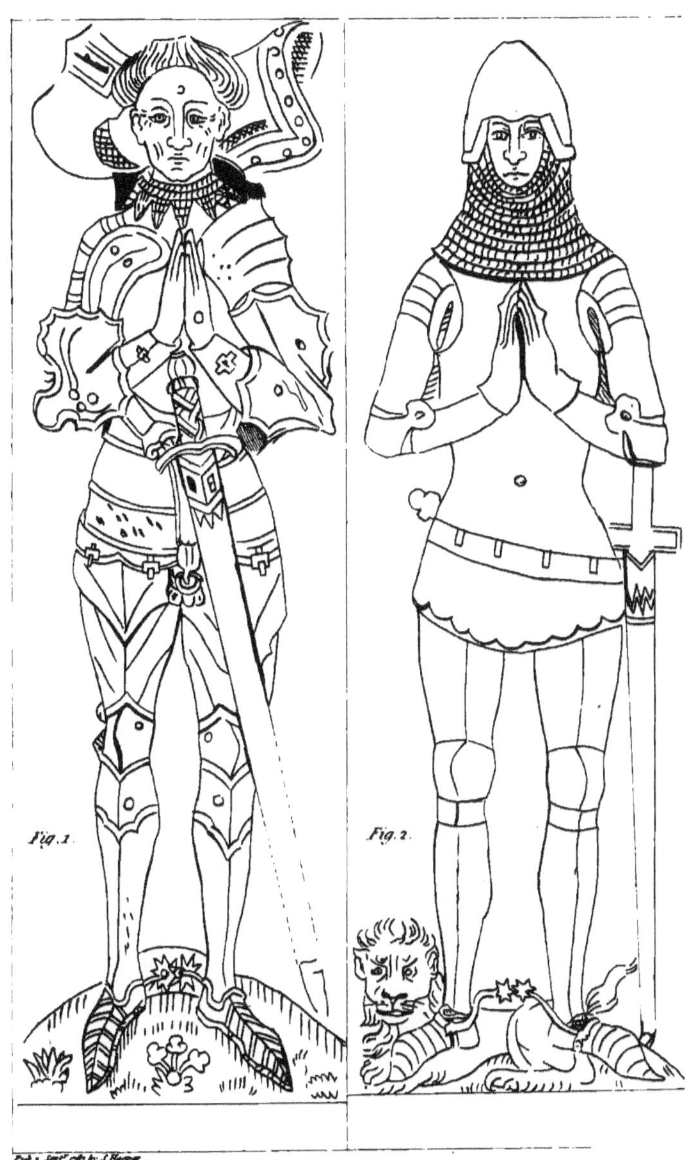

MONUMENTS. Pl. VII.

Pub. 7 Sept 1787 by S. Hooper

MONUMENTS Pl. VIII.

MONUMENTS. *Pl.IX.*

Fig. 2. John Flambard, from a braſs plate in Harrow church, Middleſex; he has the following ſtrange inſcription:

Jon me do marmore numinis ordine flam tumulatur;
Barde quoque verbere ſtigis é funere hic tueatur.

PLATE VIII.

Fig. 1. From a braſs plate in Nordiam church, Suſſex, ſuppoſed to be one of the family of Tuſton.

Fig. 2. A figure on a braſs plate in Rodmarton church, Glouceſterſhire: under it is this inſcription:

Hic Jaci Johis Edward qndam dns manerii de Rodmarton et verus patronus ejuſdem, famoſus apprentici in lege pitus qui obiit vii die Januarii A° Dni mccccclxi cuj ane appicatur De ame.

PLATE IX.

Fig. 1. John Wythines, Dean of Battle, in Suſſex, from a braſs plate in that church.

Out of his mouth iſſue two labels with theſe inſcriptions:

On the right, Tædet animam meam vitæ meæ.
On the left, Cupio diſſolvi et eſſe cum Chriſto.

Under his feet.—Hic jacet Johannis Wythines in prænobili Civitate ceſtriæ natus, et in Academia Oxon Educatus, ibique Ænei Naſi Collegii ſocius, ſacræ Theologiæ Doctor, academieq. Oxon pradcae vice cancellarius, Hujuſq. Eccleſia de Batel xlij Annos Decanus, qui obijt xviii Die Martii, Anno Ætatis ſuæ 84.
Et ſalutis humanæ 1615.

On a plate below:

Vixi dum volui, volui dum Chriſte volebas
Nec mihi vita brevis, nec mihi longa fuit;
Vivo tibi moriorq. tibi, tibi Chriſte reſurgam,
Mortuus et vivus ſum maneoq. tuus.

ADDENDA

TO THE

PREFACE.

FONTS.

BAPTISM was in primitive times adminiſtered only at Eaſter and Whitſuntide, unleſs in caſes of neceſſity, and that chiefly to adults, and was performed in the open air, in fountains, lakes, rivers, and even the ſea. The perſons to be baptized were immerſed three times, on the naming of the Three Perſons of the Trinity. Sprinkling was, in ſome caſes, allowed; but perſons ſo baptized were incapable of holding any dignity in the church. It was long diſputed whether infants were originally admitted to this ceremony, and it was often delayed a long time for different reaſons. St. Ambroſe was not baptized before he was elected Biſhop of Melan, and ſome of the fathers not till near their death. It was thus performed at the time of Juſtin Martyr and Tertullian; for the latter ſpeaks of perſons going from the church to the water to be baptized. It continued to be adminiſtered in the open air till the time of the Saxons; for Paulinus, Archbiſhop of York, baptized a thouſand perſons at one time in the river Swale: for the due performance of that ceremony it was required the parties ſhould be quite naked. Baptiſtries were afterwards

wards built in churches, perhaps for the ſake of decency, and ſometimes by the biſhop's licence in private houſes; but this was however condemned by the ancient councils.

As baptiſm was only adminiſtered at ſtated periods, the baptiſtries and fonts, or baſons holding the water, were very large, on account of the great concourſe of people reſorting to them. They commonly conſiſted of two apartments; the porch or anteroom, where the catechumens made the confeſſion of their faith and renunciation of Satan; and an inner room, where the ceremony of immerſion was performed: for this there were ſeparate apartments for the different ſexes; and there were anciently a ſet of deaconeſſes, part of whoſe buſineſs it was to ſtrip the women. Baptiſtries, according to Durandus, continued till the 6th century out of the church; though ſoon after, ſome were admitted into the porch, and afterwards into the church itſelf.

These buildings were covered at the top, and ſupplied with freſh ſpring water by pipes laid into the ſuſtaining columns or walls, and were let out by cocks in the form of ſtags' heads, lambs, and other animals. The different parts of the building were alſo frequently adorned with the images of ſaints and holy men, as examples to thoſe baptized.

At firſt, baptiſtries were only erected in great cities, where biſhops reſided, who alone had the right of baptizing; but in after ages, according to Blackmore, they were ſet up in country pariſhes. The monks were at firſt forbidden to baptize, unleſs they had a ſecular prieſt with them; but they afterwards found means to evade this prohibition, at firſt, by officiating at ſome pariſh church that belonged to their monaſteries; and a little before the diſſolution, fonts were ſet up in almoſt all the churches of the great monaſteries, under pretence of baptizing the children of ſervants and labourers born within their franchiſes, deemed extra-parochial. Baptiſtries were long continued in Italy, at Piſa, Florence, Bononia, and Parma. Laſſels ſays, at Florence there was, when he wrote, a public baptiſtry, where all the children of the town were baptized; and a building ftill remaining at the cathedral of Canterbury, is fuppofed by Mr. Gofling to have been a baptiftry.

INFANT baptifm at length becoming univerfal, and immerfion having been found in the northern countries inconvenient and dangerous in cold weather, afperfion or fprinkling was adopted in its ftead; and as this required but little water, probably the fonts began to decreafe from that time till they reached their prefent fize. Sprinkling was, it is faid, firft introduced into England about the beginning of the ninth century; but it did not entirely fuperfede immerfion: the choice of either being left to the parents, the ancient mode was fometimes retained; for it is recorded by William of Worcefter, of King Etheldred, that at his baptifm, A. D. 967, he bewrayed the baptiftry. On this ominous occafion the archbifhop Saint Dunftan, who performed the ceremony, exclaimed in a paffion, "By God and his Mother, he will be a cowardly fellow." Pope Leo IV. directed that every church fhould have a ftone font; and if ftone could not be had, then a veffel of fome other materials, but appropriated folely to that ufe.

BY the canons of the church of England, every parifh church is directed to have a font made of ftone; becaufe, fays Durandus, the water which typified baptifm in the wildernefs flowed from a rock; or rather, becaufe Chrift is called a Corner-ftone.

AMONG many ancient ceremonies, that of hallowing the font was performed on Eafter and Whitfun eves; the reafon for it is given in the following words by an anonymous author quoted by Strut:—"In the begynnyng of holy Chirch, all the children weren kept to be cryftened on thys even, at the font hallowing; but now for enchefone that in fa long abydynge they might dye without Cryftendome, therefore holi chirch ordeyneth to cryften at all the tymes of the year fave 8 daies before thefe eveyns, the chylde fhalle abyde till the font hallowing, if it maye be favely for perrill of deth, and ells not." See MS. Bib. Cot. Claudius, A. 2. quoted in Horda Angelcynnen, vol. iii. p. 174.

THE

THE ornaments on the fonts of the prefent eftablifhment are not always religious fubjects; we fometimes meet with huntings, grotefque figures, and the figns of the zodiac.

THE antiquity of many fonts may be difcovered by their ftyle of architecture, particularly where there are reprefentations of arches or buildings. Thus the ancient font at Winchefter has a building with circular arches, and another at Alphington in Devonfhire (engraved in the repertory) has both circular and interfecting arches. The font of St. Martin's church, Canterbury, is alfo very ancient; it is large and cylindrical; all the outfides covered with interwoven circles, ornamented with fmall pellets or balls, as is fhewn in fig. 2; fig. 2. gives a general idea of the font itfelf. The firft is undoubtedly of Saxon workmanfhip, the latter at leaft very early Norman.

ANOTHER font alfo cylindrical, and covered with bands, croffing each other lozenge fafhion, is of very antique workmanfhip; the original is in Denton church, Suffex.

ANOTHER ancient ftyle of ornaments on fonts, are the inftruments of Chrift's paffion, fuch as the fpear, nails, pincers, hammer, pillar, fcourge, and crown of thorns. The font, fig. 6. in Felix-Stowe church, Suffolk, is fo ornamented; it is octagonal, but one of its fides plain.

THE two other fonts, fig. 1. and fig. 4, are more of modern workmanfhip; the firft is in Tering church, and the other in that of Bifhopftone, both in the county of Suffex.

THE font, No. 5, in Luton church, Bedfordfhire, is in form like a baptiftry; it is neverthelefs of no very remote antiquity, probably about the time of Henry VI.

DESCRIP-

DESCRIPTION OF THE FONTS

IN THE

ADDENDA TO THE PREFACE.

FIG. 1. Font in Tering church, Suſſex.
FIG. 2. Font in St. Martin's church, Canterbury.
FIG. 3. Font in Denton church, Suſſex.
FIG. 4. Font in Biſhopſtone, Suſſex.
FIG. 5. Font in Luton church, Bedfordſhire.
FIG. 6. Font in Felix Stowe church, Suffolk.

END OF THE ADDENDA TO THE PREFACE.

Pub. 18 Sep. 1787 by S. Hooper.

FONTS. Pl. X.

COUNTY INDEX TO VOL. I.

Name of the Abbey, Castle, Monastery, Priory, or Ruin, &c.	Point of View.	When founded or built.	When refounded or rebuilt.	View when taken	View by whom taken. *N. B.* Those without a name were drawn by the author.	Page
BEDFORDSHIRE.						
The Map. - - - - -	—	—	—	—	to face Preface	142
Bedford-Bridge, - plate 1.	N. E.	921	1224	1761	- -	1
Ditto, - - plate 2.	E.	—	—	1760	- -	3
BERKSHIRE.						
The Map. - - - -	—	—	—	—	- -	4
Bustlesham, or Bysham Monastery.	—	1338	—	1760	Tho. Forrest, Esq;	4
Dunnington Castle. - - -	N. W.	—	1396	1768	- -	5
—— Plan of, with view of Gateway,	—	—	—	—	- -	5
George's (St.) Chapel, Windsor.	—	—	—	—	Mr. T. Sandby.	9
Reading Abbey, - plate 1.	—	1121	1732	1762	Mr. P. Sandby.	13
Ditto, - - - plate 2.	S.	1125	—	1759	- -	17
BUCKINGHAMSHIRE.						
The Map. - - -	—	—	—	—	to face -	21
Stivecle, or Stukeley Church. -	—	—	—	—	- -	21
CAMBRIDGESHIRE.						
The Map. - - -	—	—	—	—	- -	20
Cambridge Castle. - - -	S. E.	1066	—	1769	- -	21
Plan of, and Bird's-eye view when entire.	—	—	—	—	- -	21
Pythagoras's School. - - -	—	—	—	—	- -	23
CHESHIRE.						
The Map. - - -	—	—	—	—	to face -	26
Beeston Castle, - - plate 1.	S W.	1200	—	1760	Mr. Hamilton.	27
Ditto, - - plate 2.	S.	—	—	1773	Mr. P. Sandby.	29
Birkchedde Priory. - - -	—	1192	—	1770	Mr. Richards.	32
Chester Castle. - plate 1.	—	1100	—	1770	- -	33
Ditto, - - plate 2.	S. E.	—	—	1769	- -	35
Chester Bridge. - - -	—	918	—	1770	- -	36
—— New or Water Tower. -	—	1322	—	ditto	- -	37
CORNWALL.						
The Map. - - - -	—	—	—	—	to face -	39
Restormel Castle. - - -	—	—	—	—	- -	39
CUMBERLAND.						
The Map. - - - -	—	—	—	1774	to face -	43
Bees (St.) Monastery of. - -	N. W.	1117	—	ditto	- -	43
Carlisle Castle. - - -	N. E.	1095	—	1774	- -	46
—— Plan of, on plate with Penrith.	—	—	—	—	- -	46
Cockermouth Castle, - plate 1.	N. E.	1070	—	1774	- -	49
Ditto, - - - plate 2.	—	—	—	ditto	- -	51
Lanercost Priory, - plate 1.	N. E.	1169	—	ditto	- -	51
Ditto, - - plate 2.	W.	—	—	ditto	- -	53
Naworth Castle, - - plate 1.	—	1336	—	—	- -	56
Ditto, - - - plate 2.	—	—	—	1772	Mr. M. Griffiths	58
Penrith Castle. - - - -	N. W.	—	—	1774	- -	61
—— Plan of, on plate with Carlisle.	—	—	—	—	- -	46

DIRECTIONS for placing the CUTS, &c.

THE views, plans and maps are to be placed to each respective description as referred to in the preceding Index.

History preserving the monuments of Antiquity, frontispiece to Vol. I.

The knight and hermit to front the introduction.

The machines of war to front page 16.

The plate of armour to face page 51.

Religious orders to face page 90.

Grand door of Barfreston Church, in Kent, page 111.

Barfreston Church, page 113.

Strangers Hall, Christ Church, Canterbury, page 113.

Frize on the north and south fronts of Alderbury Church, Oxfordshire, page 112; mentioned there by mistake as in Suffolk.

The plate of architecture to front page 111.

Saxon and Gothic Architecture, to face page 125.

Druidical Antiquities to face page 135.

BEDFORDSHIRE.

Is a ſmall inland county. When the Romans landed in Britain, 55 years before Chriſt, it was included in the diſtrict inhabited by the Catieuchlani, whoſe chief or governor Caſſibelinus, headed the forces of the whole iſland againſt Cæſar, and the year following was totally defeated. In 310 the emperor Conſtantine divided Britain into five Roman provinces, when this county was included in the third diviſion, called Flavia Cæſarienſis, in which ſtate it continued for 426 years, when the Romans quitted Britain. At the eſtabliſhment of the kingdom of Mercia (one of the diviſions of the Saxon Heptarchy) it was conſidered as a part of that kingdom, and ſo continued from 582 to 827, when with the other petty kingdoms of the iſland it became ſubject to the Weſt Saxons under Egbert, and the whole was named England. In 889 Alfred held the ſovereignty, when England was divided into counties, hundreds and tythings, and Bedfordſhire firſt received its preſent name. It is in the Norfolk circuit, the province of Canterbury, and biſhoprick of Lincoln; its form is oval, being about 33 miles long, 16 broad, and nearly 73 in circumference; containing an area of about 323 ſquare miles, or 260,000 ſquare acres. It ſupplies 400 men to the national militia. Bedford,

BEDFORDSHIRE.

Bedford, the county town, is situated north-west from London about 51½ miles. It contains 124 parishes, 58 vicarages, and 10 market towns, viz. Bedford, Ampthill, Biggleswade, Dunstable, Leighton Beaudesart, Luton, Potton, Shefford, Tuddington and Woburn, and 55 villages; the inhabitants by computation are 67,350, and it has 7,294 houses that pay taxes: it is divided into 9 hundreds, sends 4 members to parliament, and pays 7 parts of 513 of the land tax.* Its principal river, the Ouse, is navigable to Bedford, and divides the county into two parts, of which that to the south is the most considerable. In its course, which is very meandering, it receives several small streams, the principal one is the Ivel, which takes its rise in the southern part of the county. The air is healthy, and the soil in general a deep clay. The north side of the Ouse is fruitful and woody, but the south side is less fertile; yet producing great quantities of wheat and barley, excellent in their kind, and woad for dyers. The soil yields plenty of fullers-earth for our woollen manufactory. The chief manufactures of the county are thread lace and straw ware.

In this county there are many remains of Roman, Saxon and Norman antiquities, but few Roman stations, viz. Sandy near Potton, and the Magiovinium of Antoninus, by others supposed to be the ancient Salenæ, containing 30 acres, where many urns, coins, &c. have been dug up. Another at Madining-bowre or Maiden-bower, one mile from Dunstable, containing about 9 acres, which Camden supposes to have been a Roman station from the coins of the emperors having been frequently dug up there, and calls it Magintum. Leighton Beaudesart is supposed to have been a Roman camp, and another is at Arlesey, near Shefford; and a Roman amphitheatre may be traced near Bradford Magna.

The Roman road, Icknield-street, crosses this county, entering at Leighton Beaudesart, from whence it passes Dunstable, where it inclines northward over Wardon hills to Baldock in Hertfordshire. The Watling-street enters this county near Luton from St. Albans, passes a little north of Dunstable, where it crosses the Icknield-street, and from thence to Stoney Stratford in Buckinghamshire. A Roman road also enters near Potton, passes on to Sandy, and from thence to Bedford, where it crosses the Ouse, and proceeds to Newport Pagnell in Buckinghamshire.

ANTIQUITIES in this COUNTY worthy NOTICE.

Bedford Bridge and Priory
Chicksand Abbey, near Shefford
Dunstable Priory, near Luton
Eaton Park House or Eaton Bray
Five Knolls, near Dunstable
Newnham Priory, near Bedford
Northill Church, 3 miles from Biggleswade
Summeris Tower, near Luton
Warden Abbey, near Shefford
Woburn Abbey
Woodhill Castle, or Odhill Castle, near Harewood.

* The number of members of parliament for England is 513, and the land tax is divided into the same number, of which this county pays 7.

2 Pl. 2

D.L. sculp

BEDFORD BRIDGE.

Pub.d by S. Hooper [illegible]

THE ANTIQUITIES OF ENGLAND and WALES.

BEDFORD BRIDGE. (PLATE I.)

THIS bridge ſtands upon the river Ouſe, which runs through, and almoſt equally divides the town. Hiſtory is ſilent both as to the founder and the time of its conſtruction. Tradition ſays it was erected with part of the materials of the caſtle demoliſhed by King Henry III. in the year 1224. It is highly probable this was built in the place of a much older bridge; as by an extract from Roger Hoveden's Chronicle, in Leland's Collectanea, it appears, that the part of the town, on the ſouthern bank of the river, was built by Edward the elder, in the year 912. It ſeems, therefore, almoſt impoſſible the inhabitants could ſo long have wanted this neceſſary means of communication between the north and ſouth parts of the town.

THE caſtle was demoliſhed on the following occaſion: King John having taken it from William de Beauchamp, beſtowed it on Falco de Brent, or Breant, raiſed by his favour from a private ſoldier to great riches and power. This man having committed divers acts of violence on the neighbouring inhabitants, and dilapidated ſeveral religious houſes and churches, particularly that of St. Paul, for the purpoſe of repairing and ſtrengthening his caſtle, was, by Martin Paterſhul, Thomas de Multon, and Henry Braybrooke, judges, then ſitting at Dunſtable, fined in the ſum of three thouſand pounds.

Falco being greatly enraged thereat, and conſidering it as an injury done him, ſent his brother to ſeize theſe judges, and bring them priſoners to Bedford. They, apprized of his intentions, fled; but Braybrooke being taken, was carried to the caſtle, where he ſuffered a thouſand inſults and indignities.

The king, highly incenſed at this audacious violation of the laws, and determined to bring the offenders to exemplary puniſhment, laid ſiege to the caſtle, which, after a reſiſtance of ſixty days, ſurrendered at diſcretion. He then cauſed the governor, William de Breant, brother to Falco, with twenty-four knights, and eighty ſoldiers, to be hanged, and the fortifications to be levelled with the ground. The ſite and dwelling-houſe he returned to William de Beauchamp; and gave the ſtones, ſome to the canons of Newenham and Chadwell; ſome to the church of St. Paul; and, according to tradition, applied the remainder to the building of the bridge. At this ſiege the king was aſſiſted by Stephen, archbiſhop of Canterbury, who brought him a conſiderable and well appointed body of men. Falco taking refuge in a church at Coventry, abjured the realm; or, as ſome writers ſay, was with his wife and child ſhortly after baniſhed.

Camden quotes the following curious account of the ſiege, from a writer contemporary with the facts deſcribed.

"On the eaſt ſide were one petrary and two mangonels daily applying upon the tower. On the weſt two mangonels battering the old tower; as alſo one upon the ſouth, and another upon the north part, which beat down two paſſages through the walls that were next them. Beſides theſe there were two machines contrived of wood, ſo as to be higher than the caſtle and tower, erected for the purpoſe of the baliſtarii, or gunners and watchmen; they had ſeveral machines, wherein the gunners and ſlingers lay in ambuſh; alſo there was moreover another machine, called cattus, under which the diggers who were employed to undermine the walls of the

Bedford Bridge Pl. I.

Published 1 May 1783. by S. Hooper.

the tower and caſtle came in and out. The caſtle was taken by four aſſaults; in the firſt was taken the barbican; in the ſecond the outer ballia; at the third attack the wall by the tower was thrown down by the miners; where with great danger they poſſeſſed themſelves of the inner ballia; through a chink, at the fourth aſſault, the miners ſet fire to the tower, ſo that the ſmoke burſt out, and the tower itſelf was cloven to that degree, as to ſhew viſibly ſome broad chinks; whereupon the enemy ſurrendered."

This bridge is one hundred and ſixteen yards in length, four and a half broad, and has a parapet three feet and a half high; this, it is ſaid, was erected in the reign of Queen Mary, out of the ruins of St. Dunſtan's church, which ſtood on the ſouth ſide of the bridge. It has ſeven arches, and near the centre were two gate-houſes; that on the north being uſed for a priſon, and that on the ſouth ſerved as a ſtorehouſe for the arms and ammunition of the troops quartered here. Theſe gate-houſes were taken down in the year 1765; and ſix lamps ſet up on poſts at proper diſtances. The bridge is kept in repair by the corporation, who have a very conſiderable eſtate. In this view taken in 1761, only the north gate-houſe appears.

(PLATE II.)

In this view both the gate-houſes formerly ſtanding on this bridge are ſhewn. In the former plate, at the point from whence it was taken, which was choſen as the moſt picturesque, only one of them could be ſeen. As theſe buildings have been taken down, it has been intimated to the author, that a view, in which they might both appear, would be agreeable to ſeveral curious perſons, as more particularly preſerving the appearance of this ancient bridge. In obedience to this opinion, he here preſents a ſecond view, happy to have it in his power to oblige the encouragers of his work. This drawing was made anno 1760.

BERKSHIRE.

BUSTLESHAM, BYSHAM MONTAGUE, or BYSHAM MONASTERY.

ROBERT de FERRARIIS, in the reign of King Stephen, gave the manor of Buſtleſham to the templars, who thereupon made here a preceptory for the knights of that order. Upon their diſſolution in the reign of King Edw. II. this ſeems not to have paſſed with the greateſt part of their eſtates to the knights of St. John of Jeruſalem, for they had before granted it away in fee to Hugh de Spencer jun. Afterwards it came to William Montacute, earl of Saliſbury who, A. D. 1338, built a priory here for canons of the order of St. Auguſtine, which was endowed 26 Henry VIII. with 285l. 11s. ob per ann. Dugdale; 327l. 4s. 6d. Speed.

THE prior and convent having ſurrendered this monaſtery July 5, 1536, King Henry VIII. in the year following, refounded and more amply endowed it with lands of the late diſſolved abbey of Chertſey, and the priories of Cardigan, Bethkelert, Ankerwike, Little Marlo, Medmenham, &c. to the value of 661l. 14s. 9d. per ann. for the maintenance of an abbot, who was to have the privilege of wearing a mitre, and thirteen Benedictine monks. But this new abbey was of ſhort continuance, being ſurrendered 30 Henry VIII. June 19, 1539, three years after its inſtitution.

THE ſite of it was granted 7 Edward VI. to Sir Edward Hoby, in whoſe deſcendants it continued till the year 1768, when the laſt of that name dying, bequeathed it to John Mill, Eſq; the preſent proprietor, who by act of parliament took upon him the name of Hoby. In the charter of the firſt foundation, this monaſtery is ſaid to be dedicated to our Lord Jeſus Chriſt, and the Bleſſed Virgin his Mother; and in that of the ſecond foundation to the Bleſſed Virgin Mary; yet in the time of Richard II. and in both the ſurrenders, it is ſtiled the conventual church of the

Holy

[illegible]HAM MONASTERY

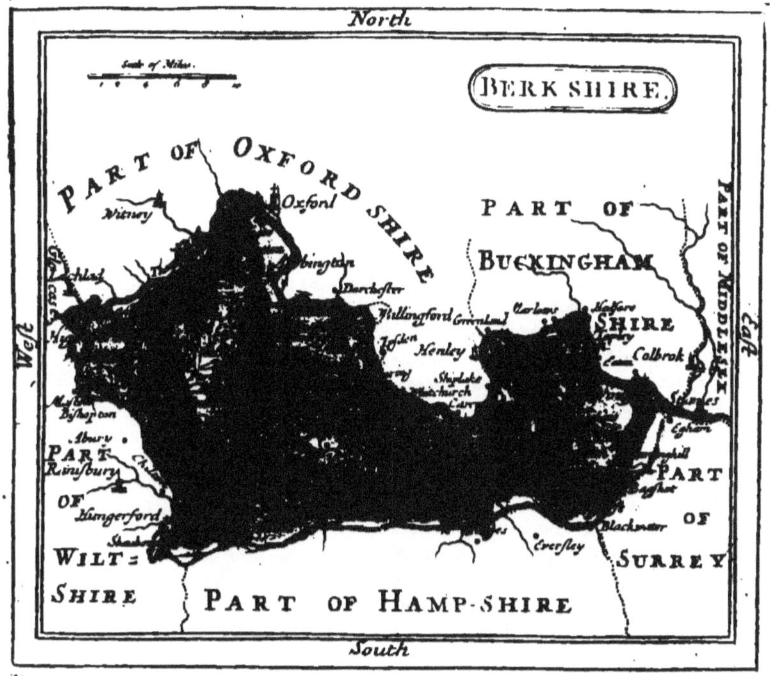

B E R K · S H I R E.

IS an inland county, that contained the whole of that Britiſh principality inhabited by the Atrebatii, who are ſuppoſed to have been originally from Gaul. When Conſtantine divided the iſland into Roman provinces in 310, this principality was included in Britannia Prima, the firſt diviſion, whoſe boundaries were the Engliſh Channel on the ſouth, and the Thames and Severn on the north. On the Romans quitting the iſland, and civil diſſentions enabling the Saxons to eſtabliſh the Heptarchy, this part of the country was included in the kingdom of the Weſt Saxons, which commenced in 519, and continued till 828, when it became the only remaining ſovereignity, having conquered all the others, and they were incorporated by the name of England, under Egbert; whoſe grandſon, Alfred, an native of Wantage in this county, in 889 divided his kingdom into counties, hundreds and pariſhes, and at that time this diviſion firſt received its appellation of Berkſhire or Berocſhire. At preſent it is in the Oxford circuit, the province of Canterbury, and dioceſe of Saliſbury. The general ſhape of it

ſome-

ſomewhat reſembles the form of a ſlipper or ſandal. It contains an area of 654 ſquare miles, or 527,000 ſquare acres, is 39 miles long, 29 broad, and is about 137 in circumference. It ſupplies 560 men to the national militia, is ſituated north-weſt from London, has 140 pariſhes, 62 vicarages, 12 market towns, but no city: 671 vilages, 135,000 inhabitants, 11,560 houſes that pay the tax, is divided into 20 hundreds, ſends 9 members to parliament, 2 for the county, 2 for Windſor, 2 for Reading, 2 for Wallingford, and one for Abingdon; and pays 10 parts of the proportion of the land-tax. Its principal river is the Thames. It alſo has the Kennet, great part of which is navigable; the Loddon, the Ocke and the Lambourne, a ſmall ſtream, which, contrary to all other rivers, is always higheſt in ſummer, and ſhrinks gradually as winter approaches. The air of this county is healthy even in the vales; and tho' the ſoil is not the moſt fertile, yet it is remarkably pleaſant. It is well ſtored with timber, particularly oak and beech, and produces great plenty of wheat and barley. Its principal manufactures are wollen cloth, ſail cloth and malt.

Its market towns are Abingdon, Farringdon, Hungerford, Eaſt Illey, Lower Lambourne, Maidenhead, Newbury, Ockingham, Reading, Wallingford, Wantage, and Windſor, remarkable for its royal caſtle, as the county is for White-horſe-hill, near Lamburne, where is the rude figure of a horſe, which takes up near an acre of ground on the ſide of a green hill, ſaid to have been made by Alfred in the reign of his brother Ethelred, as a monument to perpetuate a victory over the Danes in 871, at Aſhdown, now Aſhbury Park.

The Roman Watling-ſtreet, from Dunſtable, enters Berkſhire at the village of Streatly, between Wallingford and Reading, and croſſing this county proceeds to Marlborough. Another Roman road from Hampſhire enters this county, leads to Reading and Newbury, the Spinæ of Camden, where it divides: one branch extends to Marlborough in Wilts, and the other to Cirenceſter in Glouceſterſhire. A branch from the Icknield-ſtreet proceeds from Wallingford to Wantage.

There is a Roman camp near Wantage on the brow of a hill, of a quadrangular form; there are other remains of encampments at Eaſt Hampſtead, near Ockingham, near White-horſe-hill, near Puſey, and upon Sinodun-hill, near Wallingford. At Lawrence Waltham is a Roman fort, and near Denchworth is Cherbury caſtle, a fortreſs of Canute. Uffington caſtle, near White-horſe-hill, is ſuppoſed to be Da-[illegible], and near it is Dragon-hill, ſuppoſed to be the burying place of Uter Pendragon, a Britiſh prince. Near White-horſe-hill are the remains of a funeral monument of a Daniſh chief ſlain at Aſhdown by Alfred.

ANTIQUITIES in this COUNTY worthy NOTICE.

Abingdon Church and Abbey
Aldworth Caſtle, near Eaſt Illey
Bysham Monaſtery
Donnington Caſtle
Lambourne Church
Reading Abbey
Sunning Chapel
Wallingford Church and Caſtle
Windſor Caſtle beggars all deſcription for ſituation, &c.

PLAN OF DUNNINGTON CASTLE

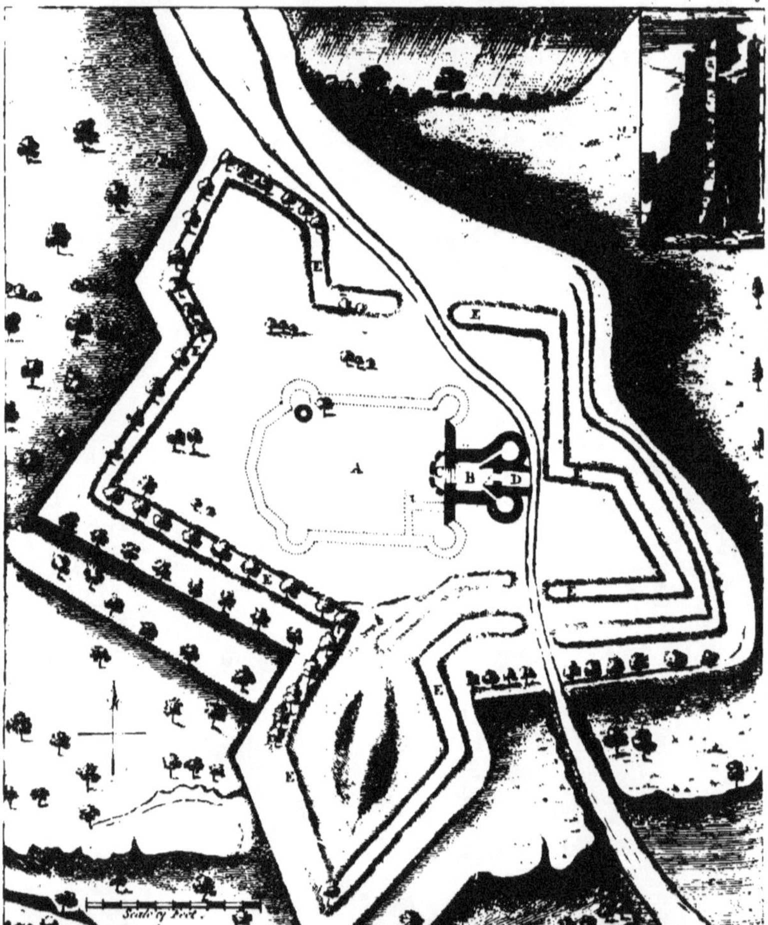

Donnington Castle.

A. *The Castle in Ruins*

B. *The entrance with the Towers standing*

C. *A Drinking Room erected by the Proprietor*

D. *Another Porch open at Top*

E. *Temporary Works thrown up in the Civil War*

• *Between the vaulted Passage B. & Drinking Room the Steps is a Vacancy for a Port Cullis*

Publish'd 9th Oct. 1783. DUNNINGTON CASTLE. By S. Hooper.

Holy Trinity. At the diſſolution a penſion of 66l. 13s. 4d. was aſſigned to abbot Cowdrey, who had, as I find (ſays Browne Willis) either voided the ſame by death or preferment before the year 1553; when only theſe following penſions remained in charge, viz. Will Walker, 7l. John Mylleſt, Will Roke, Will Byggs, John Rolfe, Edward Stephenſon, 5l. each: beſides 14l. 13s. 4d. in annuities.

Hither with the licence of Henry V. the bones of the founder, John Montacute, earl of Saliſbury were removed by Maud his widow from the abbey of Cirenceſter; and here alſo, according to Dugdale's Baronage, ſeveral others of that family lie interred.

This abbey ſtands in the eaſternmoſt part of the county, near the banks of the Thames, about two miles north of the road leading from Maidenhead to Henley. Tradition ſays, Queen Elizabeth once reſided here. Since that time the houſe has been greatly repaired and modernized, and has ſerved as a manſion for ſeveral reſpectable families. This view was drawn anno 1760.

DUNNINGTON CASTLE.

THIS caſtle ſtands on an eminence, about a mile from Newbury, half a mile from Spinham Sands (the ancient Spina of Antoninus) and a ſmall diſtance from the little village of Dunnington; it is north of all theſe places, and not far from the rivulet of Lambourne.

By a manuſcript in the Cotton library, it appears that, in the time of Edward II. it belonged to Walter Abberbury, ſon and heir of Thomas Abberbury, who gave the king C. s. for it; and towards the latter part of the reign of King Richard II. Sir Richard Atterbury or Abberbury, who was a favourite of that king, obtained a licence to rebuild it; from him it deſcended to his ſon Richard, of whom, according to Urry, it was purchaſed by that prince of Engliſh poets Geoffry Chaucer.

Hither, about the year 1397, in the ſeventieth year of his age, that bard retired, in order to taſte the ſweets of contemplation and rural quiet, having ſpent the greateſt part of his life in the hurry of buſineſs and intrigues of a court; during which time he had ſeverely experienced the mutability of fortune. Here he ſpent the laſt two or three years of his life, in a felicity he had not before known; but on the death of the king, going to court, to ſolicit the continuation of ſome of his grants, he ſickened, and died in London, in the year 1400.

Bishop Gibson, in his edition of Camden, ſays, "Here was an oak ſtanding till within theſe few years, commonly called Chaucer's oak; under which he is ſaid to have penned many of his famous poems;" and Mr. Urry, relating the above circumſtance, adds, "Mr. Evelyn gives a particular account of this tree; and ſays, there were three of them planted by Chaucer; the king's oak, the queen's oak, and Chaucer's oak. The firſt of theſe traditions, is, in all likelihood, a miſtake; as moſt, if not all, of Chaucer's poems were written before he retired to this place: but the latter (namely, that he ſtudied under an oak of his own planting at Dunnington) is an abſolute impoſſibility, ſeeing that he was not in poſſeſſion of this eſtate above three years."

His ſon, Thomas Chaucer, who had been chief butler to King Richard II. and ſeveral times ambaſſador to France, ſucceeded to the caſtle; with his daughter Alice, it went to her third huſband, William de la Pole, firſt earl, and afterwards duke of Suffolk, who reſided chiefly here and at Ewlham. This lord, abuſing the power he had over that weak prince Henry VI. enraged the commons ſo much, that they procured his baniſhment; and the partizans of the duke of York, dreading his return, ſeized him in Dover road, whilſt on his paſſage, and cut off his head on the ſide of a cockboat. His body was buried at the Chartreuſe at Hull. At his deceaſe the caſtle came to his ſon John, and from him deſcended to Edmund de la Pole, duke of Suffolk, the laſt of that name; who engaging in treaſonable practices againſt Henry VII. was executed, and his eſtates conſequently eſcheated to the crown; where Dunnington remained, at leaſt, till the 37th of Henry VIII. as appears by an act of parliament then paſſed,

whereby

whereby that king was authorized to erect his castle of Dunnington, with three other places therein named, into as many honours; and to annex to them such lands as he should think proper. It afterwards came into the possession of Charles Brandon, duke of Suffolk, probably by the grant of Henry VIII. and was entire in Camden's time, who thus describes it: "A small, but very neat castle, seated on the browe of a woody hill, having a fine prospect, and windows on all sides very lightsome."

In the reign of King James I. it belonged to a family of the name of Packer; and in the time of the civil wars, was owned by Mr. John Packer; when it was fortified as a garrison for the king, and the government entrusted to Colonel Boys, being a post of great importance, commanding the high-road leading from the west to London, and that from Oxford to Newbury.

During these troubles it was twice besieged: once on the 31st of July, 1644, by Lieutenant General Middleton, who was repulsed with the loss of one colonel, eight captains, one serjeant-major, and many inferior officers and soldiers; and again the 27th of September, in the same year, by Colonel Horton, who raising a battery against it, at the foot of a hill near Newbury, fired upwards of a thousand shot, by which he demolished three of the towers, and a part of the wall. During this attack, the governor, in a salley, beat the enemy out of their trenches, and killed a lieutenant-colonel and the chief engineer, with many private men. At length, after a siege of nineteen days, the place was relieved by the king; who, at Newbury, rewarded the governor with the honour of knighthood.

After the second battle of Newbury, the king retiring towards Oxford in the night, left his heavy baggage, ammunition and artillery here. The place was summoned by the parliamentary generals, who threatened, that if it was not surrendered, they would not leave one stone upon another. To this Sir John Boys returned no other answer than, "That he was not bound to repair it, but however would, by God's help, keep the ground afterwards." This was the favourable moment for totally ruining the

the king's affairs; but the earl of Manchefter and Sir William Waller fuffered it to efcape; for, either on account of a difagreement between them, or for fome other reafon, nothing farther was done; and the king, a few days afterwards, came unexpectedly, at the head of a body of horfe, and efcorted his artillery and baggage to Oxford.

After the civil war was over, Mr. Packer pulled down the ruinous parts of the building, and with the materials erected the houfe ftanding under it, now in the occupation of Mark Bafket, Efq. The caftle at prefent belongs to Doctor Hartley, who married the heirefs of the name of Packer.

From an accurate plan, made by an officer who refides near the fpot, I am enabled to give not only the figure and dimenfions of the caftle when entire, but alfo to defcribe the works thrown up in the civil wars; all which he carefully traced out, amongft the bufhes and briars with which they are at prefent overgrown.

The walls of this caftle nearly fronted the four cardinal points of the compafs; having the north and fouth fides perpendicular on its eaft end. Thefe fides were confequently parallel. Its weft end terminated in a femi-octagon, infcribed in the half of a long oval. It was defended by four round towers; two on the angles, formed by the concurrence of the north and fouth fides with the eaft end; and two others, placed on the angles formed by the junction of the fame fides with the femi-poligon. The length of the eaft end, including the towers, was eighty-five feet; and the extent, from eaft to weft, reckoning the thicknefs of the walls, one hundred and twenty feet. Near the north-weft tower was a well; and in the fouth-eaft angle a fquare building, whofe fides meafured twenty-four feet. Two of thefe fides were formed by the exterior wall, and enclofed the tower.

The entrance was at the eaft end, through a ftone gate-houfe, having a paffage forty feet long; at the end of which is remaining the place for the portcullis. It is flanked by two round towers: that on the fouth has a ftair-cafe. This gate is now ftanding, and is fhewn in the view. In it is held the manor-court. On its weft

C. J. Besser sculpsit

ST. GEORGE'S CHAPEL, WINDSOR.

Publish'd the 9th of June 1784 by S. Hooper.

weſt ſide a ſmall drinking room has lately been added by the proprietor. Round about, and almoſt occupying the whole eminence, are the modern works, thrown up for the defence of the caſtle. Theſe explain and juſtify the ſpeech of Sir John Boys; which otherwiſe, conſidering its ſtate at that time, would have been a mere rodomontade. Their ſhape is that of an irregular pentagon; the greateſt angle fronting the ſouth, on which was a very capacious baſtion. There was another, but ſmaller, on the north-weſt angle; and the north-eaſt was defended by a demi-baſtion, placed on its ſouthern extremity. From the gorge of the great ſouthern baſtion, to the ſalient angle of the demi-baſtion, ran a double, and from thence to the north-eaſt angle of the pentagon a triple rampart. The road paſſed through theſe works, cloſe to the gate of the caſtle. This view was taken in the year 1768.

ST. GEORGE'S CHAPEL, WINDSOR.

THIS view ſhews the chapel dedicated to St. George, the houſes of the poor knights, and at a diſtance the round tower.

TANNER, in his Notitia Monaſtica, gives the following hiſtory of this chapel:

" IN the caſtle here was an old free chapel, dedicated to King Edward the Confeſſor, in which King Henry I. placed eight ſecular prieſts, who ſeem never to have been incorporated nor endowed with lands, but to have been maintained by penſions yearly paid out of the king's exchequer. And in the park here was, in the beginning of King Edward the Second's reign, a royal chapel for thirteen chaplains and four clerks, who had yearly ſalaries out of the manors of Langley Mark and Sippenham, in Bucks. King Edward III. anno regni IV. removed thoſe chaplains and clerks out of the park into the caſtle; and ſhortly after added four more chaplains and two clerks to them. But this victorious prince, being afterwards deſirous of raiſing this place of his nativity to much greater ſplendor, refounded this ancient free chapel royal, and in A. D. 1352, eſtabliſhed it as a collegiate church, to the honour of the Virgin Mary, St. George, and St. Edward, King and Confeſſor, conſiſting of a cuſtos (ſince called a dean) twelve great canons, or prebendaries, thirteen vicars, or minor canons, four clerks, ſix choriſters, twenty-ſix poor alms-knights, beſides other officers; their yearly revenues were rated, 26 Henry VIII. at 1602l. 2s. 1d. ob. 9. This free chapel was particularly excepted out of the act for ſuppreſſing colleges, &c. 1. Edward VI. c. 14. and ſtill ſubſiſts in a flouriſhing condition." Thus far reſpecting its foundation and endowment; its preſent ſtate and form is thus accurately delineated in the work entitled "London and its Environs deſcribed."

"Among the buildings of this noble palace we have mentioned the chapel of St. George, ſituated in the middle of the lower court: this ancient ſtructure, which is now the pureſt ſtyle of Gothic architecture, was firſt erected by King Edward III. in the year 1337, ſoon after the foundation of the college for the honour of the order of the garter, and dedicated to St. George, the patron of England; but however noble the firſt deſign might be, King Edward IV. not finding it entirely compleated, enlarged the ſtructure, and deſigned the preſent building, together with the houſes of the dean and canons, ſituated on the north and weſt ſides of the chapel; the work was afterwards carried on by Henry VII. who finiſhed the body of the chapel, and Sir Reginald Bray, knight of the garter, and the favourite of that king, aſſiſted in ornamenting the chapel and compleating the roof.

The architecture of the inſide has always been eſteemed for its neatneſs and great beauty; and in particular the ſtone roof is reckoned an excellent piece of workmanſhip. It is an ellipſis, ſupported by Gothic pillars, whoſe ribs and groins ſuſtain the whole cieling, every part of which has ſome different device well finiſhed, as the arms of Edward the Confeſſor, Edward III. Henry VI. Edward IV. Henry VII. and Henry VIII. alſo the arms of England and France quarterly, the croſs of St. George, the roſe, portcullis, lion rampant, unicorn, &c.

In

In a chapel in the ſouth aiſle is repreſented in ancient painting, the hiſtory of John the Baptiſt; and in the ſame aiſle are painted on large pannels of oak, neatly carved and decorated with the ſeveral devices peculiar to each prince, the portraits at full length of Prince Edward, ſon to Henry VI. Edward IV. Edward V. and Henry VII. In the north aiſle is a chapel dedicated to St. Stephen, wherein the hiſtory of that ſaint is painted on the pannels, and well preſerved. In the firſt of theſe pannels St. Stephen is repreſented preaching to the people; in the ſecond, he is before Herod's tribunal; in the third, he is ſtoning; and in the fourth, he is repreſented dead. At the eaſt end of this aiſle is the chapter-houſe of the college, in which is a portrait at full length, by a maſterly hand, of the victorious Edward III. in his robes of ſtate, holding in his right hand a ſword, and bearing the crowns of France and Scotland, in token of the many victories he gained over thoſe nations. On one ſide of this painting is kept the ſword of that great and warlike prince.

But what appears moſt worthy of notice is the choir. On each ſide are the ſtalls of the ſovereign and knights companions of the moſt noble order of the garter, with the helmet, mantling, creſt, and ſword of each knight ſet up over his ſtall on a canopy of ancient carving curiouſly wrought, and over the canopy is affixed the banner or arms of each knight, properly blazoned on ſilk; and on the back of the ſtalls are the titles of the knights, with their arms neatly engraved and blazoned on copper. The ſovereign's ſtall is on the right hand of the entrance into the choir, and is covered with purple velvet and cloth of gold, and has a canopy and complete furniture of the ſame valuable materials; his banner is likewiſe of velvet, and his mantling of cloth of gold. The prince's ſtall is on the left, and has no diſtinction from thoſe of the reſt of the knights companions; the whole ſociety, according to the ſtatutes of the inſtitution, being companions and colleagues, equal in honour and power.

The altar-piece was, ſoon after the reſtoration, adorned with cloth of gold and purple damaſk by King Charles II. but on removing

moving the wainſcot of one of the chapels in 1707, a fine painting of the Lord's Supper was found, which being approved of by Sir James Thornhill, Verrio, and other eminent maſters, was repaired and placed on the altar-piece. Near the altar is the queen's gallery for the accommodation of the ladies at an inſtallation. In a vault under the marble pavement of this choir are interred the bodies of Henry VIII. and Jane Seymour his queen, King Charles I. and a daughter of the late Queen Anne.

In the ſouth aiſle, near the door of the choir, is buried Henry VI. and the arch near which he was interred was ſumptuouſly decorated by Henry VIII. with the royal enſigns, and other devices, but they are now much defaced by time. In this chapel is alſo the monument of Edward, earl of Lincoln, lord high admiral of England in the reign of Queen Elizabeth, erected by his lady, who is alſo interred with him: the monument is of alabaſter, with pillars of porphyry. Another, within a neat ſcreen of braſs work, is erected to the memory of Charles Somerſet, earl of Worceſter, and knight of the garter, who died in 1526, and his lady, daughter to William, earl of Huntingdon. A ſtately monument of white marble erected to the memory of Henry Somerſet, duke of Beaufort, and knight of the garter, who died in 1699. There are here alſo the tombs of Sir George Manners, Lord Roos, that of the Lord Haſtings, chamberlain to Edward IV. and ſeveral others.

Before we conclude our account of this ancient chapel, it will be proper to obſerve, that King James II. made uſe of it for the ſervice of popery; and maſs being publickly performed there, it has ever ſince been neglected and ſuffered to run to ruin; and being no appendage to the collegiate church waits the royal favour to retrieve it from the diſgrace of its preſent ſituation."

READING ABBEY, Pl. 1.

READING ABBEY. (Plate I.)

THIS was a mitred parliamentary abbey, and one of the moſt conſiderable in England, both for the magnificence of its buildings and the richneſs of its endowments. King Henry I. began to lay the foundations anno 1121, having pulled down a ſmall deſerted nunnery, by ſome ſaid to have been founded by Elfrida, mother in law of King Edward, called the martyr, in expiation of the murder of that king at Corfe Caſtle. The new monaſtery was completed in four years; but the church was either not conſecrated till the reign of Henry II. or elſe that ceremony was, for the ſecond time, performed in the year 1163 or 1164, by Archbiſhop Becket, the king and many of the nobility being preſent. It was dedicated to the honour of the Holy Trinity, the Bleſſed Virgin Mary, and St. John the Evangeliſt. Browne Willis, from divers good authorities and reaſons, to theſe adds St. James, making its tutelars ſtand in the following order; the Holy Trinity, the Bleſſed Virgin Mary, St. James, and St. John the Evangeliſt. It was however commonly called the abbey of St. Mary at Reading, probably from the extraordinary veneration paid in thoſe days to the Holy Virgin, which even exceeded that ſhewn to the name of Chriſt. It was endowed for two hundred monks of the Benedictine order, although at the inquiſition, 50 Edward III. there were only one hundred.

In this abbey was buried the body of King Henry I. its founder; but his heart, eyes, tongue, brains and bowels, according to Doctor Ducarrel, in his Anglo Norman Antiquities, were depoſited under a handſome monument, before the high altar, in the ancient priory church of Notre Dame du Pres, otherwiſe the Bonnes Nouvelles, at Rouen, founded anno 1060, and deſtroyed during the ſiege at Rouen, in 1592.

Here likewiſe was interred Adeliza, his ſecond queen; and, according to ſome writers, his daughter Maud the empreſs, mother to King Henry II. though others, with more probability, fix the place of her ſepulchre at Bec, in Normandy. Over her tomb here, it is ſaid, were the following verſes:

> Ortu magna, viro major, ſed maxima partu,
> Hic jacet Henrici filia, ſponſa, parens.

In this place was alſo buried, at the feet of his great grandfather, William, eldeſt ſon of King Henry II. likewiſe Conſtance, daughter of Edmund de Langley, duke of York; Anne, counteſs of Warwick; a ſon and daughter of Richard, earl of Cornwall; and a great number of other perſons of rank and diſtinction. King Henry I. had a tomb, on which was his effigies, as appears from a record, quoted by Tanner; and probably there were many other magnificent monuments, which were demoliſhed or removed, when the monaſtery was converted into a royal manſion; but it is not likely that the bones of the perſons buried were diſturbed and thrown out, as aſſerted by Sandford, neither was the abbey turned into a ſtable; for Camden ſays, "The monaſtery, wherein King Henry I. was interred, was converted into a royal ſeat; adjoining to which ſtands a fair ſtable, ſtored with noble horſes of the king's." The demolition of theſe monuments is thus pathetically lamented.

> ———————— Heu dira piacula! primus
> Neuſtrius Henricus, ſitus hic inglorius urna
> Nunc jacet ejectus, tumulum novus advena quærit
> Fruſtra; nam regi tenues invidit arenas
> Auri ſacra fames, regum metuenda ſepulchris.

History particulariſes only two councils held here, in the refectory, or rather the church; one in the reign of King John, by the pope's legate; the other in that of Edward I. by Archbiſhop Peckham: there is reaſon however to believe, that divers others were held at the ſame place; likewiſe in this monaſtery a parliament was aſſembled 31 Henry VI. wherein divers laws were enacted.

This abbey had funds for entertaining the poor and travellers of all ſorts; which, according to William of Malmſbury, was ſo well

well performed, that more money was ſpent in hoſpitality than expended on the monks. Yet nevertheleſs, Hugh, the eighth abbot, having, as he ſays in his grant, obſerved an improper partiality, in the entertainment of the rich in preference to the poor, (although the founder, King Henry, had directed, that hoſpitality ſhould be ſhewn indifferently to all perſons) he therefore founded an hoſpital, near the gate of the monaſtery, for the reception of ſuch pilgrims and poor perſons as were not admitted into the abbey; and likewiſe gave to the ſaid hoſpital the church of St. Laurence, for ever, for the maintaining of thirteen poor perſons, in diet, clothes, and other neceſſaries: allowing for the keeping of thirteen more, out of the uſual alms. This, in all likelihood, though done under the ſpecious pretence of charity, was only a method taken to exclude the meaner perſons from the table of the abbey, which was at that time, when inns were not ſo common as at preſent, often frequented by travellers of the better ſort. By this means alſo a conſiderable ſaving would accrue to the houſe; the fare of this hoſpital being, doubtleſs, ſuitable to the condition of the perſons there entertained.

An hoſpital for poor lepers was alſo founded near the church, by Aucherius, the ſecond abbot; it was dedicated to St. Mary Magdalen. Here they were comfortably maintained, and governed by divers rules and regulations, admirably well calculated for preſerving peace, harmony, and good order. Among them were theſe: Any one diſputing, and being ordered by the maſter to hold his peace, not obeying at the third monition, was to have nothing but bread and water that day. He who gave the lye was ſubject to the ſame puniſhment attended with ſome humiliating circumſtances: if after this he continued ſullen, or did not patiently ſubmit to his caſtigation, it was to be repeated another day: when, if he ſtill perſevered in his obſtinacy, he was to loſe the benefit of the charity for forty days. A blow was immediate expulſion; and none were to go abroad, or into the laundreſs's houſe, without a companion.

Hugh

Hugh Farringdon, the laſt abbot, refuſing to deliver up his abbey to the viſitors, was attainted of high treaſon, on ſome charge trumped up againſt him; and in the month of November, 1539, with two of his monks, named Rugg and Onion, was hanged, drawn and quartered at Reading. This happened on the ſame day on which the abbot of Glaſtonbury ſuffered the like ſentence, for the ſimilar provocation.

At the diſſolution, the revenues of this monaſtery were valued at 1938l. 14s. 3d. ob. q. Dugdale; 2116l. 3s. 9d. ob. Speed. The abbot had an excellent ſummer retirement at Cholſey, near Wallingford, called the Abbot's Place; by which name it was granted to Sir Francis Englefield, 4 and 5 Philip and Mary. The ſite of this abbey now belongs to the crown; the preſent leſſees for a term of years, are John Blagrave, Eſq; and the repreſentatives of Henry Vanſittart, Eſq.

The abbey church ſeems to have been a ſpacious fabric, built in the form of a croſs: ſome of its walls were lately remaining; they were of rough flint, and were formerly caſed with ſquared ſtone; but of this they have been ſtripped. There is likewiſe to be ſeen, the remainder of our lady's chapel and the refectory; this laſt is eighty-four feet long, and forty-eight broad: and is, according to Willis, the room in which was held the parliament before mentioned. The cloiſters have long been totally demoliſhed. About eight years ago, a very conſiderable quantity of the abbey ruins, ſome of the pieces as much as two teams of horſes could draw, compoſed of gravel and flints, cemented together with what the bricklayers now call grout, a fluid mortar, conſiſting moſtly of lime, was removed, for General Conway's uſe, to build a bridge in the road betwixt Wargrave and Henley, adjoining to his park.

This view, drawn in 1762, repreſents the great gate of the abbey, which was formerly embattled; about thirty years ago it was judged neceſſary to take off the embattlements: this has conſiderably hurt its appearance.

PLATE

READING ABBEY. PL. 2.

(PLATE II.)

This plate ſhews the ſouth view of the remains of this once magnificent abbey, majeſtic even in its ruins!

The following circumſtances relative to this monaſtery occur in Prynne's Hiſtory of Papal Uſurpations. In the year 1215, the abbot of Reading was one of the delegates appointed by the pope together with Pandulph the legate, and the biſhop of Wincheſter, for the promulgating the excommunication againſt the barons concerned in the oppoſition to King John; as alſo in the ſucceeding year, when divers of thoſe barons were excommunicated particularly and by name. In 39 Henry III. the maintenance of two Jewiſh converts, both women, was impoſed on this houſe; and in the ſame reign, the king attempting to borrow a large ſum of money from ſome of the great abbies, among which were Weſtminſter, St. Albans, Reading, and Waltham, was poſitively refuſed by the abbot of Reading.

Fuller in his Church Hiſtory has this anecdote of one of the abbots, which he ſtiles "a pleaſant and true ſtory: King Henry VIII. as he was hunting in Windſor Foreſt, either caſually loſt, or (more probably) wilfully loſing himſelf, ſtruck down about dinner time to the abbey of Reading, where, diſguiſing himſelf (much for delight, more for diſcovery to ſee unſeen) he was invited to the abbot's table, and paſſed for one of the king's guard; a place to which the proportion of his perſon might properly entitle him. A ſir-loyne of beef was ſet before him (ſo knighted, ſaith tradition, by this King Henry) on which the king laid on luſtily, not diſgracing one of that place for whom he was miſtaken. Well fare thy heart (quoth the abbot) and here in a cup of ſack I remember the health of his grace your maſter. I would give an hundred pounds on the condition I could feed ſo heartily on beef as you doe. Alas! my weak and ſqueazie ſtomach will hardly digeſt the wing of a ſmall rabbet or chicken. The king pleaſantly pledged him, and heartily thanked him for his good

 chear;

chear; after dinner departed as undiſcovered as he came thither. Some weeks after the abbot was ſent for by a purſuivant, brought up to London, clapt in the Tower, kept cloſe priſoner, fed for a ſhort time with bread and water; yet not ſo empty his body of food, as his mind was filled with fears, creating many ſuſpicions to himſelf, when and how, he had incurred the king's diſpleaſure. At laſt a ſir-loyne of beef was ſet before him, on which the abbot fed as the farmer of his grange, and verified the proverb, that two hungry meals make the third a glutton. In ſprings King Henry out of a private lobbie, where he had placed himſelf, the inviſible ſpectator of the abbot's behaviour. My lord (quoth the king) preſently depoſite your hundred pounds in gold, or elſe no going hence all the daies of your life. I have been your phyſician to cure you of your ſqueazie ſtomach; and here, as I deſerve, I demand my fee for the ſame. The abbot down with his duſt, and glad he had eſcaped ſo, returned to Reading; as ſomewhat lighter in purſe, ſo much more merrier in heart than when he came thence."

The ſucceſſion of the abbots is thus given by Browne Willis, in his Hiſtory of Mitred Abbies: " 1. Hugh prior of Lewis, co. Suſſex, was at the time of the foundation, an. 1125, made the firſt abbat by the founder Henry I. about four years after which, viz. an. 1129, he was tranſlated to the archbiſhopric of Roan in Normandy, where he died the Ides of Nov. 1134. On his quitting this abbey, he was therein ſucceeded by, 2. Auſgerus, called in the Monaſticon, Aucherius. He founded an houſe of lepers to the honour of St. Mary Magdalen; and dying an. 1134, or as Matthew of Weſtminſter ſays, 6 Cal. Feb. 1135, was ſucceeded by, 3. Edward, who died in December, an. 1154, and was ſucceeded by, 4. Reginald, made abbat the ſame year; he died 3 Nones Feb. 1158, as Matthew of Weſtminſter ſays, and was ſucceeded by, 5. Roger; in whoſe time Thomas archbiſhop of Canterbury dedicated the monaſtery of Reading anew, King Henry II. and many of the nobility being preſent: he died 13 Cal. Feb. an. 1164, and was ſucceeded by, 6. William, a religious and prudent man,

man, made archbiſhop of Bourdeaux, an. 1173, by the ſpecial favour of King Henry; whoſe ſucceſſor, 7. Joſeph, deceaſing about the year 1180, was ſucceeded by, 8. Hugh, a learned writer, and a ſpecial benefactor to this houſe. He erected an hoſpital without the gate of the abbey, to maintain 26 poor people, and all ſtrangers who ſhould paſs that way. An. 1199, being made abbat of Cluny, he quitted this abbey, and was ſucceeded the next year, viz. 1200, by, 9. Helias; who dying 12 Cal. Aug. 1212, was ſucceeded, after near a year's vacancy, by, 10. Simon. He died the Ides of Feb. an. 1226, and was ſucceeded by, 11. Adam de Latebar, or Lathbury, prior of Leominſter, co. Hereford; upon whoſe deceaſe, an. 1238, 8 Ides April, 12. Richard, ſub-prior of this houſe, was appointed abbat. He continued but a ſmall time, and was ſucceeded by, 13. Adam, who reſigned an. 1249, and was ſucceeded by another of his name, viz. 14. Adam, ſacriſt of this houſe; on whoſe death or ceſſion the ſame year, 15. William, ſub-prior of Coventry, became abbat; whoſe ſucceſſor, 16. Richard, dying anno 1261, 17. Richard de Banaſter, alias de Rading, was elected abbat. He preſided 8 years, and was ſucceeded an. 1268, by, 18. Robert de Burghare; who reſigning an. 1287, 19. William de Sutton ſucceeded as abbat: he died an. 1305, and was ſucceeded by, 20. Nicholas de Quaplode, who had his election confirmed in September 1305. He began to build our lady's chapel on the 13 Cal. of May, an. 1314; and deceaſing an. 1327, had for his ſucceſſor, 21. John de Appelford. He died an. 1341, and was ſucceeded by, 22. Henry de Appelford. He governed twenty years, and dying July 29, 1360, 35 Edward III. was ſucceeded by, 23. William de Dombleton, confirmed abbat, an. 1361. Dr. Tanner informs me, he has met with one Nicholas, abbat of Reading, an. 1362; but this ſeems to be a miſtake; for William Dombleton died poſſeſſed of this abbey, an. 1368, and was then ſucceeded by, 24. John de Sutton: upon whoſe death, which happened an. 1378, 25. Richard de Yately was elected abbat. I do not find when he died; but it appears from Saliſbury Regiſter, that he preſided an. 1396; and 'tis probable that he did ſo ſo till the year 1409, when, 26. Thomas Erle was elected. He died an. 1430, and was ſucceeded December the 1ſt, the ſame year, by, 27. Thomas Henley; who dying November 11, 1445, 28. John Thorne was preferred to this dignity January the 7th following. During his government he ſuppreſſed an old alms-houſe of poor ſiſters, near St. Laurence's church, founded in all likelihood by one of the preceding abbats of Reading, and employed the revenues to the uſe of the almoner of this abbey; which King Henry VII. being informed of, at his coming to Reading, he ordered abbat Thorne to convert both the houſe and lands to pious uſes; whereupon the abbat deſired the king that it might be made a grammar ſchool; which being aſſented to, one William Dene, a rich man and ſervant of the abbey, gave 200 marks towards the advancement of the ſaid ſchool; which, Mr. Leland tells us, appeared from his epitaph in the abbey church. This abbat died before this ſettlement was perfected, viz. an. 1486, in the ſecond year of King Henry VII. and was ſucceeded by another, 29. John Thorne; who died an. 1519, and was ſucceeded by, 30. Thomas Worceſter. He governed but a ſhort time; for in the next year, viz. 1520, he was ſucceeded by, 31. Hugh Farringdon, the laſt abbat, executed at Reading, as has before been obſerved, anno 1539. I find only 59l. 13s. remaining in charge out of the revenues of this late convent, to 13 monks and novices; the execution of the abbat probably depriving the dependants of their claims to fees and annuities. Theſe monks were Elizeus Burgeſs, whoſe penſion was 6l. as were John Fryſon, John Wright, John Harper, John Mylly, John Turner, Luke Wythorne, Thomas Taylor, 5l. each. Robert Bayner's penſion was 4l. 6s. 8d. John South's 3l. 6s. 8d. and Richard Purſer's, and Richard Butts, 2l. apiece." This view was drawn anno 1759.

STIVECLE,

BUCKINGHAMSHIRE.

IS an inland county. During the time prior to the landing of the Romans it was included in the division of Catieuchlani; and after their conquest it was included in their third province of Flavia Cæsariensis. During the Heptarchy it belonged to the kingdom of Mercia, which commenced in 582, and terminated in 827, having had eighteen kings; and it is now included in the Norfolk circuit, the diocese of Lincoln, and the province of Canterbury. It is bounded on the north by Northamptonshire, south by Berkshire, east by Bedfordshire, Hertfordshire, and Middlesex, and west by Oxfordshire. It is of an oblong form, whose greatest extent is from north to south. It contains 441,000 acres, has above 111,400 inhabitants, 185 parishes, 73 vicarages, is 39 miles long, 18 broad, and 109 in circumference. It has 15 market towns, viz. Buckingham and Aylesbury the county towns, Marlow, Newport Pagnell, Winslow, Wendover, Beaconsfield, Wiccomb, Chesham, Amersham, Stony Stratford, Colnbrook, Ivingho, Oulney, Risborough; besides the considerable villages of Eaton and Fenny Stratford, and 613 others inferior. It is divided into 8 hundreds, provides 560 men for the militia, sends 14 Parliament Men, and pays 12 parts of the land

land tax. Its rivers are the Thames, Oufe, Coln, Wicham, Amerfham, Ifa, Tame, and Loddon. Its chief produce is bone-lace, paper, corn, fine wool, and breeding rams. The moft noted places are the Chiltern Hills, Vale of Aylefbury, Bernwood-Foreft, Wooburn-Heath, and 15 Parks. The air is generally good, and the foil moftly chalk or marle.

THE Roman encampments in this county are but few, viz. at Ellefborough, near Monk's Rifborough, and at Prince's Rifborough. As to the Roman military roads, that called Watling Street croffes the Oufe into Northamptonfhire, to Lactodorum or Stony Stratford, and from thence to Verulam or St. Albans, a branch of which goes to Sandy, in Bedfordfhire, and from thence to Ravenfworth in Hertfordfhire, and thence again to Verulam or St. Albans. Newport Pagnell is a corruption of Nova Porta, a name given the Roman military ways in fome counties. Near Calverton is an eminence where was a Roman camp, and near it paffes the old road that led over the Oufe to Pafham, that ancient pafs of the river, which the Saxon hiftorians fay was maintained by Edward the Elder againft the Danes. On the difufe of this road, the bridge and road by Old Stratford was erected. Both Newport and Bedford have evident proofs of a great road going through them, fuppofed to be the Watling Street, and was the only way from Daventry to London before Edward the Confeffor's time.

ANTIQUITIES in this COUNTY worthy NOTICE.

Aylefbury Church
Bolbec Caftle, near Winflow
Cheyneis Church, near Amerfham
Colnbrook Chapel
Eaton College, near Windfor
Notley Abbey, near Winflow
Oulney Church, near Newport Pagnel
Stukely Church, near Monk's Rifborough.

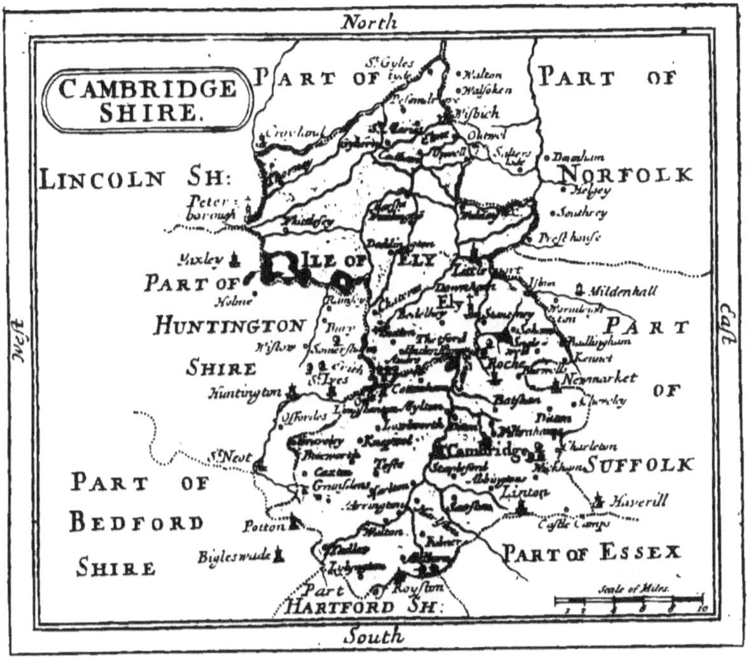

CAMBRIDGESHIRE.

Is an inland county. Prior to the arrival of the Romans it was included in the antient diviſion of the Iceni; and after their conqueſt in the third province of Flavia Cæſarienſis, which reached from the Thames to the Humber. During the Heptarchy it belonged tp the kingdom of the Eaſt Angles, the ſixth kingdom, which began in 575, and ended in 792, having had 14 kings; and it is now included in the Norfolk circuit, the dioceſe of Ely, and province of Canterbury. It is bounded on the weſt by Huntingdonſhire and Bedfordſhire; on the eaſt by Norfolk and Suffolk; on the ſouth by Hertfordſhire and Eſſex; and on the north by Lincolnſhire. It is about 40 miles in length from north to ſouth, and 25 in breadth from eaſt to weſt, and is 130 miles in circumference, containing near 570,000 acres. It has about 17,400 houſes, 140,000 inhabitants, is divided into 17 hundreds, in which are one city, Ely; 8 market towns, viz. Cambridge, which is the ſhire town and a celebrated univerſity; Caxton, Linton, Merch, Newmarket, Soham, Wiſbeach, Thorney, and part of Royſton; 220 villages, 64 pariſhes, ſends four Members to Parliament, pays one part of the land tax, and provides 480 men in the militia. Its only rivers

rivers are the Cam, Nene, and the Ouſe; but it has an innumerable number of drains in the fenny part; a ſpacious plain containing above 300,000 acres of land, which extends into the counties of Norfolk, Suffolk, Huntingdon, and Lincolnſhire. The Iſle of Ely is the north diviſion of the county, and extends ſouth almoſt as far as Cambridge. In the iſle the air is damp, foul, and unwholſome; but in the ſouth-eaſt parts it is pure and ſalubrious, and produces great plenty of bread, corn, and barley, ſaffron, fiſh, fowl, and game. The moſt noted place, beſides the univerſity and Newmarket Heath, is Gogmagog-hills. Here are five parks, with Streatham, Soham, Whittleſea, and Ramſay Meers.

The Roman, Saxon, or Daniſh encampments, are at Grantcheſter, near Cambridge; at Royſton, at Arbury near Cambridge, upon Gogmagog-hills near Cambridge, and near Audre.

The military Roman road is viſible from Cheſterton to Gogmagog-hills, where is a camp with treble ditches, ſuppoſed to be the Camboritum of the Romans. It ſtands on an eminence upon the great road from Colcheſter to Lincoln, within a few miles of the interſection of the Erming and Ikeniſng Streets, and within ſight of both. Camulodonum, now Caſtle Camps, is the next Cambridgeſhire ſtation.

ANTIQUITIES in this COUNTY worthy NOTICE.

Angleſey Abbey, near Waterbeach.
Barnwell Priory, near Cambridge
Pythagoras's School, and the different Colleges of the Univerſity and publick Schools, with the Town-Gaol, Croſs, Conduit, &c.
Cambridge Caſtle, Round Church,
Caſtle Camps, near Linton
Denny Priory, near Waterbeach
Ely Cathedral, and St. Mary's Church, near it
Grantcheſter, near Cambridge
Incleton Nunnery, near Foulmere
King's College Chapel and Bridge, in Cambridge
Ramſey Abbey Gateway
Soham Church, near Ely
Spiney Abbey, near Soham
Thorney Abbey, near Peterborough
Whittleſea Church.

Stewkley Church, Bucks

CAMBRIDGE CASTLE.

Pub.d 24 Dec.r 1783 by S. Hooper.

STIVECLE, OR STUKELY CHURCH.

THE ſolidity of this building, as well as its circular arches and zig-zag ornaments, evidently mark its great antiquity. The particular time of its erection is not known; it is however mentioned as early as the reign of Henry II. when it was given by Geffery de Clinton, chamberlain to that king, to the priory of Kenelworth in Warwickſhire, of which his father was founder. It is there called the church of Stivecle or Stiff Clay, in all likelihood from the kind of ſoil whereon it ſtood. The preſent church muſt be from its ſtile at leaſt as old as that period.

IT is a vicarage in the dioceſe of Lincoln and deanry of Mureſley; the church is dedicated to St. Mary; the biſhop of Oxford is both proprietor and patron; the certified value 68l. 19s. 8d. and rated in the king's books at 9l. 9s. 7d. the yearly tenths, 18s. 11½.

THIS plate is engraved from a drawing made at the expence of the late Dr. Littleton, biſhop of Carliſle, and communicated to the author. The original is in the library of the Society of Antiquaries of London.

CAMBRIDGE CASTLE.

IS ſituated on the north ſide of the river Cam, near the bridge; and was, with many others, erected by William the Conqueror, in the firſt year of his reign, for the purpoſe of awing his newly acquired ſubjects. It appears, by Domeſday-book, that eighteen houſes were deſtroyed for the ſite of this caſtle, which was both ſtrong and ſpacious, having a noble hall, with many other magnificent apartments. In the year 1216, in the reign of King John, it was beſieged and taken by the barons; and about the year 1291, King Edward I. was entertained here two days and two nights. He is ſaid to be the firſt king who ever honoured it with the royal preſence. And in 1299 that prince granted it with the town of Cambridge to Queen Margaret as part of her dower. In procefs of time this caftle being neglected, and falling to ruin, the materials of its great hall were given, by King Henry IV. to the mafter and wardens of King's Hall, towards building their chapel; and Queen Mary granted as much of the ftones and timber to Sir John Huddleftone, as fufficed to build his houfe at Sawfton. Great part of it was ftanding in Cambden's time, who calls it "a large antient caftle, which feemeth now to have lived out his full time;" and Mr. Arthur Agard, an ingenious antiquary, his cotemporary, fays, the JULLIET, or KEEP, was ftanding when he was a fcholar at Cambridge; but adds, that fince his time it had been defaced.

In an antient view of the town of Cambridge, printed at Strafbourg, in the year 1575, in the poffeffion of Doctor Ducarrel, which feems to belong to fome topographical book, the caftle is reprefented entire, and ftanding on an eminence; its figure, an irregular pentagon, having its north and fouth fides (which are perpendicular to that on the eaft) parallel, and much longer than the others: thefe fides are flanked by four towers; three of them fquare, and one round. The round tower is at the fouth-eaft angle, and is much larger than the reft; the entrance is through a tower, facing fouth-weft.

On the infide, adjoining to the walls, are buildings which have the appearance of dwelling-houfes, and were probably apartments for the governor, and barracks for the garrifon. As that print was publifhed abroad, and well engraved, it was in all likelihood copied from fome Englifh draught, of approved authority, and of much earlier date; and indeed it thoroughly agrees with the plan annexed, which had every mark of authenticity. In the year 1769, when this view was taken, nothing remained but the gate-houfe, which then ferved for the county prifon. At a fmall diftance from this building, is one of thofe artificial mounts, fo frequently to be found near antient caftles. Immediately under it, and oppofite the windows of the prifon, ftands the gallows for the execution of malefactors.

PYTHA-

Plan & View of Cambridge Castle, from an Ancient Drawing, formerly belonging to General Armstrong; supposed to be Drawn about the Reign of Queen Elizabeth.

B. The Julliet or great Tower mentioned by Ralp Agard vide Antiquarian discourses.

Pythagoras's School.

PYTHAGORAS'S SCHOOL.

FOR the following very ingenious diſſertation and deſcription of this ancient building, I am obliged to a clergyman in the neighbourhood of Cambridge, well verſed in Engliſh antiquities, and particularly in thoſe of the county wherein he reſides.

BEFORE I attempt to dive into the very obſcure origin of this ancient ſtructure, it may be uſeful to trace its transfer from its remoteſt owners down to its preſent proprietors; and this from authentic documents in the archieves of Merton college, to whom it now belongs.

THE priory of St. Giles's, in Cambridge, was founded about 1092, by Picot, baron of Brunne, with Hugolina, his wife, near the place where the church of St. Giles now ſtands: but the ſituation being found to be too ſtrait and confined, it was removed, ſome twenty years after, to a place called Bernewelle, on the other ſide of the river. Whether this building was any part of that foundation, I believe is more than can be aſcertained: certain it is, however, that it was part of their poſſeſſions. For Laurence de Stanfield, prior, with the convent of Bernewelle, demiſed the premiſes, formerly granted to Algar Nobilis of Cambridge, to Hervey Fitz Euſtace, of the ſame place; this was about the year 1233, as it is witneſſed by Jeremiah de Caxton, then ſheriff of the county. Much about the ſame time, Baldwin, the ſon of Baldwin Blangernun, of Cambridge, conveys this meſſuage to Hervey Fitz Euſtace, for one of the witneſſes to the conveyance was Geoffrey de Hatferd, high ſheriff of the county: now he was in that office from 1224 to 1232. The ſame perſon alſo grants the ſaid meſſuage, with an holme, to the ſaid Hervey: this was towards the end of the reign of Henry III. as Jer. de Caxton is a witneſs, together with Henry de Colvyle, then ſheriff; but as he was in that office both in 1236, 1240 and 1250, it may be difficult to aſcertain the preciſe year. In the copy I have ſeen of this conveyance, the ſheriff is called Hen. de Colȳ; but as no ſuch

ſuch perſon ever was ſheriff, and a Hen. de Colvyle, an old family, ſtill in being, was evidently ſo about this time, I have no difficulty to ſuppoſe him to be the perſon meant, and that the tranſcriber made a miſtake. Together with the meſſuage was conveyed an holme: this I make no doubt, are the ſwampy low grounds and pond-yards, lying on the bank of the river, and extending towards the library of St. John's college, on this ſide of the river.

About the year 1256, John Shotley, prior of Bernewelle, with his convent, demiſed the ſaid premiſes to Euſtace Fitz-Hervey, probably ſon of the former, which formerly had been in the occupation of Henry, the ſon of Edward Froſt, whom I take to have been the original founder of St. John's Hoſpital, in Cambridge, about 1210, by giving the ſite on which the hoſpital was built. So that the college of St. John the Evangeliſt, now grafted on that hoſpital, and ſtill enjoying its poſſeſſions, may juſtly be accounted the firſt of our preſent colleges.

By an indenture, dated at Cambridge 41 Henry III. anno 1256, Euſtace, the ſon of Hervey Dunning of Cambridge, leaſes to Mag. Guy de Caſtro Bernardi, the meſſuage that belonged to his father Hervey, and in which he lived, with other lands, &c. except the capital meſſuage which he had purchaſed of Baldwin Blangernun: and in the ſame year the ſaid Euſtace mortgaged his eſtate, together with this capital meſſuage, to the aboveſaid M. Guy de Caſtro Bernardi, an ancient family in Cambridge; on whoſe deceaſe, Richard, ſon and heir of Euſtace Fitz-Hervey Dunning, ſeiſed, as lord of the manor, the ſaid premiſes into his hands: whereupon William de Maneſend, nephew and heir of the ſaid M. Guy, brought it into the King's Bench, where it was tried before Sir Robert Fulco, chief juſtice of that bench, where the cauſe was traverſed, and given againſt the ſaid Richard Dunning. This happened about 1270, and probably brought on, on purpoſe to create a clear and legal title to the eſtate: for in the ſame year, this William de Maneſend conveyed the ſame to the preſent proprietors. About the year 1256, it appears that the houſe was in the occupation of St. John's Hoſpital, in Cambridge;

bridge; for about that time the mafters and brethren of that hofpital grant to Henry Fitz-Euftace, and his heirs for ever, two beds with their neceffary coverlids, for the ufe of infirm perfons, in their ftone houfe, obliging themfelves to find a chaplain, and to celebrate mafs, efpecially for the foul of Euftace Fitz-Hervey, in acknowledgment for the lands granted by him to their hofpital, lying in Cambridge, Chefterton and Madingley. No doubt he was a confiderable benefactor to that religious houfe, though omitted as fuch, by the worthy Mr. Baker, in his excellent hiftory of that foundation; for fo late as the year 1284, when Richard Cheverel was mafter, they oblige themfelves to find and maintain a chaplain, one of their brethren, for the above purpofe, within their own houfe. This was after Merton college was in poffeffion of the meffuage, but yet for the lands which he had conveyed to them, they were obliged to celebrate for him as a benefactor. The manor was fettled on the college by bifhop Walter de Merton in 1270, as appears by this defcription of it by the founder in his fecond charter, and the title he added to it. Terr. et Red. quondam Rici Dunning & Wilkelmi de Manefeld, quos ipfi in Cantebrigia & Portibus adjacentibus mihi dimiferunt. And they were the chief perfons the college was concerned with in the purchafe.

The great difficulty is ftill behind, I mean the original ufe and deftination of the building and by whom erected. That it was not defigned for any religious purpofe is plain, for its having no one part of it proper for an altar to be placed in, and its having only one entrance would be equally inconvenient. My firft thoughts were, and I have not altered them, that it was a part of Picot's foundation for a prior and fix canons: where the fite being found too confined, Pagan Peverel removed them to Bernewelle; whofoever looks at St. Giles's Church, which has all the marks of one of our moft ancient buildings, muft be convinced, that could not be the fite of Picot's foundation, both as the choir and church would be too fmall; but more efpecially, as it is bounded and hemmed in on two fides, the fouth and weft by the king's highway, and to the north by the precincts of and

 afcent

aſcent to the caſtle. The way alſo from them to the river, muſt conſequently have been acroſs the road to Cheſterton, which would have been inconvenient.

Possibly the priory might receive its denomination of St. Giles's from its vicinity to this pariſh church, even from the founders: in the ſame manner as Corpus Chriſti College acquires its uſual one from the adjoining church of St. Benedict.

But even allowing the ſituation of this priory to have been where I would rather ſuppoſe it to have been placed, ſtill they muſt have been much cramped and confined, which probably occaſioned their removal, for on one ſide was the common road, and to the eaſt, a range of buildings conſtituting the ſtreet oppoſite Magdalene College; and to the ſouth a moraſs with a branch or cut of the river by it, now filled up. At preſent I conceive, nothing poſitive can be ſaid on a ſubject too much in the dark, till farther diſcoveries are made to throw more light upon it.

However that may be, this building bids faireſt to authenticate the antiquity of the univerſity of Cambridge of any in the place, as it ſeems moſt likely to have been the ſtructure where the Croyland monks gave their lectures to their ſcholars: and from them has retained the name of ſchool, from that period to this very time.

The undercroft is exactly in the ſame ſtile of building with that given by T. Hearne for St. Grymbald's church, except in a plainer and more ſober way, conſequently more likely to be the antienter of the two; and that this has only a ſingle row of pillars which run in a line from one end to the other, which by the plan and ſection taken by Mr. Richard Weſt in 1739, and publiſhed by Mr. Maſters ſome years after, ſeem to have their plinths or baſes hidden and ſunk into the ground. Of theſe pillars there are only five round and ſhort with pilaſters on each ſide and end, oppoſite to every one of them. The arches are ſemicircular and ſpring from the pillars to the walls, which are of a great thickneſs, and contain on one ſide only four narrow windows.

Pl. I

Beeston Castle Cheshire.

Pub.d Feb.y 23, 1786 by S. Hooper.

windows. The capitals are of no poſitive order, but of the plain ſtyle of the unornamented ſort in Grymbald's crypt and that under the choir of Canterbury cathedral. It ſeems to me that the uſe of it might be in the laſt inſtance, whatever its original one was, to have been to read lectures of philoſophy and the ſciences in, and to have been made uſe of as ſchools of learning, with rooms over it for the ſame purpoſe, in various branches. If this is allowed it will carry up the date to 1109, when the Benedictine monks from Croyland Abbey came to Cambridge for that intent: ſome few years after which, about 1112, the canons of St Giles's left Cambridge for Bernewelle. On their retreat, it is no ſtrained inference to ſuppoſe, that they might accommodate theſe profeſſors with a building that would be ſo convenient to them and was of no uſe to themſelves, at their firſt coming hither they were contented with worſe accommodations.

Mr. Goſtling in his account of the crypt under the choir of the cathedral of Canterbury, as Mr. Hearne in his of that under St. Grymbald's, ſeem to aim at very high antiquity in their reſpective relations of them. I can hardly ſuppoſe either of them ſo ancient as the 10th century: Hearne has a ſyſtem to complete, which was never out of his head: but Mr. Goſtling was of a ſoberer and more rational underſtanding. However their conjectures may turn out, or whatever may be the age of either of their crypts, it muſt be in favour of Pythagoras's ſchool: for the ſame ſort of building with pillars and arches of the ſame ſtyle, will equally prove that this at Cambridge is of as high antiquity as either of the other. This view was drawn anno 1777.

BEESTON CASTLE. (Plate I.)

THIS caſtle, as appears not only from its preſent remains, but alſo from the teſtimony of Camden, was once ſtrongly fortified by art, as well as almoſt inacceſſible by nature. His words are, "Beeſton caſtle, a place well guarded by walls of a great com-

" paſs,

" paſs, by the great number of its towers, and by a mountain " of very ſteep aſcent." Leland conceived ſo high an opinion of it, that he wrote, or rather repeated in ſome latin verſes, a kind of prophecy, which, however, does not ſeem very likely to be accompliſhed. Theſe verſes are thus tranſlated by Biſhop Gibſon, in his edition of Camden.

Ranulph, returning from the Syrian land,
This caſtle rais'd his country to defend.
The borderer to fright and to command.

Though ruin'd here the ſtately fabric lies,
Yet with new glories it again ſhall riſe,
If I a prophet may believe old prophecies.

The following account of this caſtle is given in the Vale Royal of Cheſhire, publiſhed anno 1656, by Daniel King, and now become extremely ſcarce.

" And ſo we cannot here but ſtay to look on the next ſtately houſe and fine demeſne of Beeſton, the name both of the houſes, the townſhip, and that famous and far-ſeen caſtle, built there by the laſt Ranulph, the famous earl of Cheſter; and, without queſtion, was a place, when ſuch ſtrong holds were in requeſt, of admirable and impregnable ſtrength. It is mounted upon the top of a very ſteep hill of ſtone, the chief tower whereof, in the very ſumitty of it, had a draw-well of an incredible depth to ſerve it with water, I have meaſured it, and, notwithſtanding that by the great number of ſtones which from the ruinated walls thoſe that repair thither do caſt in, it is ſuppoſed the well in the outward to be half ſtopped up; yet it is of true meaſure ninety-one yards deep, and the other above eighty yards deep by M. S. and from that tower, a circular wall of a large compaſs, containing a fine plat of ground, where, in the circuit of it, and in the middeſt of that, another well, which yet by the long deſcent of a ſtone before it fall down to the water, when you ſhall hear the fall of it of a huge depth; and the foot of the whole wall

CHESHIRE.

Is a maritime county, on the eaſt ſide of the Iriſh ſea. Prior to the introduction of the Romans, it was inhabited by the Cornavi, one of the principalities of the antient Britons. During the reſidence of the Roman governors, it was included in their third diviſion of Flavia Cæſarienſis: and during the Saxon Heptarchy it belonged to the kingdom of Mercia, which was the 7th eſtabliſhed, beginning in 582, and ending 827; having continued under 18 kings, till made ſubſervient to the Weſt Saxons under Egbert, who became ſovereign of the whole, when the name of England was given to the ſouth part of the Iſland, except that part inhabited by the antient Britons, now called Wales. In 889, king Alfred divided his kingdom into 32 Counties, of which Cheſhire was the 30th. He alſo ſub-divided each county into hundreds and pariſhes. After the Norman conqueſt, the kingdom was divided into circuits, in which Cheſhire was not included, being erected into a County Palatine, with its peculiar privileges, ſuch as its own judge or juſtice, court of exchequer, which it yet retains, though of a mixed kind, &c. Its dioceſe is in the province of York, and includes the counties of Cheſhire, Richmondſhire (a part of Yorkſhire) Lancaſhire, and part of Cumberland. It is bounded on the north by Lancaſhire, on the ſouth by Shrop-

Shropshire, on the east by Derbyshire and Staffordshire, and on the west partly by Flintshire, Denbigshire and the Irish sea. It is 50 miles long, 30 broad, and 112 in circumference; containing 372,000 acres, 24054 houses, 125,000 inhabitants: it is divided into 7 hundreds, in which are one city, Chester; 12 market towns, viz. Haulton, Frodsham, Altrincham, Knotsford, Nampwich, Macclesfield, Malpas, Middleswich, Northwich, Congleton, Stockport, Sanbach; 670 villages, 101 parishes, 20 vicarages, provides 560 men to the militia, send 4 members to parliament, and pays 7 parts of the land tax. Its chief rivers are the Mersey, Dee, Weelock Croke, Dan, Fulbrook, Wever, Goyte, Bollin and Ringay; with the most extensive and important inland canals in the kingdom, first begun by the duke of Bridgewater, which conveys the county products, which are corn, salt, coals, iron, millstones, allum, wood, hops, timber, cheese, &c. William the Conquerer, in 1070 made it an earldom and County Palatine, in favour of his nephew Hugh Lupus, to be held as he did the kingdom, by the sword. Chester and Parkgate are the two greatest thoroughfares to Ireland. Edgar the Saxon king of Mercia obliged eight of his tributary princes to row him and his attendants on the river Dee, from St. John's Church to his palace in Chester. The soil of the county is rich and fertile.

The Roman road enters this county from Manchester, (the Mancunium or Manucium of the Romans) which proceeds to Congleton, (the Condate) 18 miles distant; but the military way to it is not so visible, as to make one sanguine upon the discovery of it. There are 2 roads that lead from Manchester; one by Knotsford, the other nearer to Macclesfield; the first seems to have been the road, because it passes by the fortress S.W. of Manchester; whereas the other does not approach it. At Congleton there are no remains to ascertain the station; from thence you go to Chester, (Deva) which is 20 miles, and agrees with the Itnerary of Antoninus. That this hath been a colony, is proved from inscriptions and coins, and from the remains frequently discovered there: indeed here the 28 legion called Valaria Victrix was quartered. The road from Chester to Bangor, (Bovium) 10 miles has been allowed by all Antiquarians to be Roman.

ANTIQUITIES in this COUNTY worthy NOTICE.

Ashbury Church
Beeston Castle near Bunbury
Birkenhead Priory
Chester Cathedral, Chapter-house, Castle, Bridge, and Hypocaust
Combermeer Abby near Nampwich
Haulton Castle
Holt Castle
St. John's Church in Chester
Inc Ruins near Chester
Malpas Church
Norton Priory
Water Tower at Chester
Rudheath an antient Assylum
Sanbach Church
Stockport Church

BEESTON CASTLE Pl. 2.

wall ſtanding ſo deep on every ſide, that ſaving one way up to the gates of the caſtle towards the eaſt, and thoſe very fair and ſtately, men can hardly find a footing to ſtand on any part of the ſaid hill; concerning which, though I have no reaſon to fix my belief upon any, either idle prophecies, as they call them, or vain predictions of vulgar report; yet, neither will I be ſo ſcrupulous as not to make mention of the common word thereabouts uſed, that Beeſton caſtle ſhall ſave all England on a day; nor ſo envious as not to take notice of old Leland's bold conjecture of the future exalting of the head of it in time to come; whereof I only ſay this, that I wiſh every man to look upon what grounds he gives credit to any old dreams. To the place I wiſh all good, and to the name of Beeſton I could alſo wiſh a continuance as the caſtle ſtands, being now in the poſſeſſion of an ancient knight, Sir Hugh Beeſton, of much reſpect; but now, through want of iſſue male, like to paſs into another name, the heir being now married to one of the younger ſons of the honourable and aftermentioned knight and baronet Sir Thomas Savage."

ALTHOUGH the time when the caſtle was built is not here ſpecified, it muſt have been between the year 1180, when Ranulph became earl of Cheſter, and 1232, when he died. This view, which repreſents the great gate, or chief entrance into the caſtle, was drawn anno 1760.

(PLATE II.)

SINCE the printing of the firſt plate of this caſtle, in which I inſerted the account of it as given in the Vale Royal of Cheſhire, I have met with a more ancient deſcription, written by Sampſon Erdeſwicke, eſq; and printed in the year 1593. Although this ought, in point of time, to have preceded the other, yet, as the Survey of Staffordſhire, in which it is contained, is become extremely ſcarce, I imagine the reader will rather excuſe the violation of order, than want the deſcription; I, therefore, have here tranſcribed it.

" As in Staffordſhire I have begun with Trent, ſo proceeding to the deſcription of Cheſhire, I think it my readieſt courſe to begin with Weever, a fair river, which takes its firſt ſource or ſpring to Peckforton Hills, near Beeſton caſtle, and preſently runneth, firſt ſouth-eaſt, then plain ſouth, then bendeth ſouth-eaſt again, then plain eaſt, then turneth ſuddenly plain north, and ſo keepeth on its courſe, though it have diverſe windings, ſometimes weſtwards, and ſometimes eaſt, for fifteen or ſixteen miles ſtill northwards, and then returneth, as it were, ſuddenly weſt; which courſe it holdeth on, until it come into the Freet of Merſey, where it diſchargeth itſelf into a pretty little ſea, and, as Trent doth, divides the ſhire into two equal parts, eaſt and weſt; the one being called the Over ſide of Cheſhire, and the other the Lower ſide.

Not far from the fountain of Weever (as I have ſaid) ſtands Beeſton caſtle, which for that it was more eminent and famous than any particular part of the ſhire (the city of Cheſter excepted) I covet to begin withal; and you muſt ſomething bear with me, if a little I range about the head of Weever, for three or four miles on both ſides of the river; for that in that part of the ſhire the rivers be not ſo plentiful as in other places thereof: and beſides the barony of Rob. filius Hugonis, being the firſt barony which is ſpoken of in Doomſday-Book, which therefore I covet to begin withal, lieth the moſt part of it about this part of Cheſhire, and not far from Weever, between it and Dee, except ſome little of it which lies in Flintſhire, then reputed as a member of the county palatine of Cheſter.

Beeston caſtle ſtands very loftily and proudly, upon an exceeding ſteep and high rock, ſo ſteep upon all ſides but one, that it ſuffers no acceſs unto it; ſo that though it be walled about, yet (for the moſt part thereof) the wall is needleſs, the rock is ſo very high and ſteep: and where the nature of the thing admitteth acceſs, there is firſt a fair gate, and a wall furniſhed with turrets, which encloſeth a good quantity of ground (four or five acres) which lieth north-eaſtwards, ſomewhat riſeth until it come

to

to the over part of the rock, where is a great dike or ditch hewed out of the main rock, and within the ſame a goodly ſtrong gate-houſe and a ſtrong wall, with other buildings, which, when they flouriſhed, were a convenient habitation for any great perſonage. In which it is a wonder to ſee the great labour that hath been uſed to have ſufficient water; which was procured by, no doubt with great difficulty, a marvellous deep well through that huge high rock; which is ſo deep, as that it equals in depth the riveret, which runneth not far from the ſaid caſtle, through Teverton, Hocknell, and ſo on to Merſey.

THIS caſtle ſtands within the manor of Beeſton; but the ground whereon it ſtands, was procured by Randulf, the third earl of Cheſter, from the owner of the ſaid manor, to the end he might make and fortify the ſaid caſtle there, which he did accordingly.

THE manor of Beeſton, whereof this place was a member before the caſtle was builded, is within the pariſh of Bunbury, poſſeſſed at this day by Sir George Beeſton, whoſe ſon and heir Hugh Beeſton hath (as I hear) alſo purchaſed the caſtle of Beeſton of the Queen.

THE Beeſtons are deſcended paternally from the Bunberyes, who (as I take it) were lords of the whole pariſh, or the moſt of it, about Henry the Second's time; and were at the firſt known by the name of St. Peere, but (by reaſon of their habitation, and the ſeignory of Bunbury together) changed their name from St. Peere to Bunbury. As Henry of Bunbury (to whom his father had given Beeſton about King Henry the Third's time) had iſſue a ſon named David, who was called David de Beeſton by reaſon of his habitation; which David had iſſue Henry Beeſton, who had iſſue David Beeſton, William (that died without iſſue) Henry that begat Thomas, and William that had iſſue John, Rauſe, and Agnes."

FROM the accounts here given it appears, this caſtle was in decay when they were written; but its preſent ruinous condition ſhews the honourable ſcars of ſeveral vigorous attacks ſuſtained by by it during the laſt civil war. In the beginning of theſe troubles, this caſtle was ſeized for the parliament, but was attacked and taken December 12th, 1643, by the king's forces, then juſt landed from Ireland. It appears the garriſon made little or no defence; for Ruſhworth ſays, the governor, one Captain Steel, was tried and executed for a coward. The parliamentarians afterwards attempted to retake it, and it was unſucceſsfully beſieged for ſeventeen weeks, being bravely defended by Captain Valet. On Prince Rupert's approach the enemy abandoned it, March 18th, 1644. In 1645 it was again attacked; and on the 16th of November it ſurrendered on condition, after eighteen weeks continual ſiege, in which the garriſon were reduced to the neceſſity of eating cats, &c. The governor, Colonel Ballard (ſays Ruſhworth) in compaſſion to his ſoldiers, conſented to beat a parly, whereupon a treaty followed; and having obtained very honourable conditions (even beyond expectation in ſuch extremity) viz. to march out, the governor and officers with horſes and arms, and their own proper goods (which loaded two wains) the common ſoldiers with their arms, colours flying, drums beating, matches alight, and a proportion of powder and ball, and a convoy to guard them to Flint caſtle; he did, on Sunday the 16th of November, ſurrender the caſtle, the garriſon being reduced to not above ſixty men, who marched away according to the conditions.

Many traces of theſe operations, ſuch as ditches, trenches, and other military works, are ſtill diſcernible in the grounds about it.

The ſite and ruins of this caſtle at preſent belong to Sir Roger Moſtyn of Moſtyn, in the county of Flint, Bart. This plate gives a general proſpect of the ruins as they appear when ſeen from the ſouth. It was drawn anno 1773. Plate I. preſented a more particular view of the great gateway.

BIRKE-

25

BIRKHEDDE PRIORY CHESHIRE.

Published 20 Oct 1783 by S. Hooper.

BIRKEHEDDE PRIORY.

THIS priory was, as appears from different writers, alſo called Bricheved, Byrket, and Burket-wood priory. It was founded in the latter end of the reign of Henry II. or in that of Richard I. by Hamon Maſſey, third baron of Dunham Maſſey, who placed therein ſixteen Benedictine Monks. A manuſcript in Corpus Chriſti College, Cambridge, makes them canons of the order of St. Auguſtine. It was dedicated to St. Mary and St. James.

In the Monaſticon are two charters of the ſaid Hamon Maſſey. In the firſt, he grants to this monaſtery in free alms, half an acre of land at Dunham, and an acre at Lacheker, with the advowſon of the church of Bowdon; and in the other, the liberty of chooſing their own prior, granted before by Pope Alexander: from whence it ſeems, as if the papal permiſſion for ſuch election was not then ſufficient without the confirmation of the patron.

At the diſſolution, its revenues were eſtimated at 90l. 13s. per ann. according to Dugdale; 102l. 16s. 10d. Speed; its reputed value 108l. and by a M. S. in Corpus Chriſti College, Cambridge, it was only reckoned at 80l. In 36 Henry VIII. it was granted to Ralph Worſeley.

This houſe is ſaid by Leland to have been ſubordinate to the abbey of Cheſter; but Tanner does not ſubſcribe to that opinion. "The grant of free election for a prior, the diſtinct valuation of its poſſeſſions, both in Tax. Lincoln. and 26 Henry VIII. makes me doubt much, ſays he, whether this was a cell to Cheſter."

In the Vale Royal of England, publiſhed anno 1656, by Dan. King, there is a view of this priory, by which it is plain that much of the buildings have been demoliſhed ſince the time when that was drawn. Annexed to it is the following account: "Where the paſſage lies over into Lancaſhire, unto Leaverpool, we ſtep over into Berket-wood, and where hath been a famous priory, the foundation whereof I am not yet inſtruct for; but now a very goodly demean, and which is come, by deſcent from the Worſleyes, men of great poſſeſſions, now to a gentleman of much worth, Thomas Powel, eſq; the heir of that ancient ſeat of Horſley, in the county of Flint; and one whom our county may gladly receive; to be added to the number of thoſe that deſerve better commendation than I am fit to give them; though unto him I am particularly bound to extend my wits to a higher reach, then here I will make tryall of."

At preſent it is the property of Richard Perry Price, eſq; whoſe grandfather, Mr. Cleveland, purchaſed it of Mr. Powel.

What is ſhewn in the view here repreſented, ſeems to have been part of the church or chapel of the priory. Towards the left hand, under the middle of the tuft of ivy, is the remains of a confeſſional ſeat, the entrance being through the Gothick arch: the ſmall window was the aperture, at which the penitents related their tranſgreſſions to the prieſt. This drawing was made anno 1770.

CHESTER CASTLE. (Plate I.)

THIS caſtle, it is ſaid, was either built or greatly repaired by Hugh Lupus, earl of Cheſter, nephew to William the Conqueror; it is twice deſcribed in the Vale Royal of England, publiſhed anno 1656, by Dan. King; as that book is extremely ſcarce, I ſhall here literally tranſcribe both paſſages.

"The caſtle of Cheſter ſtandeth on a rocky hill, within the wall of the city, not far from the bridge: which caſtle is a place having privileges of itſelf, and hath a conſtable, the building thereof ſeemeth to be very ancient. At the firſt coming in is the gate-houſe, which is the priſon for the whole county, having diverſe rooms and lodgings; and hard within the gate is a houſe, which was ſometime the exchequer, but now the cuſtom-houſe; not far from thence, in the baſe-court, is a deep well, and thereby ſtables and other houſes of office; on the left hand is a chapel, and hard by adjoining thereunto, the goodly fair, and large ſhire hall,

CHESTER CASTLE, Pl. 1

Publish'd the 1st of June 1784 by S. Hooper

hall, newly repaired, where all matters of law, touching the county palatine, are heard and judiciouſly determined; and at the end thereof the brave new exchequer, for the ſaid county palatine; all theſe are in the baſe-court. Then there is a draw-bridge into the inner ward, wherein are diverſe goodly lodgings for the juſtices, when they come, and here the conſtable himſelf dwelleth.

THE thieves and felons are arraigned in the ſhire hall, and being condemned, are by the conſtable of the caſtle, or his deputy, delivered to the ſheriffs of the city, a certain diſtance without the caſtle gate, at a ſtone called the Glovers-ſtone; from which place the ſaid ſheriffs convoy them to the place of execution, called Boughton."

AGAIN. "Upon the ſouth ſide of the city, near unto the ſaid water of Dee, and upon a high bank or rock of ſtone, is mounted a ſtrong and ſtately caſtle, round in form; the baſe-court likewiſe, incloſed with a circular wall, which to this day retaineth one teſtimony of the Romans magnificence, having a fair and ancient ſquare tower; which, by the teſtimony of all writers I have hitherto met withall, beareth the name of Julius Cæſar's tower; beſides which there remaineth yet many goodly pieces of buildings, whereof one of them containeth all fit and commodious rooms for the lodging and uſe of the honourable juſtices of aſſize twice a year; another part is a goodly hall, where the court of the common pleas and goal delivery, and alſo the ſheriffs of the counties court, with other buſineſſes for the county of Cheſter, are conſtantly kept and holden; and is a place for that purpoſe of ſuch ſtate and comelineſs, that I think it is hardly equalled with any ſhire hall in any of the ſhires in England.

AND then next unto the ſouth end of the hall is a leſs, but fair, neat and convenient hall, where is continually holden the princes highneſs moſt honourable court of exchequer, with other rooms, fitly appendant thereunto, for keeping of the records of that court. Within the precincts of which caſtle is alſo the king's priſon for the county of Cheſter, with the office of prothonotary,

thonotary, convenient rooms for the dwelling of the conſtables, or keeper of the ſaid caſtle and goal, with diverſe other rooms for ſtabling and other uſes, with a fair draw-well of water in the middeſt of the court; diverſe ſweet and dainty orchards and gardens, beſide much of the ancient building, for want of uſe, fallen to ruine and decay, and which we may well conjecture were of great ſtatelineſs and great uſe, conſidering that the ſame caſtle was, as hereafter will appear, the pallace of many worthy princes, who kept therein, no doubt, great and moſt brave retinues; and I find that the caſtle, with the precincts thereof, were reſerved out of that charter of King Henry VII. by which the city was made a county of itſelf; and accordingly, hath ever ſince been uſed for the king's majeſty's ſervice of the county of Cheſter, and eſteemed a part thereof, and not of the county of the city."

THIS caſtle is built of a ſoft reddiſh ſtone, which does not well endure the weather, and is at preſent much out of repair, ſeveral large pieces of the walls having lately fallen down into the ditch. Indeed its trifling conſequence as a fortreſs, would hardly juſtify the expence of a thorough repair. It is, however, commanded by a governor and lieutenant governor, and is commonly garriſoned by two companies of invalids. This drawing was made anno 1770.

(PLATE II.)

As this edifice cannot well be repreſented at one view, without taking it at ſo great a diſtance as would render the parts extremely indiſtinct and confuſed, this ſecond proſpect was judged neceſſary; which being drawn from the ditch within the walls of the city, ſhews ſome of the principal internal buildings, giving the beholder an idea of the antient magnificence of this venerable pile. The church ſeen in the back ground is dedicated to the Virgin Mary, and called St. Mary's of the Caſtle. In and near the angle under the great window appears the rock on which the caſtle is founded.

IN

CHESTER CASTLE, PL. 2.

CHESTER BRIDGE.

Publish'd the 23d of May by S. Harper. 1784.

In Peck's Defiderata Curiofa, Chefter caftle ftands in the lift of Queen Elizabeth's garrifons, with the following officers and falaries:

C H E S T E R.

	l.	s.	d.
Conftable of the caftle; fee - - - - -	6	13	4
Porter; fee - - - - - - - - - - - -	4	11	3
Keeper of the gardens; fee - - - - -	6	1	8
Surveyor of the works within Chefhire and Flint; fee - - - - - - - -	6	1	8
Mafter mafon; fee - - - - - - - - -	8	12	4
Mafter carpenter; fee - - - - - -	9	2	6

It ftill continues to be a royal garrifon, and has a governor and lieutenant-governor, each at 10s. per diem; and two independent companies of invalids are ftationed here.

During the civil war under Charles I. Chefter was befieged, and at length, Feb. 3, 1645, taken by the parliamentary forces commanded by Sir William Brereton; but the caftle neither made any particular defence or feparate capitulation. This drawing was made anno 1769.

CHESTER BRIDGE.

This bridge is more worthy of notice for its picturefque appearance, than remarkable for its antiquity; not but part of it is very ancient, though it appears to have been frequently repaired at different times, and with different materials; however, the greateft part of it is built with the fame reddifh ftone as the caftle. Very little is to be met with relative to this bridge in the county hiftories; it is flightly touched upon by Lee, in the Vale Royal of England, publifhed by Dan. King, anno 1656, but neither the builder, the time of its erection, nor by whom it is repaired, is there mentioned. "The bridge-gate, fays he, is at the fouth part of the city, at the entering of the bridge, commonly called Dee-bridge, which bridge is builded all of ftone of eight arches in length: at the furtheſt end whereof is alſo a gate; and without that, on the other ſide of the water, the ſuburbs of the city, called Hond-bridge."

A MS. account of Cheſter, communicated by a friend, has the following paſſage relative to this bridge. "After the death of Elfleda, her brother Edward ſucceded to the throne, who, fighting againſt the Danes, would have been taken priſoner, but for the unparalleled courage and activity of his ſon Athelſtan. In the year after this engagement he viſited his territories in Cheſhire, and greatly ſecured them, by erecting fortreſſes at Thelwell and Mancheſter. He likewiſe finiſhed the bridge over the river Dee at Cheſter, which was begun by his ſiſter Elfleda, before which time there was a ferry for paſſengers under St. Mary's Hill, at the Ship Gate. This view was drawn anno 1770.

NEW OR WATER TOWER, CHESTER.

THIS tower ſeems to have been built for the defence of a quay on the river Dee, which once flowed cloſe to it, but is now ſo choaked up by ſands, as to render it entirely uſeleſs for that purpoſe. It was built, according to the account given of it in King's Vale Royal of England, anno 1322, at the expence of the city, by one John Helpſtone, a maſon, who contracted to complete it, according to a given plan, for the ſum of one hundred pounds. The indenture or agreement is preſerved among the archives of the city.

THE following deſcription of it is given in another part of the ſame book: "From the north gate, ſtill weſtward, the wall extendeth to another tower, and from thence to the turning of the wall ſouthwards; at which corner ſtandeth another fine turret called the New Tower, and was pitched within the channel of Dee-water; which new tower was built, as it is reported, in or near to the place in the river which was the key, whereunto veſſels of great burden, as well of merchandize as others, came cloſe up, which may the rather ſeem probable, as well by a deeper foundation

Sparrow sculp.

The NEW or WATER TOWER CHESTER.

Published Nov. 3. 1785, by S. Hooper.

foundation of ftone work yet appearing from the foot of that tower, reaching a good diftance into the channel, as alfo by great rings of iron here and there faftened to the fides of the faid tower, which, if they ferved not for the faftening of fuch veffels as then ufed to approach to the fame key, I cannot learn what other ufe they fhould be for."

AND again another paffage in the fame book fays: "The Water-gate is in the weft fide of the city, whereunto, in times paft, great fhips and veffels might come at full fea, but now fcarce fmall boats are able to come, the fands have fo choaked the channel; and although the citizens have beftowed marvellous great charges in building this new tower, which ftandeth in the very river between this gate and the north gate, yet all will not ferve; and therefore all the fhips do come to a place called the New Key, fix miles from the city."

THE form of this tower is extremely fingular, its outfide being broken into a variety of angles, and thofe neither encreafing its beauty, ftability, or powers of defence. This view was drawn anno 1770.

CORNWALL.

RESTORMEL CASTLE.

WILLIAM of Worcester, a monk who wrote an Itinerary the latter end of the fifteenth century, mentions this castle by the name of Reformel Castle, all he says of it is, that it is situated between the towns of Lastydielle and Lanceston.

IT is also described by Leland in his Itinerary, vol. iii. page 17. thus: "The park of Restormel is hard by the north side of the town of Lostwithiel.—Tynne workes in this Parke.—Ther is a castel on an hill in this park, wher sumtymes the erles of Cornewal lay. The base court is sore defaced. The fair large dungeon yet stondith. A chapel cast out of it a newer work then it, and now onrofid. A chapel of the Trinitie in the park not far from the castelle." And in vol. vii. p. 122. a. "The little round castel of Lestormel standith in the kinge's park ny to Loswithiel."

BORLACE in his History of Cornwall, gives an elevation of the inside of this castel fronting the entrance, accompanied with a plan and the following description, "One of the principal houses of the earles of Cornwall, was Restormel Castle, about a mile north of the town of Lostwythiel. This castle stands not on a factitious hill, for the architect finding a rockey knoll on the edge of a hill overlooking a deep valley, had no more to do than to plane the rock into a level, and shape it round by a ditch, and the keep would have elevation enough, without the trouble of raising an artificial hill, (like that at Trematon) for it to stand on." The base court was sore defaced, as Leland says, in his time; some few ruins were to be seen in the lower part, (in Mr. Carew's

time)

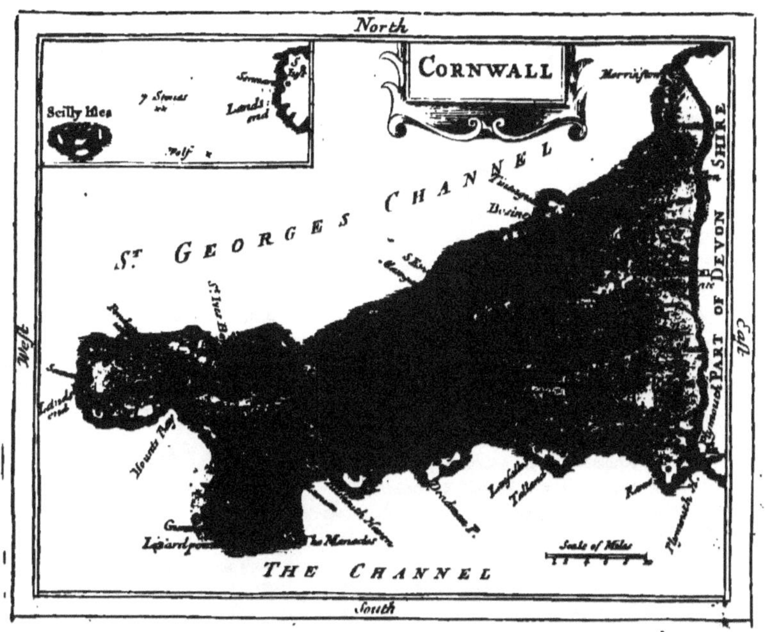

CORNWALL.

Is a maritime county on the extreme western point of the island, included in the principality of Danmonii of the antient Britons, and of Britannia Prima of the Romans. Hither the antient Britons (as well as in Wales) retired on the intrusion of the Saxons, where they opposed their further conquests. In this part of the island they formed a kingdom that existed for many years after, under different princes, amongst whom were Ambrosius Aurelius, and the justly celebrated Arthur; nor were they subdued till the middle of the 7th century, from which time Cornwall was considered as subject to the West Saxon kings, who begun their sovereignty in 519, and continued it till 828, under 18 sovereigns, the last of whom was the great Egbert, who subdued all the others, and by uniting them, formed the kingdom of England, when this county was included in the county of Devon, then the 9th division; and that accounts for Alfred's not mentioning Cornwall, which on forming the circuits after the Norman conquest, is included in the western circuit. Ever since Edward III. in 1337, who created his son Prince of Wales and Duke of Cornwall, it has been under the Prince's jurisdiction, who not only appoints the sheriff, but all writs, deeds, &c. are in his name, and not in the king's; and he has also peculiar royalties and prerogative distinct from the crown,

for

for which he appoints the officers. It is included in the diocese of Exeter, is bounded on all sides by the ocean, except on the east by Devonshire; it is 80 miles long, 40 broad, and 250 in circumference; containing 960,000 acres, 126,000 inhabitants, is divided into 9 hundreds, has 27 market towns, viz. Launceston, Truro, Falmouth, Helston, Saltash, Bodmyn, St. Ives, Tregony, Camelford, Fowey, St. Germains, Penryn, Callington, St. Austle, East-Looe, Padstow, St. Colomb, Pensance, Grampond, Leskard, Lestwithiel, St. Mawes, St. Michael, Newport, Market Jew, Stratton and Redruth; 1230 villages, 161 parishes, 89 vicarages, provides 640 men to the militia, sends 44 members to parliament, and pays 8 parts of the land-tax. Its chief rivers are the Tamer, Fale, Cober, Looe, Camel, Fowey, Haile, Lemara, Kense and Aire. Its principal capes or head-lands are the Land's-end, the Lizard, Cape Cornwall, Deadman's-head, Rame-head, &c. and a cluster of islands, 145 in number, called the Scilly Isles, supposed formerly to have been joined to the main land, though now 30 [illegible] distant [illegible]unding with antiquities, particularly Druidical.

As the Romans had but 2 stations in this co[illegible] [illegible]ised on by Antiquarians, little can be said concerning [illegible] [illegible]ne of them is supposed to be Totness, (the Nidum of the Romans[illegible] [illegible]er Launceston, (the Bomium of the same people) but as this is merely [illegible] [illegible]tle dependance can be lain on it. Dr. Stukely mentions a Roman am[illegible] [illegible]iles from Redruth. The reason Roman antiquities have been neglecte[illegible] [illegible]ed in this county is, that all this part of the island has been a forest [illegible] the conquest; for in king John's time it was appointed to be disforested; but yet it is allowed to have been habitable before by the Britons, who retired here on the inroad of the Romans, and the incroachment of the Saxons.

ANTIQUITIES in this COUNTY worthy NOTICE.

Boscajall Castle in the Parish of St. Just
Bosiney Castle near Camelford
St. Burien's Church near Pensance
Carn Brea Castle near Redruth
The Cheese-ring near St. Clair
Choon Castle near Morva
Ethy Church near Fowey
Fowey Castle
St. Germain's Priory near Saltash
The Giant's Hedge near West-Looe
The Holed Stone near Pensance
The Hurlers near Bodmin
Kernejack Castle in the Parish of St. Just
Kimick Castle near Bodmin
Launceston Castle
Lestormel Castle near Lestwithiel
Lestwithiel Palace

St. Mawe's Castle, Falmouth-Harbour
St. Michael's Mount
St. Neot's Church near Leskard
Pellin Castle near Lestwithiel
Pendennis Castle, Falmouth-Harbour
Pengersick Castle near Helston
Pentilley Castle near Saltash
The Rocking-stone near St. Levan
Roundago near Pensance
The Sister's Druidical Monuments near Wadebridge
Stone Deities in the Village of Men Perbeen
Tintagal Castle near Bosiney
Trematon Castle near Saltash
Treceen Castle near St. Levan
Wadebridge near Padstow

There are Saxon or Danish encampments at Trereen, near the Barton of Hall, and in the Parish of Sancred; and on St. Mary's island, one of the isles of Scilly, are several antiquities, particularly a Druidical temple, consisting of immense stones placed upon one another, called the Giant's Castle, the Giant's Cave; and several tumulis. There are some antiquities on the other islands.

Reſtormel Caſtle Cornwal .

time) where the ditch is very wide and deep, and was formerly filled with water, brought by pipes from an adjoining hill; on the higher ſide alſo leading to the principal gate, there are traces of building to be found. The keep is a very magnificent one; the outer wall or rampart is an exact circle, a hundred and ten feet diameter within, and ten feet wide at the top, including the thickneſs of the parapet, which is two feet ſix. From the preſent floor of the ground-rooms to the top of the rampart is twenty-ſeven feet ſix, and the top of the parapet is ſeven feet higher, garretted quite round. There are three ſtair-caſes leading to the top of the rampart, one on each ſide of the gateway, aſcending from the court within, and one betwixt the inner and outermoſt gate. The rooms are nineteen feet wide, the windows moſtly in the innermoſt wall, but there are ſome very large openings (in the outmoſt wall, or rampart) now walled up, ſhaped like Gothick church windows, ſharp arched, which were formerly very handſome and pleaſant windows, and made to enjoy the proſpect, their receſſes reaching to the planching of the rooms: theſe large openings are all on the chamber floor (where the rooms of ſtate ſeem to have been) and from the floor of theſe chambers you paſs on a level to the chapel. This chapel is but twenty-five feet ſix, by ſeventeen feet ſix, but that it might be the more commodious, there ſeems to have been an anti-chapel. This chapel, as Leland well obſerves, is a newer work than the caſtle itſelf; and I may add, that the gateway and the large windows in the rampart wall, are alſo more modern than the keep, for they were not made for war and ſafety, but for pleaſure and grandeur; and yet, as modern as theſe compared with the reſt may appear, they muſt at leaſt be as ancient as Edmund, ſon of Richard King of the Romans (temp. Edward I.) for ſince his death, I cannot find that any earl of Cornwall reſided here. Richard King of the Romans kept his Court here, and in all probability made theſe additions temp. Henry III. The offices belonging to this caſtle, lay below it in the baſs court, where ſigns of many ruins to the north and eaſt are ſtill apparent,

parent, and with the ruins on either hand as you come towards the great gate from the weſt, ſhew that this caſtle was of great extent; there was an oven (as Mr. Carew ſays) of fourteen feet largeneſs among the ruins in the baſs court, and may ſerve to give us ſome idea of the hoſpitality of thoſe times. This noble keep ſtill holds up the ſhell of its turreted head, but within equals the ruinous ſtate of the baſs court below, over both which the following is Mr. Carew's lamentation, in his ſomewhat antiquated but nervous ſtyle: "Certes (ſays he, p. 138) it may move compaſſion, that a palace ſo healthful for air, ſo delightful for proſpect, ſo neceſſary for commodities, ſo fair, in regard of thoſe days, for building, and ſo ſtrong for defence, ſhould in time of ſecure peace, and under the protection of its natural princes, be wronged with thoſe ſpoilings, than which it could endure no greater at the hands of a foreign and deadly enemy; for the park is diſparked, the timber rooted up, the conduit pipes taken away, the roof made ſale of, the planchings rotten, the walls fallen down, and the hewed ſtones of the windows, dournes and clavels plucked out to ſerve private buildings; only there remaineth an utter defacement to complain upon this unregarded diſtreſs." (a)

"The caſtle and honour has never been alienated, as far as I have learned, from the inheritance of the dukes and earls of Cornwall. There was a park round it, well wooded, and ſuitable to the quality of the ancient owners; but with ſeveral other parks in this county (there having been formerly belonging to this earldom nine parks, and one chace or foreſt) diſparked by Henry VIII. at the inſtance of Sir Richard Pollard."

In the act of Reſumption, 4th Edward IV. it appears, that William Sayer was on the third of March, in the preceding year, appointed to the offices of conſtableſhip of the king's caſtle of Roſtormell and parkerſhip of the ſame.

(a) I think this caſtle muſt have been built ſince the Norman conqueſt; for in the Exeter Domeſday it is not named, nor in a liſt of the earl of Moreton's lands and caſtles, communicated by Francis Gregor, Eſq; from a MS. in the Aſhmolean library among the Dugdale MSS.

This

Monastery of St Bees, Cumberland.

Pub. 10 March 1784, by S. Hooper

This castle and park is held of the dutchy of Cornwall, under a lease for three lives, by William Masterman, Esq; member of parliament for Bodmyn; his immediate predecessor in this possession, Thomas Jones, Esq; was at a considerable expence in clearing the building from the rubbish and bushes with which it was encumbered and over-run; a laudable example he has strictly followed by giving great attention to the protection and preservation of this venerable piece of antiquity, which before had, for time out of mind, been abandoned to the depredations of the under-tenants.

This view was drawn from an original picture the property of Mr. Masterman.

CUMBERLAND.

MONASTERY OF ST. BEES.

THE following account of the foundation and endowment of this house is in substance given in the History of Westmoreland and Cumberland, by Joseph Nicholson, Esq; and the Reverend Richard Burn, L. L. D.

St. Bees had its name from Bega, an holy woman of Ireland, who is said to have founded here, about the year 650, a small monastery, where afterwards a church was erected to her memory; this church was formerly called Kirkby Begock or Begoth, from the British words beg and og, signifying little and young.

This house being destroyed by the Danes was restored by William de Meschiens, son of Ranulph, and brother to Ranulph de Meschiens first earl of Cumberland, after the conquest, who made it a cell to the abbey of St. Mary's at York, consisting of a prior

prior and six Benedictine monks, and by his charter granted to God and St. Mary of York, St. Bega and the monks serving God there, all the woods within their boundaries, and every thing within the same, except hart and hind, boar and hawk; and all liberties within their bounds, which he himself had in Copeland, as well on land as water, both salt and fresh.

Ranulph de Meschiens, son to the said William, granted and confirmed to the abbey of St. Mary, York, all his father's grants, and namely the church of St. Bee, and seven carrucates of land there; and the chapel of Egremont; and the tithe of his demesne in Copeland, and all his men inhabiting therein, and of all his fisheries in Copeland, and the tithe of his hogs, and of his venison throughout his whole forest of Copeland, and also of his pannage, and of his vaccaries throughout all Copeland; and also the manor of Anendale: and the grant which Waltheof made to them of the church of Steinburn: and Preston, which they have by the gift of Ketel: and two bovates of land, and one villein in Rotington; which Reiner gave unto them: and the churches of Whittington and Botele, which they have of the gift of Goddard: and Swarthoft, given to them by William de Lancastre, son of Gilbert: and he grants to them all the woods within their boundaries, from Cunningshaw to the sike between Preston and Hensingham, which runs to Whiteshoven and there falls into the sea: and whatever they can take in those woods, except hart, hind, boar and hawk.

And William de Fortibus earl of Albermarle, by his charter grants and confirms to God and the Church of St. Bees in Copeland, and the monks serving God there, all his ancestors grants, that is to say, fourteen salmons, which they have by the gift of Alan, son of Waltheof; and by the same gift half a carrucate of land in Aspatric; and six salmons, which they have by the gift of Alice de Romely; and half a mark of silver by the same donation, out of the fulling mill at Cockermouth, and one messuage in the same ville. He further grants to them one mark of silver out of the said fulling mill yearly.

It

C U M B E R L A N D.

IS a maritime county, which prior to the arrival of the Romans, was included in the diviſion of the Brigantes; and after their conqueſt was compriſed in their fourth province of Maxima Cæſarienſis, which extended from the Humber to the Tine. During the Heptarchy it belonged to the kingdom of Northumberland, which was the 5th eſtabliſhed, begining 547 and ending 827, having had 31 kings: and is now included in the northern circuit, in the province of York and dioceſe of Carliſle. It is bounded on the north by Scotland, on the ſouth by Lancaſhire and Weſtmoreland, eaſt by Northumberland and Durham, and weſt by the Iriſh ſea. It is 78 miles long, 30 broad, and 200 in circumference, containing 1040000 ſquare acres, has 75000 inhabitants; one city, Carliſle, and 14 market-towns, viz. Penrith, Cockermouth, Whitehaven, Egremont, Keſwick, Ravenglaſs, Alncaſter, Holme, Brampton, Alſton-Moor, Ireby, Kirk-Oſwald, Longtown, and Wigton; it has 56 pariſhes, 77 vicarages, 447 villages; is divided into 6 wards, provides 320 men to the national militia; ſends 6 members to parliament, and pays one part of the land-tax. Its rivers are the Eden, Aln, Irt, Petterel, Caude, Derwent, Cocker, Duddon, Levin, Wiza, and Tyne. The moſt noted places are Hard-knot-hill, Mole-hill, Dent-hill, Skiddow-mount, The Fells, Penrith-fell, Newton-beaoon, Derwent, Uller, and Broad-water; Weſtward, Copeland and Inglewood foreſts, Wrynoſe, Sol-

way-

way-mofs, &c. Its chief products are black-lead, copper, iron, coal, lapis, calaminaries, fuftians, courfe broad-cloth, linen, falmon, cattle, fowls, game, fifh, &c. In this county are many remarkable and beautiful views, particularly on or near its lakes, meers and high-grounds.

Near Carlifle began the Picts wall, built by the Emperor Adrian in 121, which croffed the whole ifland from fea to fea, about 100 miles. It was 8 feet broad and 12 high, with 25 ftrong caftles, the foundation of many of of them are yet vifible; befides which, there are Roman, Saxon, or Danifh encampments to be feen at Morefby, Thirlwall, Bankhead, Little Chefters, Houfe-ftuds, between Seavenfhale and Little Chefters, at Carrow-burrough, Seavenfhale, Portgate near Hexham, Elenborough, Wigton, Burgh, Penrith, Netherby, Brampton, Lanecroft, at Alfton-moor called Whitley Caftle, near Rofe Caftle, at Bewcaftle, at Deerham, near Denton, and at Liddle Strength.

The Roman military-road upon which the fecond journey of Antoninus is made, commences and leads through this county, from Carlifle to Old Penrith, and another vicinal way we have from Old Penrith to the wall. The Roman road leading hither from York, may be traced to Rippon, and from thence to Merton, at the confluence of the Tees and Greta. There are five ftations from Merton to Walwick; but to Carlifle there are but 3, Brough in Weftmoreland (Lavatris) and is the firft; Old Penrith, (Veteris) the fecond; and Carlifle, (Brovoniacis) the third. A road goes alfo by the wall to Caer Vorren and Luguvallain near Walwick, and thence to Old Penrith: the laft ftation in this county is (Alone) Bewcaftle, the ftation of the 3d. cohort of the Nervians.

ANTIQUITIES worthy NOTICE in this COUNTY.

St. Bees Priory near Egremont,
Bewcaftle and the Crofs in the Church-Yard,
Boulnefs Font,
Bride Church Fort.
Calder Priory near Egremont,
Carlifle Cathedral and Caftle
Caftle-Studs in Old Penrith,
Cockermouth Caftle,
Corby Caftle near Carlifle,
Dacre Caftle near Penrith,
Danifh Chapel at ditto.
Deerham Church near Cockermouth,
Drumburg Caftle, 5 miles from Whitehaven,
Dunwalloght Caftle near Nether-Denton,
Egremont Caftle near St. Bees,
Ewanrigg near Elneburgh,
Grotto near Penrith,
Hay Caftle near Morefby,
High-head Caftle near Ireby,
Holme Cultram Abbey,
Ifis Parlifh, a Grotto near Penrith
Kirk Ofwald near ditto.
Lanecroft Priory near Naworth,
Long Meg and her Daughters near Kirk Ofwald,
Millum Caftle
The Moat near Brampton
The Monument near Caftle Rigg,
Naworth Caftle,
Nunnery near Kirk Ofwald,
Pap Caftle,
Penrith Caftle,
Old Penrith near Kirk Ofwald,
Picts Holes near Morefby,
Picts Wall,
Rofe Caftle 6 miles from Carlifle,
Scaleby Caftle,
Warwick Church,
Wetherall Priory and Cells,
Wigton Church.

It was endowed at the diſſolution with 143l. 17s. 2d. ob per annum according to Dugdale; 149l. 19s. 6d. Speed; and in the ſeventh year of the reign of King Edward VI. was granted to Sir Thomas Chaloner, knt. (amongſt other particulars) the manor, rectory and cell of St. Bees, with all its rights, members and appurtenances, and all the poſſeſſions belonging to the ſame, in St. Bees and Enerdale, and elſewhere in the county of Cumberland (not before granted away by the crown) to hold to the ſaid Thomas Chaloner, his heirs and aſſigns, in fee farm for ever, of the king, his heirs and ſucceſſors, as of his manor of Sheriffs Hutton in Yorkſhire, in free and common ſoccage, by fealty only, and not in capite; paying to the crown yearly the fee farm rent of 143l. 16s. 2d.

In the 4th and 5th of Philip and Mary, the king and queen granted to Cuthbert biſhop of Cheſter and his ſucceſſors, the ſaid yearly rent, paying thereout to the crown yearly 43l. 8s. 4d.

The manor and rectory came afterwards into the poſſeſſion of the Wyberghs, a very ancient family at St. Bees, who being great ſufferers in the civil wars in the reign of Charles I. they mortgaged St. Bees to the Lowther family, and in the year 1663, Sir John Lowther foreclosed the mortgage, and obtained a decree in chancery of the eſtate, in whoſe family it ſtill continues.

Anno 1705 the church of St. Bees was certified at 12l. a year, by James Lowther of Whitehaven, then impropriator.

This monaſtery lies in a bottom about four miles ſouth-weſt from Whitehaven, and about one north from Egremont, the chief remains are thoſe of the conventual church, which is now uſed as a parochial one. The arches of this building are all pointed, except that over the weſt door which is circular, and has zig-zag mouldings and ornaments of heads ſimilar to thoſe on the door of Iſley Church in Oxfordſhire. The key-ſtone ſeems to have repreſented the head of Chriſt, the windows in the chancel are long and extremely narrow.

Within the body of the church on the ſouth ſide is an effigy in wood of Anthony the laſt Lord Lucy of Egremont, which if a true portraiture, ſhews him to have been a large bodied man, upwards of ſix foot high and proportionably corpulent.

THE vicarage houſe appears to have been conſtructed out of the ruins of the monaſtery, and ſtands a little to the ſouth-weſt of it. Southward of the church are many foundations, which make it probable the offices extended that way. In the church yard, on the ſouth ſide of the church, are the almoſt ſhapeleſs trunks of the figures of two knights; one holding a ſhield, and the other with his hands joined, as in the attitude of praying. They are broken off at the knees, and much defaced by time.

A SMALL diſtance eaſt of the church ſtands the grammar ſchool, founded by Dr. Edmund Grindal, archbiſhop of Canterbury. It has a library to it, and has been much improved by the donations of Dr. Lamplugh, late archbiſhop of York, Dr. Smith, late biſhop of Carliſle, Sir John Lowther, and others. The right of nominating the maſter, is in the provoſt and fellows of Queens College, Oxford.

THE village of St. Bees lies a quarter of a mile ſouth of the monaſtery. The way to it is over a bridge lately repaired, but having on it the date 1588, with the initials R. G. This view, which ſhews the north-weſt aſpect of the church, was drawn 1774.

CARLISLE CASTLE, CUMBERLAND.

THIS Caſtle ſtands on the north-weſt ſide of the city of Carliſle, which it is ſaid exiſted before the coming of the Romans; being, according to our ancient Chroniclers, built by a king named Luel, or Lugbul; whence it was ſtiled by the ancient Britons Caer-Luel, or Luel's city. It is encompaſſed on the north ſide by the river Eden, on the eaſt by the Petterel, and on the weſt by the Caude. Probably a ſpot ſo ſtrong by nature was not deſtitute of a fortreſs during the time of the Romans, when, as appears from the many inſcriptions and ancient utenſils digged up hereabouts, Carliſle was a place of much eſtimation: but the preſent caſtle was the work of William Rufus, built

about

Carliſle Caſtle.

about the year 1093, two hundred years after the city had been deſtroyed by the Danes.

King William at firſt placed herein a colony of Flemings; and afterwards removing theſe to the Iſle of Angleſea, he ſent in their ſtead a number of huſbandmen from the ſouth to inſtruct the inhabitants in the art of cultivating their lands. King Henry I. is ſaid to have increaſed the fortifications of the city, and to have ſtrengthened it with a garriſon; he alſo raiſed it to the dignity of an epiſcopal ſee, granting it many privileges and immunities, with intention to render it ſtrong and populous, it being an important barrier againſt the incurſion of the Scots. In the reign of Henry III. that prince gave the cuſtody of the caſtle and county to Robert de Veteri Ponte, or Vipont.

According to Camden, the caſtle was rebuilt, or much repaired by King Richard III. whoſe arms, he ſays, were ſet up againſt it. Probably theſe repairs became neceſſary from the damage it ſuffered in the great fire, anno 1292, in which, the Chronicle of Lanercoſt Abbey ſays, it was burned down, together with the cathedral and ſuburbs: or it might, at length, have become ruinous from the aſſaults it had ſuſtained from the Scots, by whom it was often beſieged, and twice taken; once in the reign of King Stephen, and retaken by King Henry II. and again, in the time of King John.

King Henry VIII. cauſed ſeveral additions to be made to the fortifications of this town and caſtle: and Queen Elizabeth built the chapel and barracks, as appears by her arms placed thereon. This caſtle is of an irregular figure, having a ſtrong gate-houſe, and three ſmall ſquare towers, of little or no uſe in the preſent mode of defence. Theſe communicate with a rampart and parapet, for the aſcent of which there are ſeveral flights of ſteps.

The keep ſtands on the eaſt ſide. It is built of reddiſh ſtone, and now uſed for a ſtore-houſe. It is ſeparated from the caſtle-yard by a ditch on its weſt ſide; which ditch is defended by a curious round baſtion. In the inner gate of the caſtle is ſtill to be ſeen the old portcullis. Here are likewiſe ſeveral ancient guns mounted

mounted on rotten and unſerviceable carriages. This fortreſs ſuffered ſome injury during the civil wars in the reign of King Charles I. and was battered and taken by the duke of Cumberland in the rebellion of 1745. The breach cauſed by the duke's batteries, which were planted on a riſing ground to the weſt, at near five hundred yards diſtance, are now repaired; for which purpoſe the inſide of the ſouth wall has been ſtripped of its facing.

HERE were ſeveral embraſures raiſed with earth, moſt of the batteries being originally en barbette. Here the unfortunate Mary Queen of Scots lodged, when ſhe fled from Scotland. Her apartments are ſtill ſhewn among the admiranda of the caſtle.

IT is ſaid (ſays Burn) that King Henry VIII. built the citadel of Carliſle, however be that as it may, it is certain both that and the reſt of the fortifications were greatly gone to decay in the reign of Queen Elizabeth, as appears by the following return to a commiſſion of enquiry for that purpoſe, viz.

"CERTIFICATE of the decays of the caſtle, town and citadel of Carliſle, by Walter Strykland, Richard Lowther, John Lamplugh, Anthony Barwick, Alan Bellingham and Thomas Denton, Eſqrs, appointed commiſſioners for the ſame, June 12, 1563.

DECAYS within CARLISLE CASTLE.

FIRST, the dungeon tower of the caſtle, which ſhould be principal part and defence thereof, and of the town alſo, on three ſides is in decay, that is to ſay, on the eaſt and weſt ſides in length ſixty-ſix foot, and on the ſouth ſide ſixty-ſix foot in decay, and every of the ſame places ſo in decay, do contain in thickneſs twelve foot, and in height fifty foot: ſo as the ſame dungeon tower is not only unſerviceable, but alſo in daily danger to fall, and to overthrow the reſt of the ſaid tower.

ITEM, there is a breach in the wall in the outer ward, which fell 12 March, 1557, containing in length ſixty-nine foot and a half, in thickneſs nine foot, and in height with the battlement eighteen

COCKERMOUTH CASTLE.

Pub.d 1st Dec.r 1783 by S. Hooper.

eighteen foot; through which breach men may eaſily paſs and repaſs.

ITEM, the captain's tower and other principal defence wanteth a platform, and the * vawmer about forty-four foot, in breadth forty foot, and in thickneſs eight foot.

ITEM, three parts of the walls of the inner ward is not vawmer containing in length three hundred and forty-four foot, and in thickneſs twelve foot, and in height three foot, with one half round.

ITEM, the caſtle gates are in decay and needful to be made new.

ITEM, there is not in the ſaid caſtle any ſtorehouſe meet for the ordnance and munition; ſo as the ſame lieth in the town very dangerouſly for any ſudden enterprize.

ITEM, there is decayed the glaſs of two great windows; the one in the great chamber, and the other in the hall of the ſaid caſtle.

THE ordnance, artillery, and munition in the caſtle at that time were, ſagers 2, fawcons 4, all diſmounted: fawconets 2, whereof one not good; one little pot-gun of braſs: demi-bombarders 2: baſes double and ſingle 12, lacking furniture: half ſtaggs 39, not ſerviceable: bows of yew, none: arrows, 6 ſcore ſheafs, in decay: moris-pikes 30, not good: ſager ſhot of iron 58, ſager ſhot of lead 70. This view, which ſhews the north-eaſt aſpect, was drawn anno 1774.

COCKERMOUTH CASTLE, CUMBERLAND.

(PLATE I.)

THIS was the baronial caſtle of the honour of Cockermouth, built, as is ſuppoſed, ſoon after the conqueſt, by William de Meſchines, who poſſeſſed that honour by gift of his brother Ranulph, earl of Cumberland, to whom the conqueror gave all that part of Cumberland, called Copeland, lying between the

* Avantmur, the parapet.

Dudden and the Darwent. From the ſaid William, this honour, for want of heirs-male, came to Gilbert Pipard; and from him, for the like cauſe, to Richard de Lucy; whoſe daughter and co-heireſs marrying Thomas de Moulton, had iſſue a ſon Anthony, who took upon him the name of Lucy; and to him, as appears in Madox's Baronia, this honour, together with the manor of Pappe caſtle, were granted by Edward III. in the ſecond year of his reign. This Anthony dying without iſſue, his eſtates devolved to his ſiſter Maud, who firſt married Gilbert de Umfraville, and afterwards Henry de Percy, earl of Northumberland. She did, by a fine levied in the Octaves of St. John Baptiſt, in the reign of King Richard II. A. D. 1384, ſettle the caſtle and honour of Cockermouth, with a large proportion of her inheritance, upon her huſband and his heirs male, with diverſe remainders to the family of the Percy's, upon condition that they ſhould always bear the arms of Lucy, which are gules, three luces or pikes, hauriant, argent, in all ſhields, banners, enſigns, and coats of arms whatſoever, quarterly, with their own. In this family it continued till Joceline, the laſt earl, leaving only a daughter, ſhe carried it in marriage to Charles Seymour, duke of Somerſet; and by the death of Algernon (the laſt duke) without heirs male, it deſcended, together with the title of earl of Egremont, to Sir Charles Windham, bart. whoſe ſon is the preſent proprietor.

Other accounts attribute the building of this caſtle to Waldof, firſt lord of Allerdale, ſon of Goſpatrick, Earl of Northumberland, cotemporary with William the Conqueror. Waldof, it is ſaid, reſided firſt at Pappe caſtle, in this neighbourhood; which he afterwards demoliſhed, and with the materials erected this edifice. This caſtle ſtands on the weſt ſide of the Coker, on a mount, ſeemingly artificial, near the Darwent. The dimenſions of the walls, which form nearly a ſquare, are computed about ſix hundred yards in compaſs; they are flanked by ſeveral ſquare towers. The entrance is on the eaſt ſide over a bridge. Over the outer gate are five ſhields of arms; four of them are ſaid to be thoſe of the Moulton's, Umfraville's, Lucy's, and Percy's. In this gate are

Cockermouth Castle, Pl. 2.

Publish'd Oct. 1 1783, by S. Hooper

are ſome habitable rooms, wherein the auditor holds a court twice every year.

WITHIN the walls are two courts: in the firſt are ſome ſmall modern tenements inhabited by a perſon who takes care of the caſtle. From this court through a gate, is the entrance into the ſecond. On each ſide of this gate are two deep dungeons, each capable of holding fifty perſons; they are vaulted at the top, and have only a ſmall opening in order to admit the priſoners, who either deſcended by a ladder, or were lowered down with ropes. On the outſide of the gate, juſt even with the ground, are two narrow ſlits; one on each ſide, ſloping inwards. Down theſe were thrown the proviſions allotted for the wretched beings confined there, who had no other light, or air, but what was admitted through theſe chinks.

WITHIN the ſecond court ſtood the manſion, now in ruins. The kitchen, as it is called, makes a picturesque appearance; it has one of thoſe monſtrous chimneys, ſo common in old manſions, which ſerve to give an idea of the ancient hoſpitality, Under it is a groined vault, ſaid to have been the chapel, ſupported near the middle by a large polygonal column, and lighted by only one window.

DURING the civil wars it was garriſoned, anno 1648, for the king; and being beſieged and taken, was burned, and never ſince repaired; although the preſent earl has cauſed the outer walls to be new pointed, and the rubbiſh to be removed from the inner court. This caſtle, Burne ſays, was kept in repair till the year 1648, when it was made a garriſon for the king. This view, which repreſents the north-eaſt aſpect, was drawn anno 1774.

(PLATE II.)

THE former view exhibited the outſide of this caſtle; this ſhews the inſide of its inner court, viewed nearly in the contrary direction. The great room called the kitchen is here very perſpicuous. Towards the right hand, and near its top, appear the remains

remains of a ſtair-caſe. The ſmall door near the middle of the plate, with an inner arch appearing juſt above the wall, is that which leads to the ſtair-caſe, deſcending into the chapel. Under the largeſt of the two pointed arches, towards the right hand, lies the paſſage to and from the outer court. This view was drawn anno 1774.

LANERCOST PRIORY, CUMBERLAND.

(Plate I.)

THIS was a priory of canons regular of the order of St. Auguſtine, dedicated to the honour of God and St. Mary Magdalene. It was founded by Robert, ſon of Hubert de Vallibus, lord of Gilleſland. The church was dedicated by Bernard, biſhop of Carliſle, anno 1169.

Robert de Vallibus, the founder, by his charter granted to theſe canons diverſe valuable parcels of land, whoſe boundaries are therein deſcribed; alſo the church of Walton, with the chapel of Treverman, the churches of Erchinton, of Brampton, Karlaton and Farlam, with all their appurtences and dependencies.

He likewiſe gave the paſturage for thirty cows, and twenty ſows, in his foreſt of Walton; with all the bark of the timber-trees, and the dry wood in the foreſts of his barony; and free paſſage for themſelves and ſervants through his eſtates to their different churches and houſes, &c. to Brampton, Walton, Traverſman, Warboleman, and Roſwrageth, Danton, and Brenkibeth.

He moreover beſtowed on them certain lands in his wood at Brampton, for the building of a barn to collect their tythes: he alſo permitted them to make themſelves a fiſh-pond any where within his demeſnes, provided that it did not injure his mill. All theſe, with many other donations, were confirmed by the charter of King Richard I.

Anno 1315 Henry de Burgh, prior of this houſe, dying, Robert de Meburn was elected in his ſtead. The MS. chronicle of

Pl. I. 20

LANERCOST PRIORY CUMBERLAND.

Published Nov.r 3, 1780, by S. Hooper.

of Lanercoſt preſerved in the Britiſh Muſeum reports that this Henry de Burgh was a famous poet.

In 1337 on the death of prior William de Southayke, the convent choſe John de Bowethby for his ſucceſſor.

In the year 1354 John de Bothceſter having on account of his age and infirmities reſigned the office of prior, when Thomas de Hextildeſham was choſen in his place, to whom the Biſhop of Carliſle, beſides adminiſtering the uſual oath of cannonical obedience, likewiſe obliged him by ſolemn promiſe not to frequent publick huntings, nor to keep ſo large a pack of hounds as he had formerly done, he alſo directed that decent lodging in the priory, and a competent allowance of the neceſſaries and conveniences of life ſhould be made for the former prior, which the convent by an unanimous ſubſcription bound themſelves to perform.

On the death of Thomas de Hextildeſham great diſſentions aroſe reſpecting the election of a ſucceſſor, inſomuch that the biſhop thought it neceſſary to ſend letters requiſitory commanding them under pain of the greater excommunication during the vacancy of the prior, to pay canonical obedience to the ſub prior, who with his party declared themſelves for Richard de Rydal, a canon regular of St. Mary's of Carliſle, whilſt another faction inſiſted on having duly choſen John de Nonyneton a canon of their own houſe. The biſhop was appealed to, who gave ſentence in favor of John de Rydal. Anno 1360 John de Rydal abſenting himſelf from his priory, the biſhop conſtituted Martin de Brampton guardian during his abſence. Which is the laſt account of the priory to be found in the regiſter of the biſhop of Carliſle.

Robert de Vallibus, dying without iſſue, was ſucceeded by his brother Ralph, whoſe great-grand-daughter Maud marrying Thomas de Multon, carried the barony into that family. Their grand-daughter and heireſs Margaret in like manner conveyed it to the family of the Dacres.

After the diſſolution King Henry granted this priory to Thomas Dacre of Lanercoſt, Eſq; commonly called Baſtard Dacre (as being the illegitimate ſon of Thomas lord Dacre of the north) to him and his heirs male for ever, reſerving the church and church yard with ſome buildings for the reſidence of the vicar. To this grant King Edward VI. afterwards added the rectories and advowſons formerly belonging to the monks, to him and his heirs in general.

THE priory continued in the Dacre family for ſeveral deſcents, till James Dacre dying without male iſſue, it reverted to the crown, and was anno 1777 held on leaſe by Frederic earl of Carliſle.

"THE conventual church, ſays Burn, has been large and ſomewhat magnificent; a ſmall part of it is now only uſed by the pariſhioners, the reſt in ruins, having been wholly appropriated to the priory, it remains only a perpetual curacy, and was certified to the Governors of Queen Anne's bounty at 14l. 5s. and hath ſince received an allotment of 200l. from the ſaid bounty. The earl of Carliſle is patron (probably by purchaſe from the Dacres.)"

AT the ſupreſſion, the annual revenues of this houſe were eſtimated at 77l. 7s. 11d. Dugdale; 79l. 19s. Speed; at which time, here were a prior and ſeven canons. This view, which repreſents the north aſpect of the priory church, was drawn anno 1774.

(PLATE II.)

THIS priory is ſituated in a romantic valley, a ſmall diſtance north of the river Irthing, and a little to the ſouthward of the Picts wall. Its remains conſiſt of the priory church, and ſome few of the offices of the monaſtery, now fitted up for a farmhouſe.

THE chancel is in ruins, where, amidſt ſhrubs, brambles, and nettles, appear ſeveral very elegant tombs of the Dacre family, but much damaged by the weather: the way into one of the vaults beneath is laid ſo open, that the ſtairs leading down are viſible.

Pl.II.

LANERCOST PRIORY, CUMBERLAND.

Published as Oct.1,1783 by S. Hooper.

visible. Here are two stories or series of arches, the under ones circular, supported by columns of great thickness, some cylindrical, and some polygonal. About the ruined parts of this building many ash-trees have taken root, and flourish among the disjointed stones, affording a very picturesque appearance. The nave is in good repair, and serves for the parish-church: it has two side aisles divided by pointed arches of a very considerable span.

On a stone on the inside of the east wall is the following inscription:

"Robertus de Vallibus filius Huberti Domini de Gisland
Fundator Prioratus de Lanercost, A.D. 1116. Ædergaini Uxor ejus sine prole,
Reverendus G. Story hujus Ec. Pastor
Grato animo hunc lapidem posuit 1761."

Which may be thus translated: "Robert de Vallibus, the son of Hubert, lord of Gisland, founder of the priory of Lanercost, A. D. 1116. Ædergane his wife had no children. The Rev. G. Story, A. M. minister of this church, out of gratitude placed this stone 1761." According to this date, the monastery was founded fifty-three years before the dedication of the church. At the east window, under a coat armorial of three cockle-shells, are the following lines:

"Mille & quingentos ad quinquaginta novemque,
Adjice; & hoc anno condidit istud opus.
Thomas Daker, Eques, sedem qui primus in istam
Venerat, extincta religione loci.
Hoc Edvardus ei dederat, devoverat ante
Henricus longæ præmia militiæ."

"To one thousand and five hundred add fifty and nine, and in that year Thomas Daker, Esq; built this work. He was the first who came to this seat after the dissolution of the priory. It was given him by Edward, though before promised by Henry, as a reward for his long military services."

Probably the work here alluded to, was the window whereon the inscription is placed; which in the outrageous zeal of the times

times might have been demoliſhed at the ſurrender. The church itſelf is apparently too ancient to be meant.

THE weſt front of this building was neatly finiſhed, and in a niche near the top is an elegant female figure. A ſmall diſtance weſt of the church, in what was the church-yard wall is the remains of a handſome gate, whoſe arch is a ſegment of a large circle. About a mile ſouth-eaſtward on an eminence ſtands Naworth Caſtle, which is plainly ſeen from hence. This was formerly alſo the property of the Dacre family.

THIS monaſtery at preſent belongs to the earl of Carliſle, into whoſe family it came by a marriage with the ſiſter and co-heir of the laſt Lord Dacre.

IT is by ſome related that this priory was founded as an expiation for the death of one Giles Bueth, who pretending to have a right to the barrony of Gilliſland, was ſlain by Robert de Vallibus, or Hubert his father. But as no ſuch motive is mentioned or hinted at in the charter of foundation, probably it is a groundleſs ſtory.

IN the year 1306, as appears in Leland's Collectanea, King Edward the Firſt remained here ſome time, whilſt he ſent his Juſtices to Berwick, who there, according to Stowe, tried hundreds and thouſands of breakers of the peace and conſpirators, many of whom were hanged; "and the counteſſe of Bowen was cloſed in a cage, whoſe breadth, length, height, and depth, was eight foote, and hanged over the wals of Berwike." This view, which repreſents the weſt aſpect of the priory church, was drawn anno 1774.

NAWORTH CASTLE, CUMBERLAND.

(PLATE I.)

THIS caſtle is ſtill intire and inhabited; for the annexed account of it and its furniture, I am indebted to Thomas Pennant, Eſq; who permitted me to tranſcribe it from his memorandums. A viſit I made to it in Auguſt, 1774, enables me to bear teſtimony

NAWORTH CASTLE, CUMBERLAND.

Published 15 Oct. 1783, by S. Hooper.

teſtimony to the faithfulneſs of the deſcription, which here follows in his own words:

" Two miles from Brampton viſit Naworth Caſtle, once belonging to the Dacres, afterwards the property (I think by marriage) of William Lord Howard, commonly known by the name of Bauld-Willey.

It is a large pile, ſquare, and built about a court. In the ſouth ſide is a gateway, with the arms of the Dacres; over the door, thoſe of the Howards. On the north it impends over the river Ithing, at a great height; the banks ſhagged with wood. The whole houſe is a true ſpecimen of ancient inconvenience, of magnificence and littleneſs; the rooms numerous, accceſſible by ſixteen ſtair-caſes, with moſt frequent and ſudden aſcents and deſcents into the bargain. The great hall is twenty-five paces long, by nine and a half broad; of a good height; has a gallery at one end, adorned with four vaſt creſts carved in wood, viz. a griffin and dolphin, with the ſcollops; an unicorn, and an ox with a coronet round his neck. In front is a figure in wood of an armed man; two others, perhaps vaſſals, in ſhort jackets and caps; a pouch pendant behind, and the mutilated remains of Priapus to each; one has wooden ſhoes. Theſe ſeem the Ludibrium Aulæ in thoſe groſs days.

The top and upper end of the room is painted in ſquares, to the number of one hundred and ſeven, repreſenting the Saxon kings and heroes. The chimney here is five yards and a half broad. Within this is another apartment, hung with old tapeſtry, a head of Anne of Cleeves; on one ſide of her a ſmall picture of a lady full length, &c. and many others.

A long narrow gallery.

Lord William Howard's bed-room, arms and motto over the chimney; his library, a ſmall room in a very ſecret place, high up in one of the towers, well ſecured by doors and narrow ſtair-caſe; not a book has been added ſince his days, i. e. ſince thoſe of Queen Elizabeth. In it is a vaſt caſe, three feet high, which opens into three leaves, having ſix great pages paſted in, being an account of St. Joſeph of Arimathea, and his twelve diſciples, who founded Glaſtonbury; and at the end, a long hiſtory of ſaints, with the number of years or days for which each could grant indulgences.

The roof is coarſely carved; the windows are high, and are to be aſcended by three ſtone ſteps; ſuch was the caution of the times. It is ſaid, Lord William was very ſtudious and wrote much; that once when he was thus employed, a ſervant came to tell him that a priſoner was then juſt brought in, and deſired to know what ſhould be done with him: Lord William vexed at being diſturbed, anſwered peeviſhly, Hang him. When he finiſhed his ſtudy, he called and ordered the man to be brought before him for examination; but found that his orders had been literally obeyed. He was a very ſevere, but moſt uſeful man at that time in this lawleſs place. His dungeon inſtills horror; it conſiſts of four dark apartments, three below and one above, up a long ſtair-caſe, all well ſecured; in the uppermoſt is one ring, to which criminals were chained, and the marks where many more have been.

Close by the library is an ancient oratory, moſt richly ornamented on the ſides of the cieling with coats of arms and carvings in wood, painted and gilt. On one ſide is a good painting on wood, in the ſtile of Lucus Van Leyden; it repreſents the Flagellation of our Saviour, his Crucifixion and Reſurrection. Here are alſo various ſculptures in white marble; an abbeſs with a ſword in her hand waiting on a king who is ſtabbing himſelf; a monk with a king's head in his hand and ſeveral others. This place is well ſecured; for here Lord William enjoyed his religion in privacy.

The chapel is below ſtairs; the top and part of the ſides are painted in panels like the hall; and on one ſide are the creſts of arms and pedigree of the Howards, from Fulcho to 1623 and 1644. Under a great ſprawling figure of an old man, with a branch riſing from him on the cieling is written Pictor, MDXII. On the great window in glaſs are repreſented a knight and a lady kneeling;

NAWORTH CASTLE, CUMBERLAND.

Published 10 Nov. 1783 by S. Hooper.

kneeling; on their mantles pictured theſe arms, three eſcallops and chequers."

(PLATE II.)

TRADITION ſays this caſtle was built by the Dacres, but by which of them is not aſcertained. One of them, Robert de Dacre, from a quotation in Madox's Hiſtory of the Exchequer, ſeems to have been ſheriff of Cumberland, 39 Henry III. and another, Ranulph de Dacre, 14th of Edward I. conſtable of the tower.

THE firſt mention of this caſtle is in the reign of Edward II. when in the 18th of that reign, it appears from Madox's Baronia, that William de Dacre, ſon and heir of Hugh de Dacre, who was brother and heir of Ranulph de Dacre, held it, with the manor of Irchington, to which it belonged; alſo the manors of Burgh, near Sandes, Laſingby and Farlham, and other lands, by the ſervice of one entire baronia, and of doing homage and fealty to the king, and of yielding to him for cornage at his exchequer at Carliſle yearly, at the feaſt of the Aſſumption of St. Mary, 51s. 8d. By what feoffment, old or new, ſays Madox, does not appear; neither in what king's reign Ranulph de Dacre, anceſtor of William here named, was feoffed; but it is plain ſome anceſtor, under whom Ranulph claimed, was enfeoft to hold by baronia.

IT continued in the family of the Dacres till the year 1569, when on the 17th of May, according to Stowe, " George Lord Dacre of Grayſtoke, ſonne and heir of Thomas Lord Dacre, being a child in yeeres, and then ward to Thomas Lord Howard, duke of Norfolk, was by a great miſchaunce ſlayne at Thetford, in the houſe of Sir Richard Falmenſtone, Knt. by meane of a vauting horſe of wood ſtanding within the ſame houſe; upon which horſe, as he meant to have vauted, and the pinnes at the feet being not made ſure, the horſe fell upon him, and bruiſed the brains out of his head."

IN

In the January following, Leonard Dacre, Esq; of Horsley, in the county of York, second son to Lord William Dacre of Gisland, being dissatisfied with a legal decision, by which his nieces were adjudged to succeed to the estate of their brother the Lord Dacre, whose tragical death was just here related; he entered into a rebellion, with design to carry off the queen of Scots; but being disappointed by her removal to Coventry, and having the command of three thousand men, which he had been entrusted to raise for the queen's service, he seized several castles, among which were those of Greystock and Naworth; but being attacked and defeated by Lord Hunsdon at the head of the garrison of Berwick, he fled to Flanders, where he died.

This castle next came into the possession of Lord William Howard, the third son of Thomas duke of Norfolk, in right of his wife Elizabeth sister of George, the last Lord Dacre before mentioned. In 1607, when Camden visited it, it was under repair; and bishop Gibson says, it was again repaired, and made fit for the reception of a family by the Right Honourable Charles Howard, great great grandson to the Lord William Howard before mentioned.

I shall here transcribe another description of this castle and furniture, sent me by a gentleman who viewed it anno 1732, which, though it repeats many things mentioned in the former account, yet it hath also divers circumstances worthy observation, not there taken notice of.

" This is an ancient stone building; the front long, with a square tower at each angle, then you enter a court. In the noble hall the pictures of the Anglo-Saxon kings, &c. painted on wooden square panels, make the cieling and part of the wainscot at the further end of the room; they were brought from Kirk Oswald castle when that was demolished. The chapel has a cieling and part of its wainscot of the same kind, being paintings of patriarchs, Jewish kings, &c. Here is also painted a genealogy of the family from Fulcho, with their arms. It has a floor of plaister of Paris, as have some other of the rooms. Some of the apartments

apartments are very large and ſpacious; the ceiling of one conſiſts of ſmall ſquare panels of wood, black and white interchangeably; the white has two different carvings, the black is unwrought. The very little popiſh chapel is above ſtairs; the inſide work curiouſly carved and gilt; here are ſome ſmall figures of the paſſion, &c. Joining to this chapel is the library, which has a good wooden roof; the books are old; there are not above one or two of the manuſcripts here now. Vide Cat. Librorum MS. Angl. & Hib. Tom. 2d, p. 14, &c. The earl of Carliſle never lives here, but at Caſtle-Howard in Yorkſhire. In the garden walls are ſtones with Roman inſcriptions, collected probably from the Picts wall; a general account of theſe ſtones is given in Horſley's Britannia Romana."

CAMBDEN, who alſo mentions theſe ſtones, gives the following copy of ſome of the inſcriptions; one is,

IVL. AVG. DVO. M SILV. . VM.

On another,

. I . O . M . . . . II . AEL . DAC . . C . P . . . EST
VRELIVS. FA. L. S. TRIB. PET. VO. COS.

On a third,

LEG. II. AVG.

On a fourth,

COH. J. AEL. DAC. CORD. . ALEC . PER . . . .

THESE ſtones were by the late earl of Carliſle given to Sir Thomas Robinſon, who married his ſiſter, and were by him removed to his muſeum at Rookſby.

BURNE ſays that this caſtle was enlarged and improved out of the ruins of Irthington and Kirk Oſwald, and adds "Dr. Todd ſays, there were brought from Kirk Oſwald and put up on the roof or wooden ceiling of the great hall here, the heads of all the Kings of England from Brute to Henry VI. elegantly painted in good and laſting colours." This view, which repreſents the entrance into the caſtle, was drawn anno 1772.

PENRITH CASTLE.

THIS caſtle ſtands near the weſt end of the town: both its builder and the time of its conſtruction are unknown. Leland, who mentions it in his Itinerary, calls it "A ſtrong caſtel of the kinges;" an appellation it does not from its remains appear to have deſerved.

CAMDEN alſo ſpeaks of it, but neither mentions the date of its erection, nor its founder: he, indeed, ſays, it was repaired in Henry the Sixth's time, out of the ruins of Mabürg. This is by his laſt editor juſtly deemed a miſtake, and contradicted in a marginal note.

IT is built of a coarſe reddiſh ſtone, and was nearly ſquare, each ſide meaſuring about one hundred and twenty-five feet. All but a ſmall fragment of the north wall is tumbled down. There ſeems to have been a ſmall baſtion-like projection on the ſouth-weſt angle, but by much too trifling to ſerve for a defence. The ſouth-eaſt and north-eaſt angles have no ſuch addition; and whether or not there was one on the north-weſt cannot be diſcovered, that angle being entirely demoliſhed. In the middle of each face was a ſmall projection like a buttreſs or turret, and round the top of the walls run brackets, ſuch as uſually ſupport machicolations; but theſe ſeem to have been intended rather for ſhew than uſe. Neither the height nor thickneſs of the walls are extraordinary; the former no where exceeding thirty, nor the latter five feet.

THIS building ſeems to owe its preſent ruinous ſtate to more violent cauſes than the ſlow depredations of time and weather: yet hiſtory does not mention it as the ſcene of any great military atchievement; neither was its form deſtitute of flanks, by any means calculated to ſuſtain a ſiege; perhaps the value of its materials may have conduced to its deſtruction; for ſuch a propenſity have our farmers to deſtroy an ancient monument, that they will beſtow more labour to disjoint a few ſtones to mend their

Penrith Castle, Cumberland

[illegible] by S. Hooper

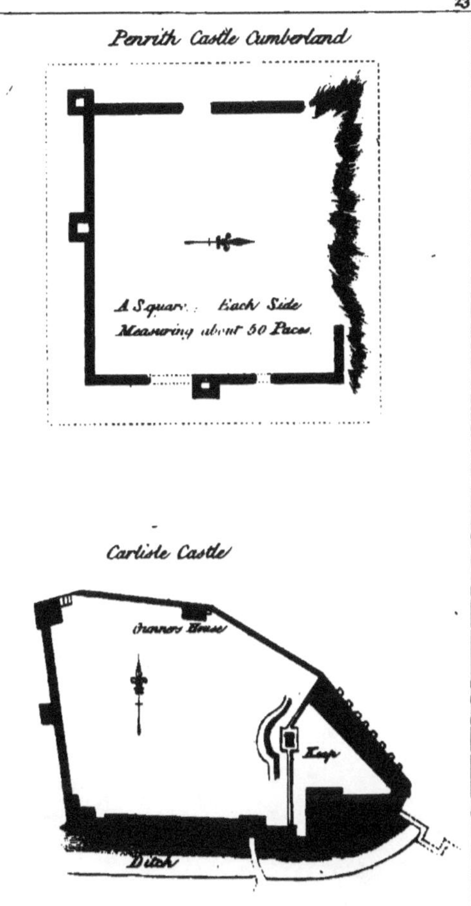
Penrith Castle Cumberland
A Square Each Side
Measuring about 50 Paces.
Carlisle Castle
Gunners House
Keep
Ditch

their buildings, than would earn them money enough to purchase three times the quantity.

THIS castle, it is said, continued in the crown till the reign of King William III. when that prince granted it, together with the honour of Penrith, to William Bentinck, earl of Portland, ancestor to the present duke of Portland.

IN a pleasing description of this part of the country, entitled, "An Excursion to the Lakes," there is the following agreeable portrait of this castle:

"WE viewed the ruins of Penrith castle:—it is said to have arose on the foundations of a Roman fortress, the traces of which are not now to be discovered.—The buildings form a square, and are situate on a rising ground surrounded with a ditch. The site towards the town is much more elevated than on any of the other quarters. This front consists of the remains of an angular tower to the east, which now stands separated from the rest by the falling of the walls: the centre, which projects a little from the plane of the front, is hastening to decay, presenting to the eye broken chambers, passages, and stairs.—This part of the building is still connected with the western angular tower, an open hanging gallery forming the communication.—Below this gallery a large opening is made by the falling of the building, forming a rude arch, through which, and the broken walls to the east, the interior parts of the ruin are perceived in a picturesque manner.—Nothing remains within but part of a stone arched vault, which, by its similitude to places of the like nature, which we had formerly seen, we conceived to have been the prison."

BURNE in his History of Cumberland, does not suppose this castle to have been built before the reign of Henry III. his description of it, and his reasons for this supposition, are as follows:

"ON the west side of the town stands the castle of square stone, inclosed within a ditch, which by its largeness and ruins seems to have been a place of some strength and consideration. But

But it ſeems not to have been very ancient, for when the two hundred librates of land (as is * aforeſaid) of which Penrith was part, were given to the King of Scots, there was a ſpecial reſervation, that thoſe lands ſhould not be where there were any caſtles. King Richard III. when he was duke of Glouceſter, that he might be at hand to oppoſe the Scots, and keep the country in obedience, which was generally of the Lancaſtrian intereſt, reſided in this caſtle for ſome time, and enlarged and ſtrengthened it with towers and other works. The ſtones for that purpoſe, it is ſaid, he had from an old ruin, ſuppoſed to have been a place of Druid worſhip at Mayburgh, about a mile diſtant, on the ſouth ſide of the river Eamont. In the civil wars in the time of King Charles I. this fabrick was totally ruined, and all the lead and timber ſold for the uſe of the commonwealth." This view which repreſents the north-weſt aſpect, was drawn anno 1774.

* The two hundred librates or oxgangs of land were given by Henry III. anno 1237, to Alexander King of Scotland, who thereupon relinquiſhed his claim to a contract made to his father William, by King John, who in conſideration of fifteen-thouſand marks of ſilver, covenanted to cede to him the counties of Weſtmorland, Cumberland and Northumberland, and alſo that one of his ſons ſhould marry a daughter of the ſaid King William.

END OF VOL. I.

DERBY-

www.ingramcontent.com/pod-product-compliance
Lightning Source LLC
Chambersburg PA
CBHW020248240426
43672CB00006B/662

* 9 7 8 3 3 3 7 3 2 1 4 1 3 *